Gendered Violence
in Public Spaces

Gendered Violence in Public Spaces

Women's Narratives of Travel in Neoliberal India

Edited by Swathi Krishna S. and Srirupa Chatterjee

Foreword by Shilpa Phadke

LEXINGTON BOOKS
Lanham • Boulder • New York • London

Published by Lexington Books
An imprint of The Rowman & Littlefield Publishing Group, Inc.
4501 Forbes Boulevard, Suite 200, Lanham, Maryland 20706
www.rowman.com

86-90 Paul Street, London EC2A 4NE

Copyright © 2023 by The Rowman & Littlefield Publishing Group, Inc.

All rights reserved. No part of this book may be reproduced in any form or by any electronic or mechanical means, including information storage and retrieval systems, without written permission from the publisher, except by a reviewer who may quote passages in a review.

British Library Cataloguing in Publication Information Available

Library of Congress Cataloging-in-Publication Data

Names: Krishna S., Swathi, 1990– editor. | Chatterjee, Srirupa, 1979– editor.
Title: Gendered violence in public spaces : women's narratives of travel in neoliberal India / edited by Swathi Krishna S. and Srirupa Chatterjee, foreword by Shilpa Phadke.
Description: Lanham : Lexington Books, 2023. | Includes bibliographical references and index. | Summary: "This book examines the vulnerability of women in public spaces in India through the analysis of artistic representations ranging from emerging digital media, commercial Hindi films and graphic narratives to narratives of real and lived experiences of women. In doing so, the book resists gendered violence and champions women's right to mobility"— Provided by publisher.
Identifiers: LCCN 2023016081 (print) | LCCN 2023016082 (ebook) | ISBN 9781666902327 (cloth) | ISBN 9781666902334 (epub)
Subjects: LCSH: Gender-based violence—India. | Women—Violence against—India. | Public spaces—India—Safety measures. | Violence in motion pictures.
Classification: LCC HV6250.4.W65 G4867 2023 (print) | LCC HV6250.4.W65 (ebook) | DDC 362.880820954—dc23/eng/20230607
LC record available at https://lccn.loc.gov/2023016081
LC ebook record available at https://lccn.loc.gov/2023016082

Contents

Foreword: Possibilities   ix

Acknowledgments   xv

Introduction: Gendered Violence and Women in Public Spaces   1
Swathi Krishna S. and Srirupa Chatterjee

PART I: HOSTILE TERRAINS, EMPOWERING TEXTUAL SPACES: NEOLIBERAL LITERATURE AND THE FEMALE TRAVELER   17

Chapter 1: No Longer Innocent: Male Gaze, Violence, and Female Kinship in Kishwar Desai's The Sea of Innocence   19
Swathi Krishna S. and Srirupa Chatterjee

Chapter 2: Peripheral Urbanization as Queer Identity in Arundhati Roy's *The Ministry of Utmost Happiness*   33
Jana Fedtke

Chapter 3: Mirrors of Reality: Toxic Masculinity, Traveling Women, and the Representation of Acid Attack Victim-Survivors in Priya's Mirror   51
Nidhi Shrivastava

PART II: BOLLYWOOD'S TRAVELING WOMEN (I): MISOGYNY, ROADS, AND FEMALE VULNERABILITY   71

Chapter 4: Stepping Out: Global Bollywood, Gendered Landscape, and Undercurrents of Neoliberal Pleasures   73
Madhuja Mukherjee

Chapter 5: Celluloid Women Rewriting Rules of Travel in
   Contemporary Hindi Cinema   93
   Rima Bhattacharya

PART III: BOLLYWOOD'S TRAVELING WOMEN (II): VEXED DUALITIES OF FREEDOM AND FEAR   113

Chapter 6: The Conditional Promise of Empowerment and
   Pleasure: An Intersectional Analysis of Hindi Film Portrayals of
   Women Navigating Public Spaces in India   115
   Uttara Manohar

Chapter 7: Traveling Women and Their Male Companions: Framing
   Risks and Vulnerabilities in Indian Road Films   131
   Pronoti Baglary

PART IV: TROUBLES OF THE OUTDOORSY WOMAN: MULTIPLE GENRES/MULTIPLE VOICES   149

Chapter 8: Roads, Dreams, and Violence: Tracing the Mental
   Landscape of India's Domestic Workers   151
   Bonnie Zare and Ditto Prasad

Chapter 9: Negotiating Violence and Traversing the City: Female
   Vulnerability in Delhi Crime (2019) and She (2020)   165
   Shreya Rastogi and Srirupa Chatterjee

PART V: STRUGGLE FOR SURVIVAL: WORKING WOMEN AND PITFALLS OF INDIAN ROADS   183

Chapter 10: Working Night Shifts, Traversing Neoliberal Roads:
   Spatial-Temporal Confluence and the Male Gaze   185
   Sucharita Sen

Chapter 11: Women Journalists Negotiating Space in India's
   "Small" Cities   201
   Ranu Tomar

PART VI: TRAVELING SOLO, TRAVELING STRONG: WOMEN BRAVING NEOLIBERAL ROADS   221

Chapter 12: Travel with Care: Reinforcing Patriarchy through Tips
   for Solo Female Travelers in India   223
   Kiranpreet Kaur Baath

Conclusion	245
Index	249
About the Editors	253

Foreword

Possibilities

"I took the housekeeper with me to the store in West Kensington as I was afraid of going there alone as there was a wine shop near there."

—Parvati Pant, November 16, 1921

Parvati bai also known as Vahini saheb, lived in London for two years between 1921 and 1923 with her husband and two children. She frequently writes about using the tube and even exclaims about how marvelous it is, and is especially charmed by the moving staircases. She goes to the cinema and writes about watching Charlie Chaplin's *The Kid* and of watching a performance of the play, *Sally* at the Winter Garden Theatre in the company of her friends and husband. She was rather privileged as can be seen from the fact that she had a housekeeper whom she could ask to accompany her.

In the prologue to our book, *Why Loiter? Women and Risk on Mumbai Streets* (2011), we drew on my diary entries of travel in North India. And it was in fact these entries that enabled the rendering of my familiar commutes in Bombay, *unfamiliar* so that one might perceive that as worthy of further inquiry, and indeed as the subject of a research project. As I write this *Foreword*, I am also translating Parvati's 100-page diary written in Marathi in 1921, now more than a century ago. Parvati Pant was also my great-grandmother and this makes the project deeply personal. Reading this diary written as it is, often focusing on the everyday, provides a grounded lens to think about women and travel.

As Abhay Sardesai, my co-translator, and I read and translate, the lines quoted at the beginning of this piece, jump up at me screaming déjà vu. For during our research on the gender and space project between 2003 and 2006, more than eight decades after Parvati wrote her diary, women in Mumbai,

India demonstrated via a mental mapping exercise, that they too prefer to avoid wine shops where many men might be hanging about. One hundred years later it might seem as if little has changed. However, while, we, that is Sameera Khan, Shilpa Ranade and I often bemoan the fact that 12 years after it was published our book continues to be as relevant as ever, and women's access to public space continues to be circumscribed, with victim-blaming alive and kicking; we are also cognizant of the ways in which the discourse of access to public space has transformed. While women may continue to strategize and use subterfuge in order to access public space, feminist scholarship on gendered public spaces are grown exponentially as has feminist activism in relation to claims to public space. When we talked of loitering in 2006 as we formulated the ideas of *Why Loiter?* feminist academics and activists, often asked why we would want to loiter, because *even* good men did not loiter. Now nobody is asking that question anymore. Loitering has become part of a feminist lexicon of access to public space.

As a young undergraduate student in the 1990s I traveled with three women friends in Tamil Nadu, India. We had no train or hotel reservations and our only 'safety net' was that one of us called home each day in rotation using the STD booths that had proliferated widely by then to check in and confirm we were fine. Dozens of people in trains and buses warned us about the dangers of four young women traveling on our own but nobody tried to harass us. We met with a lot of perhaps unwanted concern but beyond that little. In fact we met with a bus accident. We navigated the Thanjavur Medical College Hospital speaking no Tamil. People were very considerate. The proprietor of our hotel sent food for one of our friends who had to spend a night at the hospital with a broken nose. My father on the phone after ascertaining that we were all mostly ok, nonchalantly told me we should continue our holiday and have fun. This narrative is not intended to suggest that women are not harassed or even assaulted, but rather to indicate that this experience was as much my reality of travel, as the story of my travels as a woman in her twenties in the North of India which included an inordinate amount of planning and which I recount in the prologue to *Why Loiter?*

In this sense then, anxiety and anticipation are perhaps for most women the two sides of traveling. On a recent holiday I was witness to two separate scenes which demonstrated this, both of which were evocative and so much part of what we know to be women's experiences of engaging the public and especially travel.

In the first of the two episodes, I was standing on the banks of the Ganga, my then seven-year-old daughter trying her best to convince me to bathe in the icy water as she was doing. A group of young men from our hotel were hanging around waiting for their raft to arrive so they could go rafting on the rapids. When the raft arrived, it had in addition to the guy who was in charge of the raft, two women tourists who seemed to be in the late twenties. Their expressions when they saw that a group of all men were to join them were a study in concern, apprehension, and resolve. I heard one woman tell the other—we have our phones, we will be fine. The other nodded resolutely but neither looked very happy about the situation—basically sharing a raft with six men they did not know. As the raft left, the six men laughing raucously, I watched the expressions on the faces of the two women as they tried to look unconcerned and I felt their unspoken anxiety.

In the second episode on the same holiday, I was sitting in a cafe in Landour (in Uttarakhand, India), drinking hot chocolate, shamelessly eavesdropping on a conversation between two women travelers who were not together but were sharing a table. Their conversation revealed that they were both professionals. One of them had just finished an assignment in Mussoorie (again, in Uttarakhand, India) and was looking for accommodation as she took some time out for fun. The other was in between jobs and on vacation by herself. The latter phoned her hotel to ask about accommodation for the former. There was instant recognition of the quest the other was on. Both women looked comfortable and exuded a sense of belonging as they sipped their coffees.

Both stories ring true for women's engagements with public spaces as citizens of cities and towns and as travelers in the country. Of course, it is true that only a few women in this country can afford to travel, much less on their own, but nonetheless these are narratives worth recounting. If we are to go by media reports we would assume that only the first story represents the realities of women traveling on their own or with each other. There is constant strategizing, apprehension, and fear. But there is also in equal measure, simultaneously, joy, unconcern, and the pleasure of being with oneself in the world. Even just commuting within a city or a town brings with it a sense of competence and even sometimes liberation. This is the reason why paeans have been sung to Mumbai's local trains especially the women's compartments which even has a documentary film, *Ladies Special* (2003) directed by Nidhi Tuli made on it.

Many narratives of women and travel evoke a sense of possibility. Ira Mukhoty, for instance, in her glorious book *Daughters of the Sun: Empresses, Queens and Begums of the Mughal Empire* (2018) chronicles the lives of Mughal women. One highlight is the narrative of the Mughal women's Hajj trip led by Gulbandan Bano in 1578 that lasted seven years. Ira Mukhoty describes the unusual nature of such a voyage but also the sheer pleasure of it, the staying in and around Mecca for the fun of it, as also the power of being on their own and controllers of their own destiny so to speak. In her book, *Women Travellers in Colonial India: The Power of the Female Gaze* (1998) Indira Ghose records narratives of European women traveling in India. More recent accounts of travelogues by women writers include: *A Field Guide to Getting Lost* (2005) by Rebecca Solnit, *Looking for Transwonderland: Travels in Nigeria* (2012) by Noo Saro-Wiwa, *Wild: From Lost to Found on the Pacific Crest Trail* (2012) by Cheryl Strayed, *What I Was Doing while You Were Breeding: A Memoir* (2014) by Kristin Newman, *Flaneuse* (2017) by Lauren Elkin, *Around the World in 80 Trains* (2019) by Monisha Rajesh, *Shadow City: A Woman Walks Kabul* (2019) by Taran Khan, and *Elsewhere: One Woman, One Rucksack, One Lifetime of Travel* (2019) by Rosita Boland.

Neoliberalism, the period and ethos this book focuses on, additionally frames the world and its opportunities for women in particular ways. It is perhaps telling that so many of the essays in this book focus or draw on fiction in print or in the audio-visual medium. Much of women's travel takes place in our imaginations and in the creative worlds we inhabit. An engagement with these narratives in textual and graphic novels, films and web series illuminate a world of fears, dreams, adventures and aspirations. Engagements with and by women professionals, solo travelers and bikers open windows through which one might reflect on the phenomenon of women commuters and travelers. This book contributes to a growing body of literature on women and travel, historical and contemporary.

Shilpa Phadke
Mumbai, India
February 2023

The right to the city is far more than the individual liberty to access urban resources: it is a right to change ourselves by changing the city. . . . The freedom to make and remake our cities and ourselves is . . . one of the most precious yet most neglected of our human rights.

—David Harvey

Women's access to public space is fundamentally linked to the access of all citizens. The litmus test of this right to public space is the right to loiter, especially for women across all classes.

—Shilpa Phadke, Sameera Khan, and Shilpa Ranade

Acknowledgments

As editors of this book and as women living in postmillennial India, we are indebted to several people, moments, and experiences that helped and inspired us in crafting this volume. Looking back, we can happily claim that we grew up with the benefits of educational and professional freedoms that neoliberal India offers contemporary women. And yet, despite these privileges which were indeed denied to many women of earlier generations, we experienced profoundly disturbing moments of gendered threat as we traveled literally and metaphorically through public spaces in pursuit of our personal and professional engagements. This book, then, is a product of our intimate and instinctive reactions to negotiating our way through public spaces, just as it is a product of the responses of our chapter writers and perhaps of all Indian women who have traveled through the nation's roads. And we, like every Indian woman, hope and demand that public spaces and roads be transformed—sooner than later—into welcoming and safe domains as we travel through them.

To begin with, we the editors, are deeply indebted to our foreword writer, Shilpa Phadke, who is one of the greatest proponents of women's rights to mobility and public space in contemporary India. Shilpa, your scholarship on the issue of women's safety in public spaces along with the support you personally provided to our project is greatly appreciated. Thank you! We are also immensely grateful to Kaitlynn D. Mendes for her encouragement during the planning of this book project. Your support meant a lot, Kaitlynn. Further, we are profoundly thankful to all our chapter writers for providing us with their compelling insights on narratives of women's journeys and also for rigorously working with us to revise and rework their essays. In your voices our book finds its greatest strength. Thank you all. We, the editors, are also thankful to Gurumurthy Neelakantan whose scholarly input and suggestions have not only enriched us, but also helped us craft this project. And finally, we are truly grateful to Judith Lakamper of Lexington Books who supported us all the way. Whether it is about granting us extensions or guiding us out of minor roadblocks in the editorial process as we worked through the Covid pandemic years, Judith, you were patiently there with us. Thank you so much!

This acknowledgement, of course, can never be complete without mentioning names of feminist geographers and cultural activists from India and the rest of the world whose voices recursively feature in our book. While we have never personally met or interacted with Indian scholars like Sameera Khan, Shilpa Ranade, Anindita Datta, Rituparna Bhattacharyya or Himani Bannerji; and scholars from the western part of the globe like Doreen Massey, Linda McDowell, Gillian Rose, and Gill Valentine, among others, we find both scholarly and personal solidarity and familiarity in their works. These writers confirm for us that traveling women's vulnerabilities are both real and universal, and that they need to be urgently addressed. We, the editors, likewise, are also grateful to organizations such as the National Commission for Women and the National Human Rights Commission of India which along with local police forces and other social service organizations have been trying to make public spaces safe and friendly for women. We deeply appreciate their efforts at criminalizing sexual offence and sensitizing masses toward gendered violence in public spaces. Likewise, we are grateful to the many literary writers, feature film, documentary, and ad film makers, and social media influencers who have been addressing Indian women's right to safety and mobility within public spaces. To all such voices, and more, we remain ever grateful both as women and as scholars.

In addition, we are grateful to the libraries at IIT Hyderabad, IIT Ropar, and IIT Bhubaneshwar in India for helping us procure research material for our project.

And finally, Swathi Krishna S. thanks her parents, G. Sreedevi and M. R. Unnikrishnan, and her husband Akash Gupta for their invaluable support during this academic endeavor. Srirupa Chatterjee, likewise, thanks Sampa Chatterjee and Bhaskar Chatterjee, who are her parents; and Sayantan Chatterjee (her husband) whose continuous support is always a blessing.

Introduction

Gendered Violence and Women in Public Spaces

Swathi Krishna S. and Srirupa Chatterjee

Traditionally, men have had more access than woman to public spaces,[1] especially its highways, roads, and streets. This is because the presence of women in patriarchal public spaces such as roads poses a threat to traditional spatial associations of the home or domesticity with women and the roads or adventure with men. Predictably, such gender and spatial norms have always played a significant role in the construction of Indian femininity as well. Women on Indian roads have therefore been threatened with numerous and unbelievable instances of violence, some of which in the recent past have been globally and vocally condemned. Curiously, if narratives of traveling, self-sufficient women and their outdoor experiences remain scarce, what is rarer still are theoretical and critical discourses surrounding and analyzing women's predicaments on the road. No doubt, organizations such as the National Commission for Women as well as the National Human Rights Commission of India have taken powerful measures to ensure women's safety—especially in public spaces—from instances of sexual harassment, assault, and acid attacks, among others, the problem of traveling women's vulnerability needs more attention from all sectors of society, including the academia. Stressing this, academicians such as Manish Madan and Mahesh K. Nalla (2016) note that while a considerable amount of research has been done on domestic violence in India, which mostly occurs indoors in private spaces, "the treatment of women in the public sphere, particularly with regard to sexual harassment (one of the most pervasive forms of violence against women)" (1) has only received public attention after the notorious "Nirbhaya"[2] rape case (2012) due to media coverage and international outcry. While critically informed research on this issue remains scanty, a few Indian academics have been questioning the problems experienced by traveling women. Keeping mainly the Nirbhaya rape case and the gang rape of a young photo-journalist in Mumbai as contextual backdrops, Shilpa Phadke, for example, in her article "Unfriendly Bodies, Hostile Cities Reflections on Loitering and Gendered Public Space" (2013) argues that the "overarching narrative appears to be that [Indian] cities are violent spaces that women are better off not accessing at all" (50). Arguably, while empirical and data driven research has to some extent taken into account the issue of women's travel, theoretical research scrutinizing fictionalized and popular culture representations of women's road journeys in neoliberal India[3] is palpably missing. The present edited collection attempts to bridge this disturbing gap in scholarship.

At its core this book is informed by the critical and emancipatory voices of space theorists and feminist geographers, among others. It claims that space and gender have been mutually constitutive in the production of social relations and hierarchies. To begin with, this book draws upon Marxist space theorists like Henri Lefebvre who proposes key arguments on the constructions of social spaces. Lefebvre claims that "[s]pace is not . . . removed from ideology and politics; it has always been political and strategic" (1976, 31). Likewise, this volume refers to Edward Soja who envisages space as "a social product (outcome) and a shaping force (medium) in social life" (1989, 7). Further, it draws upon feminist geographers who—informed by the leftist rhetoric of space theorists—examine "the geographical implications of gender differentiation in society . . . from a feminist perspective" (Mohammad 2017, 6). Doreen Massey, for instance, in *Space, Place, and Gender* (1994) claims that "the symbolic meaning of spaces/places and the clearly gendered messages which they transmit, to straightforward exclusion by violence . . . reflect and affect the ways in which gender is constructed and understood" (179). Massey further argues that the "attempt to confine women to the domestic sphere [is] both a specifically spatial control and, through that, a social control on identity" (179). Similarly, elaborating on the engendering of travel, Linda McDowell notes:

> Travel, even the idea of travelling, challenges the spatial association between home and women that has been so important in structuring the social construction of femininity in the "West," in Western social theories and institutional practices. Because it was taken for granted for so long that a woman's place was in the home, the history of her movement was ignored. (1999, 206)

In this context, another famous cultural geographer, Gillian Rose, reiterates the gendering of spatial practices by stating how "public/private distinction is central to . . . [the] constructions of masculinity and femininity" (1993, 19) in most human societies. Feminist geographers therefore demonstrate that public spaces are governed by patriarchal power relations which very often exclude women. While most such feminist geographers named here belong to the western world, their arguments on gendered violence and public spaces are extremely relevant for neoliberal Indian women's experiences as well

When women purportedly transgress the gendered and spatial stratifications along with patriarchal boundaries to foray into male-dominated public spaces, they often experience hostility with a looming threat of sexual violence. Notably, mapping women's "geography of fear," Gill Valentine remarks that, "[u]nlike men women find that when in public space their personal space is frequently invaded by whistles, comments or actual physical assault from strange men" (1989, 386). In this regard and underscoring the specificity of female experience on the road, Trinh Minh-Ha writes:

> the general cliché by which [women] feel exiled ... is the common consensus (in patriarchal societies) that streets and public places belong to men. Women are not supposed to circulate freely in these male domains, especially after dark (the time propitious to desire, "the drive, the unnamable" and the unknown), for should anything happen to them to violate their physical well-being, they are immediately said to have "asked for it" as they have singularly "exposed" themselves by turning away from the Father's refuge. (1994, 15)

Feminist geographers including Rose Gillian and Linda McDowell have also examined women's sexual vulnerability in patriarchal public spaces. While Gillian discusses agency and embodiment in public spaces to state that sexual attacks warn women "every day that their bodies are not meant to be in certain spaces" (1993, 21), McDowell observes how urban public spaces offer liberation for some, but are "inaccessible, or places of fear and danger" (1999, 31) for others, especially women. Upholding this, British geographer Rachel Pain articulates women's fear of violent crime in public spaces when she states that "fear of attack ... constrains women's freedom of movement in towns and cities" (1997, 234). According to feminist geographers, then, public spaces such as roads are inherently gendered and restrict women's mobility with overt and covert threats of gendered violence.

For being crafted as a volume addressing women's challenging journeys in neoliberal India, this volume is informed not only by western feminist geographers but also by the voices of Indian researchers and activists alike who have been demanding women's safety in public spaces. It, for instance, draws upon the works of Rituparna Bhattacharyya (2015) who states that "public spaces of India are a male domain and suffer greatly from hegemonic patriarchy and power" (1344). Elaborating on the social construction of gender in Indian public spaces, Bhattacharyya further argues that "[c]ulturally, Indian women are expected to attend to the inner world (private space)—household chores and childcare—whereas the outer world (public space) of 'material interests' is constructed by and for men" (1344). On similar lines, Anindita Datta points out that "classic patriarchy . . . [is] near universal in India" which, along with regional contexts and economic status, shape "gendered divisions of labour and locally accepted feminine and masculine roles" (2021, 3). The above studies reiterate that public spaces are clearly gendered and women must encounter myriads of challenges while staking claim to such spaces. It is to such studies and many more that this volume is indebted. More important, it attempts to augment the critical voices surrounding women's rights to the road in neoliberal India.

In a deeply patriarchal society such as India, spatial politics along with explicit and implicit threats of violence plague millions of women who try to access public spaces, beginning with the roads. Shilpa Phadke, Sameera Khan, Shilpa Ranade in their notable and timely contribution entitled *Why Loiter?* (2011) observe how in India "women don't loiter" (vii) while men "may stop for a cigarette at a paanwalla or lounge on a park bench . . . or drink cutting chai at a tea stall . . . even wander the streets late into the night" (vii). Based on the findings of their three-year-long "Gender and Space" research project in the city of Mumbai, India, the authors argue that "despite the apparent visibility of women, even in urban India, women do not share equal access to public space with men" (2011, viii). If at all women wish to access public spaces, the authors argue, they must "conform to the larger patriarchal order by demonstrating respectability and legitimate purpose" (2011, 36) by "carrying of large bags, by walking in goal-oriented ways and by waiting in appropriate spaces where their presence cannot be misread" (34). Shilpa Ranade, likewise, in examining women's everyday practices in gendered public spaces remarks that "[w]omen occupy public spaces essentially as a transit between one private space and another" (2007, 1521) and points out how if women are to loiter in public without any apparent purpose, they will be construed as "being 'available' and 'loose' at best, and soliciting at worst" (2007, 1523). Hence, women in Indian public spaces are often forced to manufacture legitimate purpose and respectability to ensure safety. Yet, despite many precautions, women continue to face harassment every fifty-one minutes in Indian public spaces (Bhattacharyya, 2016). According to the recent data by National Crime Records Bureau, incidents of crimes against women in India has a "19.7% increase since 2014" (Roy and Bailey 2021, 1). A 2021 study by a Delhi-based NGO on women's safety in India found that "78.4 percent respondents . . . experienced violence in public spaces" ("78% Women" 2021). The rising incidents of harassment and violence, thus, impede Indian women's mobility and thwart their right to access public spaces as legitimate citizens.

Among the many forms of violence Indian women face on a day-to-day basis, street harassment, locally termed as "eve-teasing," is the most frequent which "manifests itself in lewd comments on the physical beauty of women or the way they dress, whistling, staring, stalking, singing songs or even some form of physical assaults such as groping, fondling and pinching" (Bhattacharyya 2015, 1345). Incidents of harassment induce intense fear and anxiety in women when they venture on to male-dominated spaces which, in turn, curtail their motility and freedom. This evident when Sanghamitra Roy and Ajay Bailey disclose how Indian women avoid "going out alone . . . staying out late at night . . . 'unsafe' streets . . . unknown places . . . crowded buses and metros" to manufacture a semblance of safety when in public, even as such decisions mean "limiting access to educational and other opportunities" (2021, 8). In addition, Himani Bannerji (2016) demonstrates that in neoliberal India "[v]iolence against women/girls has indeed taken both a quantitative and a qualitative leap" (4). Hence, even when "neoliberal reforms" offer women greater access to participate in the public space through education and work, "the lack of safety in their routine mobility remains a serious obstacle to their full participation in public life" (Bhattacharyya 2015, 1343). Thus, drawing upon the findings of both international and Indian scholars on the issue of women's safety within public spaces such as the road, the present volume examines cultures of misogyny, sexual violence, and traveling women's experiences.

This collection of essays is prompted above all else by the fact that in neoliberal India, especially after the Nirbhaya rape case, one encounters a growing engagement with women's travel narratives. Such discourses have emerged not only in Indian writing in English but also in films and several OTT (over-the-top) digital platforms including Netflix and Amazon Prime Videos, as also in several social networking and blog sites. Currently therefore there exists a growing discursive paradigm within spheres of literature and popular culture, and also within socio-legal platforms on the problem of women's vulnerability within public spaces to underscore the physical, mental, sexual, and epistemic violence that traveling women face. Imaginative literature has responded to this vexed issue and writers such as Kishwar Desai, Janhavi Acharekar, and Namita Gokhale have attempted to reveal how gendered violence systematically mars the outdoorsy experiences of many Indian women. On similar lines, web series such as *Delhi Crime* (2019) along with *The Good Girl Show* (2017) and *She* (2020) prove to be a powerful case in point. In addition, mainstream Hindi films such as *Chhapaak* (2020) in the recent past have also exposed how women are extremely vulnerable to the male gaze and to patriarchal violence, especially on the roads. Other fictionalized narratives that underscore women's promising albeit perilous road journeys include films such as Nagesh Kukunoor's *Dor* (2006), Leena Yadav's *Parched* (2015), Aniruddha Roy Chowdhury's *Pink* (2016), Ashtar Sayed's *Maatr* (2017), Ravi Udyawar's *Mom* (2017), and Gopi Puthran's *Mardaani 2* (2019). All such fictional depictions—drawing heavily upon real life experiences of women—unravel the regressive rape myths, stigma, victim-blaming, and misogyny that are etched into Indian society and channeled against women who dare to explore the world outside their homes.

It is worth noting here that there is a palpable research gap in the cultural and theoretical analysis of Indian women's fictional and real-life narratives of vulnerability on the road. If this is true, it is also true that many studies—mostly empirically driven and ethnographic—have examined the sexualization and objectification of the female body within public spaces as well as popular imagination (Prasad, 2005; Schaffer, 2006; Roy, 2012). The first name that comes to mind here is Shilpa Phadke, Sameera Khan, Shilpa Ranade's study titled *Why Loiter?: Women and Risk on Mumbai Streets* (2011) which has in the past powerfully claimed that even though women enjoy increased access to urban public spaces in twenty first century, they still do not have equal claim as men to these spaces. Other works by Phadke that deserve mention in this context are her articles titled "You Can Be Lonely in a Crowd: The Production of Safety in Mumbai" (2005) and "Unfriendly Bodies, Hostile Cities: Reflections on Loitering and Gendered Public Space" (2013) which discuss issues such as the flawed safety discourse, women's right to public spaces as citizens, and particularly, class and religious implications of women's access to such spaces. Tellingly, Phadke celebrates loitering as a radical act that could reclaim the rights and safety of city spaces for Indian women. Adding to this, noteworthy empirical studies include names such as Madan and Nalla's essay titled "Sexual Harassment in Public Spaces: Examining Gender Differences in Perceived Seriousness and Victimization" (2016) which uses multistage cluster and quota sampling methods in the capital city of India, New Delhi, to examine the pervasive presence of gender-based oppression in public spaces including bus stops, metros, roadsides, and the public transport. Further, Shilpa Ranade's study, "The Way She Moves: Mapping the Everyday Production of Gender-Space" examines how female bodies locate themselves within as well as move through gendered urban public spaces and the larger politics of women's everyday mobilties. Likewise, based on her extensive mapping of four public spaces in Mumbai, namely, Central Avenue, Zaveri Bazaar, Nariman Point, and Kalachowki, Ranade argues that "it is the male body that is normative" (2007, 1525–1526) in patriarchal public spaces while "female body becomes a marker of difference" and thus, "fraught with anxiety" (2007, 1526). Hence, in their everyday occupation of public spaces, Ranade claims, Indian women "perform their femininity and simultaneously legitimise their being 'out of place'" (2007, 1526). Similarly, Kalpana Viswanath and Surabhi Tandon Mehrotra in "'Shall We Go Out?' Women's Safety in Public Spaces in Delhi" (2007) conduct around 30 "safety-audits" around the city of New Delhi to find that high rates of violence severely hamper women from accessing the freedom that urban public spaces often offer.

In another empirical study based in New Delhi, "Street Harassment: A Qualitative Study of the Experiences of Young Women in Delhi" (2014), Megha Dhillon and Suparna Bakaya observe that the possibility of street harassment in public places "[control] several aspects of . . . [women's] lives, including their timings of travel, choice of clothing, and behavior in the public sphere" (9). The researchers demand a better monitoring of public spaces and effective redressal mechanisms to reduce instances of harassment. Cultural geographer Rituparna Bhattacharyya uses questionnaire surveys and open-ended interviews in her article "Understanding the Spatialities of Sexual Assault against Indian Women in India" (2015) to state that sexual assault against women in public space that manifests as comments on their body, stalking, and insults to "barbaric forms of rapes and gang rapes" (1350) and the fear of their occurrence severely shackles women's mobility. In another empirical study based in the city of Kolkata, "Safe in the City? Negotiating Safety, Public Space and the Male Gaze in Kolkata, India" (2021), Roy and Bailey conduct in-depth interviews and surveys to assert that women often internalize the processes of negotiation while venturing onto unsafe public spaces and prefer "avoidance and protective strategies" (3) over confronting their harassers. Reasserting the possibilities that urban public spaces offer women, Atreyee Sen, Raminder Kaur, and Emilija Zabiliūtė in "(En)countering Sexual Violence in the Indian City" (2019) bemoan that "cities such as Delhi, Mumbai and Chennai, can exacerbate gender-based violence" even as they paradoxically "provide sanctuaries of respite and resilience" (4) for women. Notably, Vinnarasan Aruldoss and Sevasti-Melissa Nolas in "Tracing Indian Girls' Embodied Orientations towards Public Life" (2019) critique the scant academic attention on young girls' lived experiences by remarking that young girls "are not impervious to everyday abuse and violence in public places such as schools and neighbourhoods" (1589), but in fact are more susceptible to them. In the light of three case studies from different socio-cultural backgrounds, the scholars note that "the violence orchestrated on female bodies in everyday mundane activities" adversely affects their "access and participation in public life" (1603). Clearly, all such studies point toward the need to make public spaces safer for women.

Among other socio-scientific studies, an edited volume titled *Violence against Women in India* (2019) by N. Prabha Unnithan and Mahesh K. Nalla draws upon criminology to examine the characteristics and degree of male violence against Indian women. Holding a larger patriarchal ethos to be the root of the problem discussed so far, Priyanka Dubey's *No Nation for Women: Reportage on Rape from India, the World's Largest Democracy* (2013) elaborates on how "[p]atriarchy is the nucleus of this problem and all other factors contributing to violence against women manifest themselves around it" (viii) while strongly condemning the brutal rape culture and the yearly rise in crimes against women. Among studies that examine cinematic representations of sexual violence, Srividya Ramasubramanian and Mary Beth Oliver's essay "Portrayals of Sexual Violence in Popular Hindi Films, 1997–99" (2003) deliberate upon how commercial Hindi films depict moderate sexual violence as fun, non-serious, and as an expression of romantic love. Likewise, Uttara Manohar and Susan L. Kline's essay "Sexual Assault Portrayals in Hindi Cinema" (2014) studies 24 Hindi films released between 2000 and 2012 to state how stereotypical depictions of sexual assault in movies perpetuate an environment of violence in society. Such studies provide a steppingstone for books such as the present one and helps investigate the outdoorsy experiences of women on neoliberal Indian roads. They inform how sexual vulnerability and misogyny go hand in hand to apparently put women in their "place" through the acts of assault and rape which turn are punishments accorded to women for venturing into patriarchal public spaces "forbidden" to them.

Cognizant of existing empirical and ethnographic studies on women's mobility and driven by imaginative and real-life narratives of women's journeys, this book is thematically divided into six sections. Each section of this book focuses on distinct journey narrative(s)—either in fact or in fiction—by deploying relevant theoretical paradigms. The first section of this book is entitled *Hostile Terrains, Empowering Textual Spaces: Neoliberal Literature and the Female Traveler* and initiates an analysis of literary depictions of outdoorsy women and the problems they face in public spaces such as roads. Appropriately, the volume opens with a chapter entitled "No Longer Innocent: Male Gaze, Violence, and Female Kinship in Kishwar Desai's *The Sea of Innocence*" by Swathi Krishna S. and Srirupa Chatterjee. The authors examine Desai's postmillennial novel that was published in 2013—a year after the notorious "Nirbhaya" gang rape case of New Delhi, India—to argue that even as contemporary India boasts of many freedoms, a larger culture of misogyny continues to threaten women who venture unattended into its public spaces. Krishna S. and Chatterjee focus upon Desai's recurring narrator protagonist, Simran Singh, who almost single handedly investigates an actual crime wherein a British teenager is raped and murdered in Goa, India in the year 2008. The chapter, thus, while grappling with a patriarchal cultural ethos, a tardy judicial system, and an indifferent police force, demonstrates how victim blaming is often the only response that violated women receive; and that women's (and right-thinking men's) solidarity is perhaps the only recourse women have toward hope as they travel through hostile public spaces. The second chapter in this section is titled "Peripheral Urbanization as Queer Identity in Arundhati Roy's *The Ministry of Utmost Happiness*" and is written by Jana Fedtke. Presenting a critical analysis of Roy's latest novel, Fedtke in this chapter examines how the narrative's transgender protagonist,

Anjum, experiences public spaces—specifically in Delhi, India—as a hijra (eunuch or hermaphrodite). Fedtke not only underscores how the so-called third gender inhabits the intersections of space and gender, but also vocally critiques how if people with alternate gender identities have found legal recognition, within the nation's cultural imagination they continue to be treated as the abominable "other." With the help of Teresa Caldeira's thesis on peripheral urbanization, Fedtke therefore speaks of social construction of spaces while examining the threats and perils Anjum (presenting herself as female) faces within public spaces and also questions heteronormativity and spatial construction in neoliberal India. Continuing with fictional depictions of women's experiences of gendered public spaces, the third chapter of this section entitled "Mirrors of Reality: Toxic Masculinity, Traveling Women, and the Representation of Acid Attack Victim-Survivors in *Priya's Mirror*" by Nidhi Shrivastava explores graphic narratives that foreground gut-wrenching accounts of acid attack victims. An acid attack, as Shrivastava points out, is a crime rampant against women especially in South Asia. Describing the life of "acid attack victim-survivors" as "social death," Shrivastava crafts her essay in consultation with Monica Singh, Ram Devineni (the creator of the *Priya's Shakti* series), and Paromita Vohra to argue that acid attack victim-survivors are living testimonials to horrors defining misogynistic public spaces even in neoliberal times. If the chapter showcases how graphic narratives such as *Priya's Mirror* can be educational tools toward gender sensitivity for Indian children and adults alike, it also powerfully condemns acid attack which often happens in public spaces as a heinous crime against women while also urging society to accept instead of stigmatizing survivors of such gendered violence.

The second section of this edited collection is titled *Bollywood's Traveling Women (I): Misogyny, Roads, and Female Vulnerability*. This forms the first segment of essays on narrative analysis of Bollywood cinema which is legendarily entwined with the nation's popular imagination. This section and the next focuses on Bollywood cinema that has variously attempted to represent women's experiences of travel, both in the twentieth century as well as in postmillennial India. The first chapter of section two is titled "Stepping Out: Global Bollywood, Gendered Landscape, and Undercurrents of Neoliberal Pleasures" and is written by Madhuja Mukherjee. Known for her astute writings on Indian cinema, Mukherjee in this essay attempts a narrative analysis of Bollywood films, starting with productions of the post-independence era and concluding with contemporary Hindi cinema. More important, Mukherjee underscores the issue of travel in Hindi cinema by deploying the trope of the female wanderer or the *flaneur/flaneuse* in popular films to reveal how women's freedom of movement is often compromised. The wandering female protagonist of Hindi films, claims the author, is mostly viewed as an anomalous being who is at best an ethereal and at worst an eroticized creature—either fetishized or punished—but is never granted normalcy. Rightly, then, if Mukherjee's essay historicizes Hindi cinema by foregrounding its megacities and the perils faced by traveling women therein, the next chapter in this section titled "Celluloid Women Rewriting Rules of Travel in Contemporary Hindi Cinema" by Rima Bhattacharya examines two recent Hindi films where the issue of women's vulnerability in public spaces is presented with disturbing urgency. Bhattacharya in this chapter close reads the narratives of two postmillennial Hindi films, namely, *Mardaani 2* (2019) and *Chhapaak* (2020) with the help of feminist geographers who have contested gendering of spaces and the ensuing perils women face due to such spatial demarcations. The author claims that postmillennial Hindi cinema, like the ones she examines, present a clarion call against sexual and other crimes Indian women face when on the road. Bhattacharya ends the chapter with the hope that new age Hindi films which showcase instances of gendered violence in public spaces may not only sensitize the audience toward the problem but also represent the evolving landscape of neoliberal India where women (and in fact everyone) may traverse freely. Bhattacharya's chapter, then, adds to the much-needed voice addressing the popular medium of Hindi cinema and how it can impact enabling discourses on women's safety in public spaces.

Carrying forward the discussion on both cinema's connections with and its role in defining popular perception on women and public spaces, the third section of this edited volume is entitled *Bollywood's Traveling Women (II): Vexed Dualities of Freedom and Fear*. The first chapter in this section, "The Conditional Promise of Empowerment and Pleasure: An Intersectional Analysis of Hindi Film Portrayals of Women Navigating Public Spaces in India" by Uttara Manohar, presents an interesting take on films produced in neoliberal times which have variously represented women navigating public spaces. Borrowing from both Indian and western feminist geographers and women's rights theorists, Manohar in this essay focuses on "hierarchies of caste, religion, geography, and class" as they "are represented in Hindi film depictions of women's experiences in public spaces." Hence, if Manohar views public spaces as sites of neoliberal freedom for women in some films, she argues how in others the same freedoms are often transformed into fears. In sum, Manohar claims that most contemporary Hindi films, either implicitly or explicitly, demonstrate that gender and cultural hierarchies govern women's movements within public spaces. The next chapter in this section is entitled "Traveling Women and Their Male Companions: Framing Risks and Vulnerabilities in Indian Road Films" and is written by Pronoti Baglary. In this essay Baglary outlines an interesting duality with the help of two Hindi films produced in neoliberal times, namely, *Dil Se* (1998) and *Mr. and Mrs. Iyer* (2002). Focusing on the sharply contrasting experiences of men and women as they travel, Baglary in this essay not only examines India's public spaces for the rich diversity of caste, class, gender, and community they exhibit, but also compares how traveling women experience such diversity when they travel alone and when they are accompanied by male companions. More important, Baglary points out that roads and public spaces remain specifically male dominated and while male companions often help and protect their female counterparts, the possibility of them turning into sexual predators also often lurks in the background. Simply put, the author in this essay examines narrative plotlines of Hindi cinema to advocate freedom and safety for women within the nation's public spaces.

Following a comprehensive discussion on Hindi cinema vis-à-vis women's experiences of public spaces, the fourth section of this collection entitled *Troubles of the Outdoorsy Woman: Multiple Genres/Multiple Voices* examines once again the representations of women within neoliberal public spaces and emphasizes how several hurdles befall the lone woman on the road. Far from simply romanticizing travel as an emancipatory or an adventurous act alone, this section with the help of women's narratives selected from various genres examines how women—even when they access public spaces to fulfill their day-to-day tasks and responsibilities—are beleaguered by several challenges. It begins with and essay entitled "Roads, Dreams, and Violence: Tracing the Mental Landscape of India's Domestic Workers" by Bonnie Zare and Ditto Prasad which powerfully captures experiences of women belonging largely to the nation's working class, both in fact and in fiction. Zare and Prasad undertake an analysis of the figure of the house maid or the domestic worker who forms a sizeable portion of the nation's impoverished sections. Further, by drawing upon India's regional and Hindi cinema along with fictional and real-life instances, the authors treat journey not only as moments of physical travel but also view it as a metaphor for domestic workers and house maids whose dreams and aspirations maybe compared to journeys they make toward a better life. With the help of space theorists and social research surrounding the nation's labor force, the authors in this chapter therefore assert that roads—both in reality and in imagination—are hostile and often cruel spaces for women, especially those hailing from the unorganized sector among the working classes. The next chapter in this section, "Negotiating Violence and Traversing the City: Female Vulnerability in *Delhi Crime* (2019) and *She* (2020)" by Shreya Rastogi and Srirupa Chatterjee, undertakes a scrutiny of two immensely popular recent Hindi web series that address the vexed issue women's journeys. The writers focus on *Delhi Crime* and *She*, web series which are based on the infamous Nirbhaya rape case of 2012 and the sexual perils faced by an undercover lady officer, respectively. The authors note how public spaces, specifically the roads and specifically at night, are perilous sites for the woman traveler. In both web series, which have received significant critical acclaim, Rastogi and Chatterjee point out how a lone woman out on the streets at night is not only an easy target for the notorious male gaze and male lust, but also is an easy target for societal misogyny which blames the woman, should any harm befall her. In all, the authors in this chapter with the help of feminist geographers and gender rights activists claim that a rape culture and a shockingly rampant display of misogyny undo the hard-won freedoms of women in neoliberal times and prevent them from fearlessly exploring the nation's roads.

Having examined multi-generic fictional representations of women's experiences of public spaces, the next section of this edited volume turns toward the real-life predicaments of women across Indian cities as they access public spaces, and is accordingly titled *Struggle for Survival: Working Women and Pitfalls of Indian Roads*. Based on narratives of real women who were interviewed through the last decade by the authors, this section makes a powerful case for women's uninhibited and free access to public spaces including the road. The first chapter in this section is entitled "Working Night Shifts, Traversing Neoliberal Roads: Spatial-Temporal Confluence and the Male Gaze" and is written by Sucharita Sen. In this chapter Sen uses an ethnographic lens to interview women working in Business Process Outsourcing (BPO)" industry in Kolkata, India. Sen points out that while Kolkata boasts of being a modern metropolitan city in neoliberal times, its public spaces continue to be governed by hegemonic patriarchal gender norms and sexual codes. Using narratives of pseudonymous woman participants as case studies, the author in this essay points out how women employed in the BPO sector often shoulder the economic burden of their dependent family members while also managing a demanding professional life defined by odd work hours and nightly commutes through hostile cityscapes. Sen points out that if such women are compelled to dodge the threatening male gaze that especially haunts them at night, they are also obliged to defend themselves against social stigma which chastises women for going out to work at night. In sum, the author in this essay argues that working women deserve roads devoid of threats of gendered violence such that they may fully engage with and find true fulfilment in their professional (and personal) lives. Adding to narratives on neoliberal India's working women and the threats they experience within gendered public spaces, the next chapter in this section entitled "Women Journalists Negotiating Space in India's 'Small' Cities" by Ranu Tomar presents a persuasive take on women journalists who often battle sexism and sexual vulnerability as they perform their routine professional duties. Like Sen, Tomar in this chapter uses narratives of pseudonymous woman participants who are variously engaged in the field of journalism, a profession which essentially demands that one functions outdoors. The author deliberately locates her cases in "small" towns of central India where age old traditions on gender roles define the socio-cultural ethos. Tomar claims that not only do women journalists hailing from "small" towns face gender discrimination at work but also find public spaces—where they must find their newsworthy "beats"—extremely hostile. This, claims Tomar, is often accompanied by a general apathy toward gender sensitization in "small" towns where sexism and sexual harassment is both normalized and accepted in most cases. Tomar sums up the essay with questions on women's rights as citizens of neoliberal India, and demands safer and friendlier public spaces for women.

The final section of this book provides a fitting closure to the overall debates generated by the preceding segments and the constituent chapters. It is entitled *Traveling Solo, Traveling Strong: Women Braving Neoliberal Roads* and includes an essay, "Travel with Care: Reinforcing Patriarchy through Tips for Solo Female Travelers in India" by Kiranpreet Kaur Baath. While this chapter underscores the exploratory freedoms that modernity has to offer contemporary women, it also highlights the pitfalls that women on the move are susceptible to. Hence, if Kaur in this essay presents a deglamorized account of solo women who undertake travel and adventure for pleasure and fulfilment, she also outlines how in braving the roads solo women travelers must grapple with many uncertainties and threats of violence. Drawing her data from social media posts, online resources, and guidebooks for solo women travelers which are inundated with "tips" on women's safety, Kaur not only questions masculinization of public spaces such as roads but also demands unconditional freedoms for enabling women's mobility. In conclusion, the author posits hope in possibilities of women reclaiming roads for themselves and enjoying uninhibited movement that modern avenues of travel offer.

By bringing together a multitude of critical voices that assess, question, and reframe conditions of women's access to public spaces in contemporary India, this book hopes to add to the much needed and ongoing debate around women's rights to the road and other non-domestic spaces. It draws upon feminist geographers, cultural theorists, space theorists, and gender rights activists, among others, from India and the rest of the world to assert that as lawful citizens women need and deserve an unquestioned right to their mobility. Essentially, then, this book intends to augment not only the efforts of organizations such as the National Commission for Women and the National Human Rights Commission of India in making public spaces safe for women, but also to question and change a culture of sexism and misogyny that challenges the rights and privileges of traveling women. It brings together essays that attempt critically informed analyses of literature, graphic novels, films, web series, and other popular culture representations of Indian women's experiences on the road, and ultimately initiate localized feminist interventions against gendered violence. In bringing together various genres with critically nuanced fictional and factual narratives of traveling women, this book therefore becomes a platform for a multitude of voices that demand safe and congenial public spaces and roads for contemporary Indian women. Thus, entitled *Gendered Violence in Public Spaces: Women's Narratives of Travel in Neoliberal India* this book hopes to strengthen the much-needed and ongoing scholarly discussion on women and their experiences on the road. By focusing on the complex negotiations that women undertake while moving through public spaces, this edited volume compiles critical and scholarly voices that together address a deep rooted and pressing problem fettering Indian women's mobility today and concludes with the hope that one day public spaces, especially the roads, will become both welcoming and empowering for one and all.

REFERENCES

"78% Women Experienced Violence in Public Places, Reports Survey." 2021. *Deccan Chronicle*, March 6, 2021. www.deccanchronicle.com/nation/current-affairs/060321/78-of-women-experienced-violence-in-public-places-study.html.

Armstrong, Elisabeth. 2014. *Gender and Neoliberalism: The All-India Democratic Women's Association and Globalization Politics*. New York: Routledge.

Aruldoss, Vinnarasan and Sevasti-Melissa Nolas. 2019. "Tracing Indian Girls' Embodied Orientations towards Public Life." *Gender, Place and Culture: A Journal of Feminist Geography* 26, no. 11 (May): 1588–1608. doi.org/10.1080/0966369X.2019.1586649.

Bannerji, Himani. 2016. "Patriarchy in the Era of Neoliberalism: The Case of India." *Social Scientist* 44, no. 3/4 (March–April): 3–27. www.jstor.org/stable/24890241.

Bhattacharyya, Rituparna. 2016. "Street Violence against Women in India: Mapping Prevention Strategies." *Asian Social Work and Policy Review* 10, no. 3 (July): 311–325. doi.org/10.1111/aswp.12099.

———. 2015. "Understanding the Spatialities of Sexual Assault against Indian Women in India." *Gender, Place & Culture: A Journal of Feminist Geography* 22, no. 9 (October): 1340–1356. doi.org/10.1080/0966369X.2014.969684.

Chandrasekhar, C.P. 2021. "Indian Neoliberalism: A Toxic Gift from Global Finance." *Frontline*, September 6. frontline.thehindu.com/cover-story/indian-neoliberalism-economic-reforms-at-30-a-toxic-gift-from-global-finance/article36290562.ece.

Datta, Anindita, ed. 2021. *Gender, Space and Agency in India: Exploring Regional Genderscapes*. New York: Routledge.

Dhillon, Megha and Suparna Bakaya. 2014. "Street Harassment: A Qualitative Study of the Experiences of Young Women in Delhi." *Sage Open* 4, no. 3 (July): 1–11. doi.org/10.1177/2158244014543786.

Dubey, Priyanka. 2018. *No Nation for Women: Reportage on Rape from India, the World's Largest Democracy*. New York: Simon and Schuster.

Harvey, David. 2008. "The Right to the City." *New Left Review* 53, no. 2 (September/October). newleftreview.org/issues/ii53/articles/david-harvey-the-right-to-the-city.

Lefebvre, Henri and Michael J. Enders. 1976. "Reflections on the Politics of Space." *Antipode* 8, no. 2 (May): 30–37. doi.org/10.1111/j.1467-8330.1976.tb00636.x.

Madan, Manish and Mahesh K. Nalla. 2016. "Sexual Harassment in Public Spaces: Examining Gender Differences in Perceived Seriousness and Victimization." *International Criminal Justice Review* 26, no. 2 (March): 80–97. doi.org/10.1177/1057567716639093.

Massey, Doreen. 1994. *Space, Place, and Gender*. Minneapolis: University of Minnesota Press.

McDowell, Linda. 1999. *Gender, Identity and Place: Understanding Feminist Geographies*. Minneapolis: University of Minnesota Press.

Minh-Ha, Trinh. 1994. "Other Than Myself/My Other Self." In *Traveler's Tales: Narratives of Home and Displacement*, edited by George Robertson et al., 9–26. New York: Routledge.

Mohammad, Rubina. 2017. "Feminist Geography." In *The International Encyclopedia of Geography*, edited by Douglas Richardson et al., 1–12. Hoboken, NJ: John Wiley & Sons.

Pain, Rachel H. 1997. "Social Geographies of Women's Fear of Crime." *Transactions of the Institute of British Geographers* 22, no. 2: 231–244. www.jstor.org/stable/622311.

Phadke, Shilpa. 2013. "Unfriendly Bodies, Hostile Cities: Reflections on Loitering and Gendered Public Space." *Economic & Political Weekly* 48, no. 39 (September): 50–59. www.jstor.org/stable/23528480.

Phadke, Shilpa, Sameera Khan, and Shilpa Ranade. 2011. *Why Loiter? Women and Risk on Mumbai Streets*. New Delhi: Penguin Books.

Prasad, Kira, ed. 2005. *Women and Media: Challenging Feminist Discourse*. London: The Women's Press.

Raju, Saraswati and Tanusree Paul. 2018. "Public Spaces and Places: Gendered Intersectionalities in Indian Cities." In *India's Contemporary Urban Conundrum*, edited by Sujata Patel and Omita Goyal, 128–138. London: Routledge.

Ranade, Shilpa. 2007. "The Way She Moves: Mapping the Everyday Production of Gender-Space." *Economic and Political Weekly* 42, no. 17 (May): 1519–1526. www.jstor.org/stable/4419518.

Rose, Gillian. 1993. *Feminism and Geography: The Limits of Geographical Knowledge*. Cambridge: Polity Press.

Roy, Sanghamitra and Ajay Bailey. 2021. "Safe in the City? Negotiating Safety, Public Space and the Male Gaze in Kolkata, India." *Cities: The International Journal of Urban Policy and Planning* 117 (October): 1–11. doi.org/10.1016/j.cities.2021.103321.

Roy, Subhas Singha. 2012. "Portrayal of Women in Indian Media in the Era of Neo-Liberal Economy." *Global Media Journal* 3, no. 1 (June): 1–5. www.caluniv.ac.in/global-mdia-journal/Commentaries/C4%20S%20S%20ROY.pdf.

Schaffer, Sharada J. 2006. *Privileging the Privileged-Gender in Indian Advertising*. New Delhi: Promila and Company.

Sen, Atreyee, Raminder Kaur, and Emilija Zabiliūtė. 2019. "(En)countering Sexual Violence in the Indian City." *Gender, Place and Culture: A Journal of Feminist Geography* 27, no. 1 (May): 1–12. doi.org/10.1080/0966369X.2019.1612856.

Soja, Edward W. 1989. *Postmodern Geographies: The Reassertion of Space in Critical Social Theory*. London: Verso.

Valentine, Gill. 1989. "The Geography of Women's Fear." *Area* 21, no. 4 (December): 385–390. www.jstor.org/stable/20000063.

Viswanath, Kalpana and Surabhi Tandon Mehrotra. 2007. "'Shall We Go Out?' Women's Safety in Public Spaces in Delhi." *Economic and Political Weekly* 42, no. 17 (May): 1542–1548. www.jstor.org/stable/4419521.

NOTES

1. Historically, the terms space and place have been theorized as disjoined binaries with space being "static, fixed, and bounded" while place as the realm of "lived experiences" (Raju and Paul 2018, 129). However, cultural and feminist geographers, over time, reconceptualized space/place as interconnected milieus claiming that "space provides the physical locale through which meanings and subjective positioning, with implications for lived experiences, are expressed" (129) Focusing on the differences as well as convergence between space and place, Doreen Massey claims, "space and place are constructed in the same manner as, and both reflect and affect, the contemporarily dominant western modes of conceptualizing gender" (1994, 13).

2. The notorious "Nirbhaya" case refers to the violent gang rape and murder of a twenty-two-year-old physiotherapy student named Jyoti Singh on a moving bus in the capital city of India, New Delhi in 2012. The incident and the mass public outrage and media outcry that followed "induced the issue of VAW [violence against women] to the core of political discourse" (Bhattacharyya 2015). In many ways, the Nirbhaya incident was a watershed event that led to fundamental judicial and legislative changes wherein the Government of India "announced a total non-lapsable Nirbhaya fund of INR 20 billion to escalate women's safety in public spaces" (Bhattacharyya 2015). Considering the centrality of the case in the discussions on women's safety in Indian public spaces, Nirbhaya features in a number of chapters of this book.

3. This volume focuses on women's narratives of travel in neoliberal India, a period that roughly is associated with the early 1990s when massive financial, political, and cultural changes were initiated within the nation. As mentioned, the liberalization of Indian economy (or the beginnings of neoliberalism) can be traced back to the 1990s when the government redistributed "income and assets in favour of financial capital and big business" and with this, the "inflow of foreign capital enhanced, exports success ensured, and growth accelerated" (Chandrasekhar 2012). However, the pitfalls included increased poverty, deprivation, and social degeneration. Feminist scholar Elisabeth Armstrong tellingly notes that the "precarious social value of women eroded further in these patriarchal economic regimes" under the Indian "variant of neoliberalism" (2014, 1).

PART I

Hostile Terrains, Empowering Textual Spaces

Neoliberal Literature and the Female Traveler

Chapter 1

No Longer Innocent

Male Gaze, Violence, and Female Kinship in Kishwar Desai's
The Sea of Innocence

Swathi Krishna S. and Srirupa Chatterjee

"Was it a larger problem that an apparently modernizing India did not know how to deal with female sexuality, assumed that normal, friendly behaviour and western clothes meant that the women were available?" (26), asks a concerned Kishwar Desai in her investigative crime thriller, *The Sea of Innocence* (2013). Desai dedicates this novel to Jyoti Singh of the infamous Delhi gang rape of 2012 and to thousands of women raped and murdered in modern India. Narrated from the perspective of Simran Singh, a feminist social worker turned investigator who appears in the writer's other works such as *Witness the Night* (2010), *Origins of Love* (2012), *The Sea of Innocence* bemoans the disturbing dispensability of women in India's misogynistic public spaces by presenting the rape and murder of a British teenager, Liza Kay, in the seemingly tranquil beaches of Goa, India. Liza's story has obvious parallels with the assault and murder of fifteen-year-old Scarlett Keeling from Devon, England at Anjuna beach in Goa after a Valentine's Day beach party in 2008. When the partially clad and drugged body of Scarlett surfaces from the ocean, mainstream Indian media is quick to scrutinize Keeling's addictions and "reckless" lifestyle which it claims are antithetical to Indian "values." Writing at a time when the nation was embroiled in protests for Nirbhaya's justice, Desai questions a faltering judicial system and foregrounds the intricacies of women's complex negotiations (irrespective of their nationality) with India's misogynistic public spaces. This essay studies the vicious male gaze and the resultant violence that mar women's experiences of public spaces and then examines how the female kinship that emerges from shared experiences of victimization often proves to be the only solace against female vulnerability within public spaces.

GENDERED SPACES AND MODERN FEMALE TRAVELERS: LIZA, SIMRAN, SCARLETT, AND NIRBHAYA

While explaining how her book engages with the shocking reality of gender-based violence in contemporary India, Desai poses urgent questions on the declining status of Indian women: "why was the Indian state silent while its women were being attacked, within families and out on the streets? Where was the justice and the sympathy? And why didn't Indian women speak out more strongly against what was being done to them?" (Desai 2013b). *The Sea of Innocence* is the writer's attempt to address this complex reality in order to "[disturb] and [mobilise]" the readers against "gender-based violence" (Desai 2013b) in modern India. When the novel begins, Desai's feminist heroine Simran finds her holiday in Goa with her adopted teenage daughter Durga ruined when she receives a disturbing video clipping of a teenaged white girl being molested by a group of young beach boys. The narrative informs: "a pale flame flickering amongst four dark-skinned boys who crowded around her" (Desai 2013a, 1). Simran distressingly notices how the girl struggles against the boy "who continue[s] to grope her" (2013a, 2). The video is sent to her by Amarjit, a senior police officer from Delhi and Simran's ex-boyfriend, who seeks her help to investigate about the British girl, identified as Liza Kay, who has gone missing. Amarjit urges Simran to conduct discreet investigations about Liza since a high-profile case involving a British girl here is likely to "hurt the image of the country, and even affect tourism" (2013a, 29) and the government didn't want Goa "to look unsafe" (2013a, 31) for women. The sexual overtures of the video clipping and the apparent vulnerability of the underage girl upset Simran and she disconcertingly realizes how Goa is no longer "an oasis of safety" (44). Instead, Simran finds groups of Indian men "ogling at western women, photographing their bodies . . . [as] their privacy . . . [gets] intruded upon" (44). Simran berates herself for her "foolish assumption" that the "Goan beaches would be safer than the streets of Delhi for women and young girls" (13). Here she clearly refers to the brutal gang rape and torture resulting in the death of a physiotherapy student Jyoti Singh, widely referred to as *Nirbhaya* (the fearless one). Globally infamous now, Nirbhaya was gang raped on a wintery night on a moving bus in Delhi in 2012. Desai cleverly incorporates the most horrific details of the Nirbhaya incident in her novel which even mainstream newspapers were reluctant to print (Byrnes 2013). With graphic details the writer narrates how the victim "whose intestines had been ripped out with an iron rod, lay unconscious on the [Delhi] street" (2013a, 42) on the night of the fateful event. Defending her multiple references to the Nirbhaya case in *The Sea of Innocence*, Desai insists that she never "pushed that case into the book" and instead "it all seemed to be telling a larger story of the kind of society we live in and . . . what happens to a lot of women in this country" (qtd. in Bhattacharya 2013). Undoubtedly, Delhi and most cities, towns, and villages of contemporary India remain governed by patriarchal values that often treat women merely as sexual objects who can be violated and discarded at will.

Notably, feminist geographer Doreen Massey affirms how "spaces and places, and our senses of them . . . are gendered through and through . . . [and] this gendering of space and place both reflects *and has effects back on* the ways in which gender is constructed and understood in the societies in which we live" (1994, 186; italics in the original). She further notes that the "limitation of women's mobility, in terms both of identity and space, has been in some cultural contexts a crucial means of subordination" (179). Similarly, Rose Gillian remarks how "fears of attack" (1993, 71) can turn spaces as "enemy itself" and "[t]his fear is partly about being defined as a woman" (71). Theorizing women's "geography of fear" (1989, 385), Gill Valentine contends that unlike men women in public experience their personal space invaded by whistles, comments or sexual overtures and according to her, "[w]omen's inhibited use and occupation of public space is . . . a spatial expression of patriarchy" (1989, 389). Such experiences have a universality for women, and Indian women are especially vulnerable to the nation's "geography of fear." Reasserting such views for the Indian context, Dhillon and Bakaya (2014) in their study on street harassment against young women in Delhi claim that harassment and violence "[reduce] the physical and geographical mobility of women, preventing them from appearing alone in public space and in the process accomplishing an 'informal ghettoization' of women to the private space of the home" (7). Likewise, examining the intersections of "public space, gender, women and fear," Bhattacharyya asserts that "public spaces of India are a male domain and suffer greatly from hegemonic patriarchy and power" (2015, 1344). The above studies reiterate that public spaces are thoroughly gendered and women's restricted access in such spaces sustains and perpetuates time-worn gender hierarchies.

Women's studies expert, Holly Jennifer Morgan, observes that given the writer's journalistic training, Desai's works "bridge the gaps between fiction and reality as she draws parallels between real and fictional cases and fictionalizes real events to support her narratives" (2020, 11). Hence, in addition to Scarlett Keeling and Nirbhaya, Desai alludes to the mysterious death of a nineteen-year-old Russian girl Elena Sukhanova on a railway track leading to Mumbai from Goa and notes that "more than eighty women [are] raped in the country every day" and that in Goa the "highest number of victims [are] British, followed by Russians" (2013a, 103). Observing Desai's references to real life rape cases in the course of the narrative, reviewer Madeline Clements remarks how Desai makes "[n]o attempt . . . to hide her determination to use literature to expose real social issues, particularly the (violent, sexual) use and abuse of young women, and their worrying dispensability in 'modern' India" (2013). Delving deeper into the vulnerability of women in patriarchal public spaces in India, Desai's heroine narrates the dichotomy of life on Goan beaches which appears "serenely cosmopolitan on the surface" but with "a looming darkness around the edges. Like a hungry nocturnal sea animal . . . seeking victims" (2013a, 14). Obviously, if such spaces simulate conditions of women's safety, they do so largely for the purposes of promoting tourism. In reality, such spaces are in no manner free from threats of gender and sexual violence. In the narrative therefore Simran during her frantic search for the whereabouts of Liza Kay herself experiences intense sexual threats as she attracts the unwanted attention of a group of Indian men in a beach shack. Naturally, Simran begins questioning her own choice of attire for attracting such unwanted attention and ruminates: "Perhaps it was my off-the-shoulder cotton dress and the fact that I was sitting alone [that led to this situation]" (40). However, she disconcertingly realizes that it is her second encounter with the young men who salaciously used a cheap pick-up line on her while she was floating on the waves. Even though their impudence infuriates Simran, she is quick to realize that "present day India offers little room for arguments on the street, and even less on the beach, especially for single women . . . even more so if she was in a swimsuit" (2013a, 41–42). With this sad realization, Simran makes a quick retreat with her daughter to the safety of her hotel room.

TO TRAVEL OR NOT TO TRAVEL? WOMEN'S FORAY INTO INDIA'S HOSTILE PUBLIC SPACES

Simran's fear and insecurity on the beaches of Goa can be contextualized in the light of postulations by feminist academician Shilpa Ranade who maps women's everyday negotiations of public spaces in Mumbai, India in her article, "The Way She Moves: Mapping the Everyday Production of Gender-Space." Ranade claims that "access to space is socio-culturally determined" (2007, 1520) and also notes that within male dominated public spaces in India such as paan-shops (shops selling betel leaf), tea shops, lottery shops, and bars, women feel a sense of "discomfort" (Ranade 2007, 1522). Addressing the pathetic state of affairs, Ranade also asserts:

> While safety is too closely associated to actual, physical violence, discomfort falls in the in-between space of implied threat—a sense of being made to feel that you are in the wrong place/time. This is done through being looked at, verbally assaulted (cat-calls), and very often through self-policing by women themselves. In their daily negotiation of the street, we realised, women were making implicit and often unconscious decisions about where to walk in a way that they could manufacture this comfort for themselves. (Ranade 2007, 1522)

In a similar vein, Kalpana Viswanath's and Surabhi Mehrotra's surveys and safety audits in the city of Delhi reveal how women access public spaces differently when compared to men due to higher rates of gendered violence against them. The duo find that women feel "uncomfortable in male dominated spaces such as cigarette shops, "'dhabas' (roadside tea and food stalls), taxi stands, certain street corners, helmet stands in car parks, liquor shops, and certain parks" where they "not only hesitate to use any of these spaces but also are reluctant to be near them for fear of harassment" (Viswanath and Mehrotra 2007, 1546). Clearly, women's everyday access to public spaces remains hugely threatened in contemporary India.

Unfortunately, Indian women regularly face street harassment, commonly known as "eve-teasing" which is rampant in public spaces such as parks, public transport, and bus stations, among others. Eve-teasing here implies "making passes, obscene gestures, whistling, staring, pinching, fondling, and rubbing" (Dhillon and Bakaya 2014, 2). It often begins with milder cases of mental harassment but can easily escalate into painful instances of sexual molestation. According to Dhillon and Bakaya street harassment is "a key factor in determining how women negotiated their lives in the city, how safe they felt, and the amount of freedom they had in accessing public spaces, particularly at certain times" (2014, 2). Simran in Desai's novel negotiates her fear of assault with "a hasty retreat" (Desai 2013a, 42) from the potential situation of violence and as researchers Roy and Bailey note "[w]omen in most cases resist responding to the harassments in fear of retaliation" (2021, 3), and instead they "continually engage in self-regulation, limit their mobility, avoid going to particular places, avoid wearing particular dresses, avoid going out alone at night, take family or friends along, and carry protective gadgets" (2021, 3). Drawing upon the theoretical positions discussed so far, it is apparent that women's fear of sexual harassment and violence curtail their mobility and freedom and affect their access to public spaces (Phadke 2007; Bhattacharyya 2015; Dhillon and Bakaya 2014) regularly and recurrently.

THE MYTH OF SAFETY?
LIZA'S RAPE IN COSMOPOLITAN GOA

Despite her fear of sexual victimization as a lone woman traveler, in *The Sea of Innocence* Simran's decision to stay back on the beaches to find Liza strengthens when she receives another disturbing video clipping of the victim's rape. Simran witnesses how a drugged Liza stumbling along the beach with "her clothes . . . torn, and a streak of something dark, perhaps blood, . . . visible on one leg" (Desai 2013a, 97) moves painfully after being assaulted. As she staggers on the sand, a man appears and forces himself upon Liza and Simran notes: "[h]e pulled her legs up towards him and pushed his hands between them. In pain she screamed, 'No, no . . . don't'" (98). Simran horrifyingly witnesses another man joining the first to assault Liza saying "Come on, come on, baby. You know you want it" (99). The two men brutally rape Liza until she goes limp and Simran notes how "her head fell to one side and her arms flopped down like a rag doll" (99). The explicit footage of the teenage girl's rape makes Simran "sick and nauseous, as though it was [she] who had been molested" (99) and she feels more determined than ever to find Liza. Simran kick-starts her investigations by interrogating Liza's distraught sister Marian who informs her that Liza is an "independent . . . [,] headstrong" girl (49) who "[l]ed her own life, even though she's only sixteen" (55). Marian narrates the incidents leading to Liza's disappearance after the sisters were given spiked drinks during a party at a beach shack named Fernando's. Marian and Liza visit Fernando's to finalize Liza's job offer on a floating casino, tellingly named the *Tempest*, owned by a minister in the union cabinet. Here we are told that Liza wanted to "enjoy herself and get a good job, make some money" (85) and "see the world" (310). However, on that fateful night at Fernando's, Marian loses her consciousness and she wakes up the next morning in her own room only to find Liza is missing. Sadly, it is Liza's ambition to earn, travel, and enjoy the freedoms of life that lands her in one complex situation after another in Goa. Goa here ironically represents a complex paradox where gendered public spaces are concerned: on the one hand with its casinos and sprawling beaches it perpetuates the myth of safety for women hailing from various backgrounds, it on the other hand is as much driven by misogynistic beliefs as any other part of the country. Dhillon and Bakaya succinctly point out that despite women's increased participation in public life in neoliberal India, the threat of violence mars ambitious women's experiences of public spaces. They assert: "while more urban Indian women than ever before are taking up higher studies and careers, are dating and pursuing social lives, and thus stepping into public spaces, these spaces are becoming increasingly dangerous for women" (2014, 3). Likewise, Shilpa Phadke notes how in millennial urban India "women have become more visible than ever before" (2012, 54); and yet, she claims that such positive strides "do not translate into an increased access to public space" (2012, 54–55). Corroborating these arguments, Sen, Kaur, and Zabiliūtė (2019) state that "the mobilisation of professional middle-class women outside the domestic sphere becomes associated with improvements in their lives" but "neo-liberal political economies do not necessarily entail women's empowerment" (6). Hence, it can be concluded that zealous women's foray into the public space in an increasingly market-driven and outwardly cosmopolitan urban India is often impaired by the experiences of street harassment and sexual violence.

A PALE FLAME? THE WHITE WOMAN IN MISOGYNISTIC LANDSCAPES

Contextualizing the violence meted out to Liza Kay, it can be stated that within India's popular imagination white women are often associated with sexual libertinism and promiscuity. Film critic Meraj Ahmed Mubarki notes that even in contemporary Hindi films the "white woman [i]s (re)configured as a symbol of erotic longings, and . . . disparate modes of representation and 'gaze' constitut[es] the white woman and converg[es] on her [so called] wayward sexuality" (2016, 165). Mubarki historicizes this representation and connects it to the image of the white *memsahib* from the colonial era and the larger nationalist discourse. Similarity, Mrinal Pande in her study of early Hindi films, observes how the white woman's body "be[comes] a titillating presence for the Indian [male] libido" (2006, 1650). In Desai's novel, Simran disturbingly notes how "Goa was overrun by Indian men who regarded it as one large beach party, overflowing with bikini-clad women" (Desai 2013a, 40) and how even the female beach vendors sexualize and objectify the white female body. In an instance from the novel, a tactful vendor Veeramma alludes to a young blonde woman in a bikini: "she new catch . . . some beach boys like fish . . . They sell in market" (11). Quite naturally, Simran is unnerved by her derision and the possibility of "young men snaring women like fish" (12) on the beach. On the course of her investigations about Liza, Simran encounters other local women who share Veeramma's sentiments about foreign girls: "Girls come and go . . . [w]hite white legs, golden golden hair. English passport. French passport. German passport . . . [s]poil our boys" (195). Desai here demonstrates how such prejudices stem from gross racial stereotyping of Caucasian women in Indian media. Critiquing the sustained portrayal of white women as "morally deficient" (Delaney 2013), Alexandra Delaney maintains that the "image of the sexually liberated and 'easy' white woman runs deep in the Indian imagination, a perception which is drip-fed by the country's all-pervading mainstream media" (2013). She further questions the offensive typecasting of East European cheerleaders in the extremely popular Indian Premier League (IPL) cricket matches in "tight, revealing clothing, caged off like animals from leering spectators clicking photographs of them" (Delaney 2013). With such crude portrayal of white women in IPL marketing and Bollywood, Delaney wonders if we should "really be surprised that white women get harassed, leered at and photographed on the streets of Delhi, Mumbai and Chennai by the exact men who flock to consume these highly reductionist films and mentally undress the provocative, vamp IPL dancers" (2013). The dehumanizing oriental male gaze, thus, objectifies white women's body equally and probably even more aggressively than of his brown female counterpart and Indian media clearly contributes to this undue sexualization.

Simran's investigations to unravel the truth behind Kay's disappearance leads her to the inner workings of Goa's drug trade and the complex network of politicians, police officers, shack owners, beach vendors, and drug dealers. She unearths how the oppressors of Liza used the minor girl as a drug mule by offering her free drugs, drinks, and a job at the floating casino owned by union minister, Vinay Gupta. Another sexually exploited female employee at Gupta's casino, Vicky, informs Simran how Gupta offered Liza a "well-paid job" and an opportunity to "travel" (Desai 2013a, 310) which Liza was "ambitious enough to agree" (310) with. To Simran's chagrin, Vicky claims: "Vinayji is very good at spotting girls who are eager to move ahead . . . you can't refuse him anything" (311). Simran learns from Vicky how Liza gradually became less obedient to Gupta and "she had to be taught a lesson" (Desai 2013a, 322). On the night of Liza's disappearance, Marian and Liza are drugged by Gupta's men and Gupta punishes Liza by raping her first and later commanding his bodyguards to gang rape her on the beach. Thus, from Vicky Simran finally learns the truth behind the video footage and the events leading up to Liza's gang rape and disappearance. With each new evidence Simran discovers her hope of finding Liza alive waning, and yet despite the threats due to the involvement of high-profile people in Liza's case, Simran continues her investigations.

ON THE ROAD TO JUSTICE: FEMALE KINSHIP VIS-À-VIS PATRIARCHY AND CORRUPTION

In her frantic search for Kay, we encounter in Simran a passionate need for justice coming out of an identification with and a sympathetic reaction to violated women. Simran's hope for help from law-enforcement authorities to seek justice for Liza simmers when she uncovers the close-knit web of panchayat heads, police, politicians, and the media in Goa who have "known each other for far too long to betray each other over the rape or death of an 'outsider'" (Desai 2013a, 185). In addition to this, Simran gets drugged while she investigates about a local MLA's (Member of the Legislative Assembly) son who appeared in one of the video clippings with Liza. With her troubles mounting, Simran feels "hunted . . . intruded upon . . . [v]iolated and assaulted" (133). However, she never backs down from her search for Liza since she likens the teenage girl with her own daughter. We find Simran intensely apprehensive about raising her rebellious daughter in a country which is turning increasingly unsafe for women with each passing day. Simran's concern is reflective of the anxiety of all Indian mothers who raise girl children and this becomes apparent when Simran claims: "[t]he more I learnt about Liza, the less secure I felt about Durga" (57). Researchers Aruldossa and Nolas examine how young girls relate to public life in India and disclose that the fear of sexual violence "(re)orients [their] understanding of public life in restrictive ways" or that girls feel "vulnerable on two counts—being young and being a girl. The affect of fear is sustained in the body as well as being embodied. Fear shrinks the usage of space . . . restricting their movement and the opportunity to inscribe themselves on the world" (2019, 1597–1598). Clearly, male gaze and violence affects young girls' "access and participation in public life" (Aruldossa and Nolas 2019, 1603). Notably, Liza's harassers use Durga as a pawn to terrorize Simran when they send her an image of Durga's tattoo "to remind [her] that [she] too was the mother of a young, vulnerable girl" (Desai 2013a, 182). However, Simran cannot concede defeat as she takes it upon herself to seek justice for Liza and through her, she vicariously connects with the victimized womanhood of her country. This is evident when she reveals: "I heard Liza's voice in a non-stop loop in my head, begging the man to stop . . . when I shut my eyes, I could hear the screams of the girl in the Delhi bus" and a disgruntled Simran asks, "Why had these young girls become the innocent targets of such bizarre violence?" (105). The novel in many ways celebrates this female bonding in the face of terrible male violence and powerfully foregrounds the issue of female sexual vulnerability in Indian public spaces.

Desai's novel not only uncovers the helplessness of young women but also of "poor and thus marginalized young men in this country" (Desai 2013a, 247) through the character of computer technician Vishnu who is falsely accused and jailed for molesting Liza while all he does is protect her from the assault of MLA's son Curtis. The "welts and scars covering [Vishnu's] face" from police brutality depresses Simran and she laments over the victimization of helpless good men like Vishnu. Madeline Clements appreciates Desai's attempt to bring "an important sense of balance . . . [and] humanity . . . to her story" (2013) by demonstrating the vulnerability of marginalized young men in India through "the shy and shuffling character" of Vishnu. Notably,

Shilpa Phadke, Sameera Khan, and Shilpa Ranade in their topical work *Why Loiter? Women and Risk on Mumbai Streets* (2011) question the "fallacious opposition between the middle-class respectable woman and the vagrant male (read: lower class, often unemployed, often lower caste or Muslim)" (19) while framing the safety of women in Indian public spaces. They claim that by "creating the image of certain men as the perpetrators of violence against women, women's access to public space is further controlled and circumscribed" (2011, 19). Confronting the intricacies of this exclusion, the authors of *Why Loiter* assert: "[w]omen's open access to public space . . . cannot be sought at the cost of the exclusion of anyone else" (2011, 21), instead it is the "state's responsibility to protect its citizens' right to be in public space" (190). It is this message that Desai's novel powerfully drives home while also calling out a regressive culture of misogyny that corrupts the nation's landscape. Further, in *The Sea of Innocence* Desai posits hope in a few good citizens like the character of Vishnu (tellingly named after the Hindu God who is the preserver of life) who turns out to be the hero of the narrative as he helps Simran uncover the truth about Liza's rape and disappearance.

As the novel comes to a close, Simran learns about Vishnu's and Marian's elaborate ploy to snare Vinay Gupta by sharing the videos of Liza's assault and rape from her email account to the chief officials in Indian police force. Vishnu reveals that it is he who recorded Liza's rape accidently while filming Liza who he was in love with. Simran also learns the harsh truth about Liza's murder when Vishnu sends her photographs of Liza's dead body from the morgue. Liza's battered and abused body horrifies Simran, who notes that: "Her cheek had been cut and roughly stitched up. . . . The soft blond hair lay in contrast on her cheek . . . her pubic area . . . showed an inflamed labia and bruised vaginal area . . . [which] clearly indicated that she had been raped or molested very cruelly" (324). Simran receives the news of Liza's death "like a body blow" (320). Later, her investigations with the help of the incorruptible local superintendent of police, Robert Gonsalves, unveil that Liza's body was misidentified as another UK resident, Vira Jennings,' who died of a drug overdose at Vagator beach and immediately shipped to London to be buried there before Liza's missing-case was even registered. To her distress, Simran learns that the oppressors of Liza and the drug mafia continued to exploit Liza even after her death by using her dead body to smuggle drugs to London. Simran informs the readers how the foolproof plan to protect Vinay Gupta was "made possible . . . with the complicity of the police, the forensics department and the technicians in the morgue, as well as the customs officials" (Desai 2013a, 337). Thus, exposing the intricate network of corruption and malfeasance, Desai lays bare the inner workings of a highly biased patriarchal law enforcement system that shatters any hopes of justice for victimized women. Examining others cases from across the country, Desai notes that "patriarchal attitudes are now manifest in . . . those in positions of power, especially the police. . . . There are far too many cases in which the police have been complicit—both as the perpetrator of sexual violence and also as the entity that hushes it up" (Desai 2013b). In the face of such structural failures, Simran laments how "thousands—perhaps millions—of women who [have] been raped and molested in this country . . . [are] dead and buried. And forgotten" (Desai 2013a, 343). However, Simran and Vishnu cannot allow such a fate for Liza, and hence they avenge her by releasing a video of Vinay Gupta molesting Liza to the media which eventually leads to his downfall. With no body and no other evidence against him, Gupta could not have been charged with rape and murder; but his video with Liza creates a stir within national media and the National Commission of Women along with the British government initiate cases against the mastermind of the crime for molesting a British child. Thus, with the help of Vishnu, Simran ensures a jail term for Vinay Gupta and thereby secures justice for Liza, albeit posthumously.

CONCLUSION

Notably, women's studies expert, Holly Jennifer Morgan, observes that though Simran fulfills her duty "to the immediate victims in her cases," her "inability to effectively counteract [corruption] . . . [draws] attention to many of the larger problems in contemporary India" (2020, 13). And Morgan rightfully points out how those larger issues are "far beyond the scope of [Simran's] abilities to rectify" (2020, 13). However, as the book comes to a close, Simran, and through her Desai, expresses hope for a future India where all women, irrespective of race, ethnicity, class, caste, or any other social identity, share equal access and right to public spaces without the fear of violence. In the end Desai therefore hopes that "one day this country would finally get better policing and a better justice system" (355). Further, in *The Sea of Innocence* Desai adopts a think piece tone to educate a biased society that is quick to blame the victim for her own abuse. Debunking concepts of victim blaming, Desai asserts that: "It [does] not matter whether [a woman] [is] clothed from head to toe or [is] naked, nor [does] it make a difference if she [is] stoned, or drunk or sober. . . . She could be attacked at any time and for no reason whatsoever" (43). Thus, through the medium of fiction Desai exposes how universally debilitating male gaze and misogyny can be when it victimizes innocent and adventurous women, and also how from their shared experiences of oppression the kinship women develop often acts as a tool of resistance against instances of gendered violence.

REFERENCES

Aruldoss, Vinnarasan and Sevasti-Melissa Nolas. 2019. "Tracing Indian Girls' Embodied Orientations towards Public Life." *Gender, Place and Culture: A Journal of Feminist Geography* 26, no. 11 (May): 1588–1608. doi.org/10.1080/0966369X.2019.1586649

Bhattacharya, Budhaditya. 2013. "No Longer at Ease." *The Hindu*, April 19. www.thehindu.com/books/books-authors/no-longer-at-ease/article4633718.ece

Bhattacharyya, Rituparna. 2015. "Understanding the Spatialities of Sexual Assault against Indian Women in India." *Gender, Place & Culture: A Journal of Feminist Geography* 22, no. 9 (October): 13401356. doi.org/10.1080/0966-369X.2014.969684

Byrnes, Sholto. 2013. "Trouble in Paradise for Simran Singh." *Independent*, June 15. www.independent.co.uk/arts-entertainment/books/reviews/review-the-sea-of-innocence-by-kishwar-desai-8660269.html

Clements, Madeline Amelia. 2013. "Review: The Sea of Innocence by Kishwar Desai." *Dawn*, December 8. www.dawn.com/news/1060879

Desai, Kishwar. 2013a. *The Sea of Innocence*. London: Simon and Schuster.

———. 2013b. "India has Become Very Cruel Towards its Women." *LSE*, June 7. blogs.lse.ac.uk/southasia/2013/06/07/kishwar-desai/

Delaney, Alexandra. 2013. "White Women in the Indian Imagination." *Kafila*. June 8. kafila.online/2013/06/08/white-women-in-the-indian-imagination-alexandra-delaney/

Dhillon, Megha and Suparna Bakaya. 2014. "Street Harassment: A Qualitative Study of the Experiences of Young Women in Delhi." *Sage Open* 4, no. 3 (July): 1–11. doi.org/10.1177/2158244014543786

Massey, Doreen. 1994. *Space, Place, and Gender*. Minneapolis: University of Minnesota Press.

Morgan, Holly Jennifer. 2020. "Kishwar Desai's Simran Singh Series: Crime, Detection, and Gender." *The Journal of Commonwealth Literature* 57, no. 3 (May): 706–721. doi.org/10.1177/0021989420912294

Mubarki, Meraj Ahmed. 2016. "Brown Gaze and White Flesh: Exploring 'Moments' of the Single White Female in Hindi Cinema." *Contemporary South Asia* 24, no. 2 (August): 164–183. dx.doi.org/10.1080/09584935.2016.1195337

Pande, Mrinal. 2006. "'Moving beyond Themselves': Women in Hindustani Parsi Theatre and Early Hindi Films." *Economic and Political Weekly* 41, no. 17 (May): 1646–1653. www.jstor.org/stable/4418142

Phadke, Shilpa. 2007. "Dangerous Liaisons—Women and Men: Risk and Reputation in Mumbai." *Economic and Political Weekly* 42, no. 17 (May): 1510–1518. www.jstor.org/stable/4419517

———. 2012. "Gendered Usage of Public Spaces: A Case Study of Mumbai, Delhi." In *The Fear That Stalks: Gender-Based Violence in Public Spaces*, edited by Lora Prabhu and Sarah Pilot, 51–80. New Delhi: Zubaan.

Phadke, Shilpa, Sameera Khan, and Shilpa Ranade. 2011. *Why Loiter? Women and Risk on Mumbai Streets*. New Delhi: Penguin Books.

Ranade, Shilpa. 2007. "The Way She Moves: Mapping the Everyday Production of Gender-Space." *Economic and Political Weekly* 42, no. 17 (May): 1519–1526. www.jstor.org/stable/4419518

Rose, Gillian. 1993. *Feminism and Geography: The Limits of Geographical Knowledge*. Cambridge: Polity Press.

Roy, Sanghamitra and Ajay Bailey. 2021. "Safe in the City? Negotiating Safety, Public Space and the Male Gaze in Kolkata, India." *Cities: The International Journal of Urban Policy and Planning* 117 (October): 1–11. doi.org/10.1016/j.cities.2021.103321

Sen, Atreyee, Raminder Kaur and Emilija Zabiliūtė. 2019. "(En)countering Sexual Violence in the Indian City." *Gender, Place and Culture: A Journal of Feminist Geography* 27, no. 1 (May): 1–12. doi.org/10.1080/0966369X.2019.1612856

Valentine, Gill. 1989. "The Geography of Women's Fear." *Area* 21, no. 4 (December): 385–390. www.jstor.org/stable/20000063

Viswanath, Kalpana and Surabhi Tandon Mehrotra. 2007. "'Shall We Go Out?' Women's Safety in Public Spaces in Delhi." *Economic and Political Weekly* 42, no. 17 (May): 1542–1548. www.jstor.org/stable/4419521

Chapter 2

Peripheral Urbanization as Queer Identity in Arundhati Roy's *The Ministry of Utmost Happiness*

Jana Fedtke

In an interview with Decca Aitkenhead, Booker Prize winning author Arundhati Roy addresses the fact that she and her work have often been called "the voice of the voiceless," pointing to the inadequacy of the moniker from her perspective: "it makes me crazy . . . there's no voiceless, there's only the deliberately silenced, you know, or the purposely unheard" (2017, para. 32). One could argue that Arundhati Roy's *The Ministry of Utmost Happiness* (2017) is full of such "purposely unheard" characters, including one of the protagonists, Anjum. In this chapter, I analyze the representation of the character Anjum, a transperson, in the novel. I am specifically interested in Anjum's queer identity and her place as a hijra (eunuch or hermaphrodite) in contemporary neoliberal India. I explore how the novel situates the so-called third gender at the intersections of space and gender. Public and private spaces in India—as elsewhere—are often divided along the constructed binaries of female and male. While India officially provides a category for what is generally referred to as the third gender in official documents, public recognition and societal acceptance of queer identities have not necessarily followed suit. My paper examines such recognition and societal acceptance of non-binary people in public spaces as represented in fiction.

While other fictional representations have stereotyped transpeople or ridiculed their behavior, Roy's novel presents Anjum's queer identity as an integral part of the spatial interrelations in a contemporary Indian city, specifically the country's capital, Delhi. I propose to read *The Ministry of Utmost Happiness* as carving out a recognizable space for Anjum's queerness as a non-binary individual. Non-male identities have largely been marginalized in public spaces, which is also evident for Anjum's space in *The Ministry of Utmost Happiness*. I argue that, even though the cityscapes of Delhi in the novel are not built to include queer individuals, the text showcases Delhi as a heterogeneous space where Anjum can manage to create a space for herself. I analyze the text through the lens of urban geography, paying particular attention to Teresa Caldeira's (2017) theory of peripheral urbanization in the context of the social dimension and construction of space.

Beyond this physical representation of her home in the city, I am interested in Anjum's metaphorical journey from being born Aftab to becoming Anjum. I argue that her journey in neoliberal India presents a case of what bell hooks calls "choosing the margin as a space of radical openness" (1989, 19). Anjum embraces a life at the margins and claims the cemetery as her heterotopic space. This choice puts her in control and allows her to exercise an agency in a gendered cityscape that might otherwise not be willing to accommodate her. In this sense, Anjum's graveyard also represents a space of non-discriminatory, possibly ungendered, inclusion on the physical and metaphorical margins of society.

OF BINARIES AND BELONGING: ANJUM'S JOURNEY

After the phenomenal success of Arundhati Roy's 1997 novel, *The God of Small Things*, the author published several acclaimed non-fictional texts and eventually followed up her fictional work with her second novel, *The Ministry of Utmost Happiness*, in 2017. The novel highlights many different topics, chiefly among them the insurgency in Kashmir. For the purposes of this chapter, I will focus on the parts set in India's capital, Delhi, which showcase the character Anjum and her life as a transgender woman on the city's periphery. The very first part of the novel describes the journey of how a boy, Aftab, becomes Anjum, a hijra.

Anjum's journey toward a non-binary identity is described as confusing and sometimes painful for the people involved. The reader learns about this confusion first from the perspective of Aftab's mother, Jahanara Begum: "Yes of course she knew there was a word for those like him—*Hijra*. Two words actually, *Hijra* and *Kinnar*. But two words do not make a language" (Roy 2017, 8; emphasis in the original). Aftab's mother shows concern about her child's gender. Her attitude displays a certain distance when saying "those like him." The use of the masculine personal pronoun also indicates that she thinks of her child as a boy. Most importantly though the narrator notes the lack of linguistic features to talk about Aftab's identity. Despite the two words denoting non-binary people, there is no meaningful linguistic space for Aftab.

In addition to the lack of linguistic space, the novel also highlights a lack of societal discourse around non-binary individuals. Jahanara Begum seeks help for her child when she takes Aftab to the doctor: "After examining Aftab he said he was not, medically speaking, a Hijra—a female trapped in a male body—although for practical purposes that word could be used. Aftab, he said, was a rare example of a Hermaphrodite, with both male and female characteristics" (Roy 2017, 16–17). The medicalization of Aftab's "condition" shows the child as an "abnormality" who is somehow different from most people due to exhibiting what is characteristically thought of as female and male characteristics. The narrator's definition of a hijra carries a negative connotation when saying that they are "trapped" in a male body, interpreting this condition as something to be escaped if possible. Continuing the medicalization of Aftab's identity, the doctor recommends surgery and pills to treat Aftab, but the doctor remains skeptical about the child, telling Jahanara Begum that, "the problem was not merely superficial. While treatment would surely help, there would be 'Hijra tendencies' that were unlikely to ever go away" (16–17). The medical expert describes Aftab's identity as a "problem" and refers to it as a never-ending condition of the body with the derogatory description of "tendencies."

To help her child, Jahanara Begum hides Aftab's "secret" from their environment—until it is not possible anymore. Growing up as a boy, Aftab is fascinated by Bombay Silk, a hijra whom he has observed in the neighborhood: "Aftab had never seen anybody like the tall woman with lipstick. He rushed down the steep stairs into the street and followed her discreetly . . . He wanted to be her" (Roy 2017, 18). Aftab wishes to be not only *like* Bombay Silk, but so clearly identifies with her that he wants to be her. Aftab's fascination with Bombay Silk and her style of life is even more heightened when he learns of the hijras' home, the Khwabgah, which is also known as "the House of Dreams" (19). The narrator describes the Khwabgah as an "ordinary, broken-down home," but exaggerates Aftab's sense of it as a quasi-religious experience: "as though he were walking through the gates of Paradise" (20). Just as the gates separate Paradise from the world, the Khwabgah is also a separate space that serves as a home for some of the hijras in Delhi.

Other religious references relate to the spaces that hijras are "allowed" to enter. Like Aftab/Anjum, most of the hijras in the novel come from Muslim households and/or identify as Muslims: "they visited the Jama Masjid and those dargahs that allowed them into the inner chambers (because unlike biological women Hijras were not considered unclean since they did not menstruate)" (Roy 2017, 21). The narrator describes the spaces that hijras frequent, but also anticipates some of the readers' doubts by providing an explanation in brackets which clarifies the biological features of hijras. Hijras are also excluded from accessing spaces in the city, on the road when traveling, and in other official situations: "She, who never knew which box to tick, which queue to stand in, which public toilet to enter (Kings or Queens? Lords or Ladies? Sirs or Hers?)" (122). This highlights their status as outsiders once again due to the medicalization of their bodies, which in turn allows them to enter certain spaces in the city or which would deny them access to said spaces. Even though Aftab feels at home with the hijras, there is also some tension with regard to their understanding of religious references. To explain their existence, one of the hijras tells Aftab: "D'you know why God made Hijras? It was an experiment. He decided to create something, a living creature that is incapable of happiness. So he made us" (23). Aftab is shocked and feels the need to defend the hijras' home: "How can you say that? You are all happy here! This is the Khwabgah!" (23). To Aftab, their home is a segregated, happy place that affords the hijras a place of their own where they can be who they are and want to be without interference from the outside world.

The hijras acknowledge the spaces in the physical world as segregated from their own living conditions. This divide is also evident in their own physicality. Taking the location of their own bodies, one of the hijras compares hijras to other people: "The riot is *inside* us. The war is *inside* us. Indo–Pak is *inside* us. It will never settle down. It *can't*" (Roy 2017, 23; emphasis in the original). Political riots and in particular the real-life military conflict between India and Pakistan serve as a metaphor for the war inside the bodies of non-binary people. The novel positions this conflict as an inside struggle that will not end because it simply cannot end. It is a given that allows its "owner" no other way out, which also positions being a hijra as a "natural" condition, something that will not change and does not have to change. Despite the discomfort that this inner conflict represents, Aftab/Anjum longs to be a part of the community and aims to move into the space that they call their home. This wish finally comes true when "he was presented with a green Khwabgah dupatta and initiated into the rules and rituals that formally made him a member of the Hijra community. Aftab became Anjum, disciple of Ustad Kulsoom Bi of the Delhi Gharana" (25). To Anjum, the formal acceptance plays an important role since it indicates being a part of an existing community that offers a space to live and work.

While the narrative has so far referred to Aftab in masculine personal pronouns, it now shifts to calling Aftab Anjum and to using the corresponding feminine personal pronouns. The journey from Aftab to Anjum has been completed. Anjum can claim a sense of belonging, but her identity continues to be defined as non-binary and not-quite-belonging in the remainder of the novel.

NON-BINARY SPACES IN NEOLIBERAL INDIA

The Khwabgah represents a safe space for Anjum and the other hijras as long as they are among themselves, but as a group of non-binary people, they are still largely othered in and excluded from life in the cityscapes. Due to a lack of regular work opportunities, the hijras only option in *The Ministry of Utmost Happiness* is to perform their differences to earn a living: "they descended on ordinary people's celebrations—weddings, births, house-warming ceremonies—dancing, singing in their wild, grating voices, offering their blessings and threatening to embarrass the hosts (by exposing their mutilated privates) and ruin the occasion with curses and a display of unthinkable obscenity unless they were paid a fee" (Roy 2017, 24). Their performances are seen as traditions and blessings. At the same time, they always include elements of fear, threats, and disgust, giving their livelihood an impression of illicit behavior and extortion since the hijras are forced to make their living by blackmailing their customers. Sonya J. Nair has shown that, "The upward aspirations and the shrinking living spaces of the middle and upper middle-class Indians have limited the possibility of the trans community being able to eke out a living by performing at these occasions" (2022, 6). Due to this, Hijras are exposed to "dangerous and unsafe career paths, stigma, violence, and infection" (Nair 2022, 6). Nimmo Gorakhpuri, one of the other hijras in the novel, describes their business with a hint of an animalistic nature: "'We're jackals who feed off other people's happiness, we're Happiness Hunters.' *Khushi-khor* was the phrase she used" (24; emphasis in the original). This description turns the hijras into animals, seemingly parasites, who live off other people's feelings, but Nimmo Gorakhpuri emphasizes a more positive note by pointing out how hijras search for a happiness that they might otherwise be denied.

Invisible in the workforce and underrepresented in politics, hijras remain largely absent from the public sphere in India. Public spaces are often closed to their participation. They may even encounter gendered violence when trying to access closed spaces that are constructed around binaries such as public toilets designated for females or males exclusively rather than including unisex facilities or offering separate spaces for individuals who identify as neither female nor male. This raises the question of ownership of space in cities in India and who moves how in such spaces. According to UN Habitat, "Streets and public spaces define the character of a city . . . public space frames city image . . . Having sufficient open public space allows cities and towns to function efficiently and equitably" (2018, 3). The report points out that, "The network of open public space not only improves quality of life but also mobility and functioning of the city" (3). UN Habitat also highlights the need for "opportunities to a diversity of users; particularly for the most marginalized" (2018, 3). In this sense, "public space as a common good is the key enabler for the fulfillment of human rights" (3). The report defines public spaces as "multi-functional areas for social interaction, economic exchange and cultural expression among a wide diversity of people" (5). The role of urban planning is to "establish and organize these public spaces" (5), while urban design can "facilitate and encourage their use, in the process enhancing a sense of identity and belonging" (5). It is this sense of identity and belonging in the use of public space that is also at stake for Anjum and other hijras in *The Ministry of Utmost Happiness*. The novel shows that Anjum and the other hijras are not an accepted part of public spaces. They do not participate in life as other characters and inhabitants of Delhi do. Their work and lives are characterized by discomfort and harassment. They occasionally fear for their life and suffer abuse on a regular basis due to their stigmatized identities as non-binary people.

Various scholars have discussed the patriarchal nature of the neoliberal Indian city. Das describes how the New Economic Policy "as a capitalist class agenda is implemented through accumulation projects that involve massive restructuring of space relations, producing geographical unevenness at multiple scales" (2015, 719). Introduced in 1991, the new policy views urban space as a commodity to be shaped and sold, which necessarily marginalizes certain populations. In this process, "slums are being cleared, and peasants and aboriginal people are being dispossessed of their land" (Das 2015, 719). Space is not a given, but it is socially and economically produced. In neoliberal India, particularly in the big cities, economic interests often marginalize people by depriving them of their living spaces. Taking the 2012 Nirbhaya case and increasing violence against women into account, Bannerji argues that patriarchy and capitalism work hand in hand (2016, 4). Wilson et al. (2018) situate gendered violence in the neoliberal state. In addition, Datta uses the framework of "regional genderscape" to explore the "links between gender, space and agency in Indian contexts" (2021, 1). Datta (2021) examines regional differences in the construction of gendered spaces, being aware of the fact that "India" is not one homogeneous whole, but rather a large country that exhibits regional variety. Raju and Paul show how gendered meanings are produced in spaces in the city (2017, 128). Using the framework of feminist geography, the authors focus on women in Indian cities as they navigate their spaces in a male-dominated environment. Along with other feminist geographers, Raju and Paul point out that the terms space and place overlap: "space provides the physical locale through which meanings and subjective positioning, with implications for lived experiences, are expressed" (129). These lived experiences of the hijras in *The Ministry of Utmost Happiness* also affect how the marginalized community of non-binary people experience the city of Delhi.

While Raju and Paul (2017) focus on women, one could argue that a similar positioning and production of meaning in space holds true for hijras or non-binary people in Indian cities as they navigate the public and private spheres. Shah argues that "complicating the idea of queer and trans existence and social movements in India requires locating contemporary sexuality and transgender politics in relation to the politics of urbanism" (2015, 647). As Chakrabarty has shown, for example, in the case of Kolkata, "the ever-increasing securitization and surveillance of the urban landscape has unleashed the installation of CCTVs across prominent sites, public spaces, etc. resulting in the operation of panoptic gaze. This has heightened the discomforts of the Hijra to conduct themselves in the urban spaces" (2020, 114). Surveillance of public space can influence people's behavior. It determines who has access to public spaces and how these public spaces can be used.

Beyond traditional interpretations of the Indian city, *The Ministry of Utmost Happiness* is also invested in queering understandings of space and people in spaces. The word "queer" itself does not appear in the novel, except for in the acknowledgements, where Arundhati Roy thanks "Shohini Ghosh, beloved madcap, who queered my pitch" (2017, 441). "Queering the pitch" extends to both the representation of the Indian capital as well as Anjum's character. Tickell points to "Roy's personification of Delhi as an old woman, a 'thousand-year-old sorceress' struggling under the dual assault of Hindu nationalism, and the pressures of a neoliberalism which demands that 'she' be transformed, meretriciously and with considerable loss of dignity, into a 'World Class' city" (2018, 3). Delhi is gendered as a female city and character: "She was to become supercapital of the world's favourite new superpower. *India! India!*" (Roy 2017, 96; emphasis in the original). Non-male identities are constantly marginalized in the novel, which is most clearly demonstrated in the case of the hijra characters, specifically Anjum.

In the gendered neoliberal space of Delhi, Anjum and the other hijras in the Khwabgah are presented as a threat to patriarchy. Mendes and Lau interpret Anjum's life as a precarious existence: "Anjum haunts the interstices of the mainstream, needing to inhabit spaces of precarity which most authentically reflect her precarious positionality in order to maintain a certain authenticity to her own satisfaction" (2020, 77). Despite the precariousness of Anjum's situation, Lertlaksanaporn (2020) views Anjum's portrayal as a hijra in the novel as largely positive, especially due to the sense of community in the Khwabgah. Similarly, Tickell argues that Anjum presents a resilient character in the face of adversity: "Anjum, is the vital, often desperate human signifier of the pressures of living against the grain of an assigned gender, but she is also a defiant figure, embodying the resistant, profane energies of the *hijra* communities" (2018, 3; emphasis in the original). Tickell sees the "culturally sanctioned forms of blackmail and a kind of exaggerated burlesque sexuality as weapons against a male-oriented world in which gender ambiguity is heavily proscribed" (3). Non-binary people often find themselves marginalized in India. As described in the novel, their situation can be dire at times as they struggle to establish their identities. The communities of hijras are not homogeneous, however. Queerness finds multiple forms in the novel.

Hijra communities and people who identify as non-binary in India question ideals of heteronormativity. Narrain points out that, "the more established definitions of activist politics are now being forced to engage with new political concerns articulated by people who claim gay, lesbian, hijra, transgender, kothi, and numerous other identities under the rubric of queer" (2004, 144). Dutta and Roy caution against establishing hierarchies that would privilege "the hegemonic anglophone discourse of LGBTIQ identities recognized by the state and the development sector" (2014, 320) at the risk of neglecting "forms of gender/sexual variance that are positioned as relatively regional or local on the other" (320). Similarly, Ung Loh argues that "the framing of LGBT struggles as 'global,' the referent of the Western and thereafter universal 'LGBT' subject, and the potentially exclusionary nature of LGBT movements are significant factors in examining Indian 'LGBT' rights movements, which negotiate universalising rights-based discourses alongside particular cultural contexts" (2018, 40–41). Nair also observes a lack of engagement with the everyday experiences of hijras: "Often, the spectacular, the spectacle, the erotic, and the exotic are all that remain in the eye of the public, and the lived realities of being transgender are often ignored. Who are the transpeople and what spaces do they occupy in the civil and civic life of a country like India?" (2022, 1). A novel such as Roy's *The Ministry of Utmost Happiness* provides much-needed representation of hijras as "regular" people.

The novel presents Anjum's fame among the hijras in Delhi: "Over the years Anjum became Delhi's most famous Hijra. Film-makers fought over her, NGOs hoarded her, foreign correspondents gifted her phone number to one another as a professional favour" (Roy 2017, 26). Anjum is lauded by foreign media and NGOs. At the same time, Anjum becomes a spectacle: "The foreign tourists in turn gawked at the Hijras—at Anjum in particular" (52). When out in the streets or traveling, Anjum is often the target of people's curiosity, which is more bearable when in the company of other people to avoid harassment: "Anjum was prepared to travel with him to Ahmedabad rather than risk the harassment and humiliation (of being seen as well as of being *un*seen) that she would have to endure if she travelled back on her own from Ajmer" (43, emphasis in the original). Both praised and despised, Anjum's status is threatened by the presence of Saeeda, one of the other hijras, who is more in tune with the transnational understanding of transpeople's rights: "More importantly, she could speak the new language of the times—she could use the terms *cis-Man* and *FtoM* and *MtoF* and in interviews she referred to herself as a 'transperson.' Anjum, on the other hand, mocked what she called the 'trans-france' business, and stubbornly insisted on referring to herself as a Hijra" (38; emphasis in the original). The novel presents Anjum as seemingly old-fashioned because she is not willing to use new terms to describe her own existence.

Similarly, Anjum does not mind outdated terms for marginalized people: "Anjum used the word *Chamar* and not *Dalit,* the more modern and accepted term for those that Hindus considered to be 'untouchable,' in the same spirit in which she refused to refer to herself as anything other than Hijra. She didn't see the problem with either Hijras or Chamars" (Roy 2017, 85). Despite their equally downtrodden status, the hijras assure themselves about their identities: "There was no reason to be ashamed of anything, Ustad Kulsoom Bi told her, because Hijras were chosen people, beloved of the Almighty. The word *Hijra*, she said, meant a Body in which a Holy Soul lives" (27). This redefinition of their status in a religious sense is also echoed later in the novel when Gudiya, another hijra, relates the mythological story of Sita and Ram in Ayodhya: "Ram turned to his people and said, 'I want all you men and women to go home and wait for me until I return.' Unable to disobey their king, the men and women returned home. Only the Hijras waited faithfully for him at the edge of the forest for the whole fourteen years, because he had forgotten to mention them" (51). This marks the hijras' special status as both faithful loyal followers and as different outsiders who are neither this nor that. The space that hijras and others inhabit is also marked as different: "what most ordinary people thought of as the real world— . . . Hijras called *Duniya*, the World" (24, emphasis in the original). Their space is separate from other people and the hijras mark this difference linguistically as well. Hijras also complain about the lack of understanding of their environment: "Ordinary people in the Duniya—what did they know about what it takes to live the life of a Hijra? What did they know about the rules, the discipline and the sacrifices? . . . humiliation by humiliation . . . " (53).

Among themselves, the hijras share an understanding of who they are and how they present their role to the outside world, for example, when using the hijra clap in their performances: "Only another Hijra could decode what was specifically meant by the specific clap at that specific moment" (Roy 2017, 27). What seems the norm to them is hard to understand for other people who are not part of their community. Due to a lack of mutual understanding, "people in the Duniya spread wicked rumours about Hijras kidnapping little boys and castrating them" (53). This is presented as a common stereotype in the novel among other fears that the hijras have to face. Biopolitical advances seem to be about to change the hijras' lives in Saeeda's understanding: "because sexual-reassignment surgery was becoming cheaper, better, and more accessible to people, Hijras would soon disappear. 'Nobody will need to go through what we've been through any more.' 'You mean no more Indo–Pak?'" (409). Anjum's response of overcoming the inner conflict that resembles the wars between India and Pakistan questions their identities, although it remains unclear whether Anjum and other hijras see this as a hopeful message or as a sad event of their own disappearance. The metaphorical inner journey written on their bodies is not always respected in the "real world." When traveling to Gujarat and after the violence in that state, for example, Anjum is placed in the men's section of a refugee camp in Ahmedabad and dressed in men's clothes once again (46). Her gender identity is denied in an effort to make her conform to what others might see as her "real" gender, which again victimized Anjum violently.

Anjum remains divided about her own identity as a hijra. While she is happy with her life and community at the Khwabgah, she still feels like an outsider in society. "Her patched-together body" (Roy 2017, 29) is the source of much confusion for herself and people around her. After living in the Khwabgah for 30 years, she decides to leave her home when she is 46 years old. This move is, however, not random, but triggered by certain events during the religiously motivated Gujarat riots in 2002, which leave Anjum traumatized and marginalize her even more as she moves to a graveyard in Delhi.

PERIPHERAL URBANIZATION AS QUEER IDENTITY

Anjum's lived experience of being a hijra saves her life at a critical moment in the novel. As Arundhati Roy has pointed out: "What I love about Anjum is that when she's caught up [in the massacre in Gujarat], she's spared because she's a hijra" (Aitkenhead 2017, para. 13). Roy's interviewer, Decca Aitkenhead has shown how "having been saved by the very identity that used to exclude her" changes Anjum in profound ways (2017, para. 13).

According to Tickell, "Across the first six chapters of *The Ministry* . . . Roy presents Delhi as . . . a supremely alienating place—a predatory world" (2018, 4). In this space of marginalization for Anjum and the other hijras, Tickell identifies the Khwabgah as a space of belonging and community for Anjum: "Roy's strategy . . . is to anchor her city fiction, initially, in a space of doubly marginalised, alternative community: not the more conventional family home or workplace but the ambiguous self-fashioning sisterhood of the *Khwabgah*" (3; emphasis in the original). After the traumatizing events of the Gujarat riots, the Khwabgah cannot serve as a home for Anjum anymore. Moving to the graveyard, she is once again marginalized, but this new space becomes her home—one that she herself builds and cherishes.

In neoliberal India, processes of urbanization often disadvantage the urban poor. As Gurarani and Kennedy have shown, "compared to earlier phases of urbanization, contemporary processes are inextricably linked to India's increasing global engagement over the last decades and peripheries are being produced through multi-scalar relations and interactions of local, regional, national, and transnational flows of capital, expertise, and speculation" (2021, 2). Anjum's precarious existence in the cemetery is one such as example of life on the periphery in the Global South. This periphery is characterized by Anjum's attempt at survival and her own construction of a space that seems livable to herself. Feminist geographers have pointed out the importance of this social dimension of space. Massey, for example, proposes three major points of departure to reading people in space: to "recognize space as the product of interrelations," to "understand space as . . . coexisting heterogeneity," and to "recognize space as always under construction" (2005, 9). In light of Massey's conceptualization of space, I read Anjum's construction of her space as a work in progress: her identity as related to other people in rejection of their everyday reality, her difference from other people in carving out a space of her own, and her ongoing construction of her home in the graveyard.

This process of ongoing construction of Anjum's new home on Delhi's metaphorical periphery represents an instance of what Teresa Caldeira (2017) calls peripheral urbanization. With reference to the Global South, of which India is also a part, Caldeira shows that "many cities around the world have been largely constructed by their residents, who build not only their own houses, but also frequently their neighborhoods" (2017, 3). This construction of their own homes and neighborhoods reflects their interaction with the cities or authorities: "they operate inside capitalist markets of land, credit, and consumption, but usually in special niches bypassed by the dominant logics of formal real estate, finance, and commodity circulation" (Caldeira 2017, 3). Caldeira points out that this mode of spatial production is particularly relevant in the Global South: "I use the notion of peripheral urbanization to create a problem-space that allows us to investigate logics of the production of the urban that differ from those of the North Atlantic" (4). Caldeira further argues that "peripheral urbanization consists of a *set of interrelated processes*. It refers to modes of the production of urban space that (a) operate with a specific form of agency and temporality, (b) engage transversally with official logics, (c) generate new modes of politics through practices that produce new kinds of citizens, claims, circuits, and contestations, and (d) create highly unequal and heterogeneous cities" (4; emphasis in the original). According to Caldeira, then, "peripheral urbanization not only produces heterogeneity within the city as it unfolds over time, but also *varies considerably from one city to another*" (4; emphasis in the original).

In Anjum's new home in the graveyard, the reader can also recognize such a mode of peripheral urbanization. The narrator describes the cemetery as a space of desolation: "it was an unprepossessing graveyard, run-down, not very big and used only occasionally. Its northern boundary abutted a government hospital and mortuary where the bodies of the city's vagrants and unclaimed dead were warehoused until the police decided how to dispose of them" (Roy 2017, 58). In addition to the run-down state of the graveyard, an image of which also appears on the original cover of the novel, the narrator alludes to the temporary nature of the various graves in the cemetery: "The formally constructed graves numbered less than two hundred. The older graves were more elaborate, with carved marble tombstones, the more recent ones, more rudimentary" (58). This emphasizes the nature of temporality in peripheral urbanization (Caldeira 2017).

Upon her arrival in the graveyard, Anjum's condition mirrors the shabby existence of the cemetery: "For months Anjum lived in the graveyard, a ravaged, feral spectre, out-haunting every resident djinn and spirit, ambushing bereaved families who came to bury their dead with a grief so wild, so untethered, that it clean outstripped theirs" (Roy 2017, 63). Readers learn that "she stopped grooming herself, stopped dyeing her hair. It grew dead white from the roots, and suddenly, halfway down her head, turned jet black, making her look, well . . . *striped*" (63; emphasis in the original). Slowly but surely, Anjum develops a form of agency (Caldeira 2017): "Gradually the Fort of Desolation scaled down into a dwelling of manageable proportions. It became home; a place of predictable, reassuring sorrow—awful, but reliable" (Roy 2017, 66). While still a space of precariousness, Anjum makes it her home, providing a source of reliance. The narrator details how this change in the construction of a home in the cemetery also reflects Anjum's change in appearance: "Anjum began to groom herself again. She hennaed her hair, turning it a flaming orange" (66). Even though "her relationship with the Rest-of-Her-Life remained precarious and reckless" (66), Anjum has achieved a sense of agency in taking her life into her own hands.

Caldeira refers to this agency as an important part of peripheral urbanization: "residents are agents of urbanization, not simply consumers of spaces developed and regulated by others. They build their houses and cities step-by-step according to the resources they are able to put together at each moment in a process that I call *autoconstruction*" (2017, 5; emphasis in the original). Anjum performs this autoconstruction in "her" graveyard as well: "As the Fort of Desolation scaled down, Anjum's tin shack scaled up. It grew first into a hut that could accommodate a bed, and then into a small house with a little kitchen" (Roy 2017, 66–67). Anjum develops her home, but is also careful in disguising the progress of the construction: "So as not to attract undue attention, she left the exterior walls rough and unfinished. The inside she plastered and painted an unusual shade of fuchsia. She put in a sandstone roof supported on iron girders, which gave her a terrace on which, in the winter, she would put out a plastic chair and dry her hair and sun her chapped, scaly shins while she surveyed the dominion of the dead. For her doors and windows she chose a pale pistachio green" (66–67). The novel presents Anjum as the owner of her home, presiding over the larger graveyard and its dead residents.

Despite the elevated status on the surface, peripheral urbanization remains semi-illegal: "frequently, illegality and irregularity are the only options available for the poor to become urban dwellers, given that formal housing is not affordable and public housing is not sufficient" (Caldeira 2017, 7). Part of these processes of peripheral urbanization is a questioning of official logics: "by engaging the many problems of legalization, regulation, occupation, planning, and speculation, they redefine those logics and, in so doing, generate urbanizations of heterogeneous types and remarkable political consequences" (7). In *The Ministry of Utmost Happiness*, the official logics are represented by the municipal authorities who threaten Anjum from time to time: "every few months the municipal authorities stuck a notice on Anjum's front door that said squatters were strictly prohibited from living in the graveyard and that any unauthorized construction would be demolished within a week" (Roy 2017, 67). Anjum's defense is witty: "she told them that she wasn't living in the graveyard, she was dying in it—and for this she didn't need permission from the municipality because she had authorization from the Almighty Himself" (67). Anjum subverts the meaning of her existence in the graveyard and invokes a religious authority that nobody is willing or able to contradict: "none of the municipal officers who visited her was man enough to take the matter further and run the risk of being embarrassed by her legendary abilities" (67). The narrator endows Anjum with a voice of her own, legitimized by a higher power. Her space remains hers, no matter what municipal authorities might say. In this sense, Anjum represents "a process through which residents engage in modes of production of space that constitute themselves as simultaneously new kinds of urban residents, consumers, subjects, and citizens" (Caldeira 2017, 9).

Anjum continues the process of autoconstruction by building her home on top of existing structures: "over time Anjum began to enclose the graves of her relatives and build rooms around them. Each room had a grave (or two) and a bed. Or two. She built a separate bathhouse and a toilet with its own septic tank. For water she used the public handpump" (Roy 2017, 67–68). Enjoying her position in the process of construction, Anjum also develops the graveyard into a space for other outsiders or people in need: "Anjum began to rent a couple of rooms to down-and-out travellers (the publicity was strictly by word of mouth)" (68). Tongue-in-cheek, the narrator explains how Anjum is able to run this establishment: "The advantage of the guest house in the graveyard was that unlike every other neighbourhood in the city, including the most exclusive ones, it suffered no power cuts. Not even in the summer. This was because Anjum stole her electricity from the mortuary, where the corpses required round-the-clock refrigeration" (68). This space ultimately becomes a guest house which Anjum calls Jannat, Paradise (68): "Gradually Jannat Guest House became a hub for Hijras who, for one reason or another, had fallen out of, or been expelled from, the tightly administered grid of Hijra Gharanas." Tickell shows how "in this sense, the cemetery of the Jannat Guest House is a space of both literal and figurative exclusion: a zone where those who are not accepted or welcomed in wider society can find a kind of sanctuary" (2018, 8). Anjum's autoconstruction on the periphery has turned into a fixture for people in need. Just as Anjum found refuge in the graveyard, she can now offer help to others on the periphery who might have lost their home or a space of their own.

THE GRAVEYARD AS QUEER HOME AND SITE OF RESISTANCE

Anjum's home on the periphery welcomes a host of guests and outsiders who are not necessarily hijras or identify as queer. As Aitkenhead points out, "her Jannat Guest House becomes home to a fabulously outlandish medley of the excluded: untouchables, Muslim converts, hijras, addicts, even an abandoned baby, Zainab, whom Anjum adopts" (2017, para. 9). Tickell connects Anjum's new living space in the graveyard to the loss and painful experiences she herself had to endure: "if Roy's second novel can be categorised as a work of the living city then, it is also a work of death, one that stages the metropolis as a necropolis, and as a place of death-in-life, as much as it also explores the subjective accommodation of death and loss by the living" (2018, 2). Gopinath (2020) has shown how the cemetery as Anjum's dwelling place functions as a heterotopia in the Foucauldian sense. Anjum's new home in the graveyard frees her from the violence and abuse she would have otherwise had to endure had she stayed part of the Khwabgah. In the cemetery, Anjum is in charge and decides who is or is not allowed in.

At the very beginning of the novel, the narrator describes Anjum's position in the graveyard by comparing her to the seemingly eternal patience of a tree: "She lived in the graveyard like a tree. At dawn she saw the crows off and welcomed the bats home. At dusk she did the opposite. Between shifts she conferred with the ghosts of vultures that loomed in her high branches" (Roy 2017, 3). Anjum seems to have made the cemetery her home, although other people abuse her as they did before when she was part of the hijra community: "When she first moved in, she endured months of casual cruelty like a tree would—without flinching" (3). The insults may affect her, but she makes an effort not to show it. Anjum is still marked as an outsider: "When people called her names—clown without a circus, queen without a palace—she let the hurt blow through her branches like a breeze and used the music of her rustling leaves as balm to ease the pain" (3). Her marginalization continues, but the novel describes her in a state of acceptance and resistance.

"Marginalized" with regard to the location of the graveyard does not necessarily refer to the spatial position of the cemetery. Located in Shahjahanabad in Old Delhi, the graveyard is precisely not on the outskirts of the modern-day city of Delhi. If anything, it is centrally located. Anjum's position as an outsider manifest predominantly in her gendered identity as a hijra. Despite being marginalized in society, Anjum manages to instrumentalize the margins as her weapon in what bell hooks has referred to as "the margin as a space of radical openness" (1989, 15). Speaking about her own approach as an African American who is marginalized in the contemporary US American context, hooks highlights the importance of community in resistance: "For me this space of radical openness is a margin - a profound edge. Locating oneself there is difficult yet necessary. It is not a 'safe' place. One is always at risk. One needs a community of resistance" (19).

hooks also recognizes the significance of the margins as a space for radical openness for other oppressed groups of people: "understanding marginality as position and place of resistance is crucial for oppressed, exploited, colonised people. If we only view the margin as sign, marking the condition of our pain and deprivation then a certain hopelessness and despair, a deep nihilism penetrates in a destructive way the very ground of our being" (1989, 21). Against such hopelessness, hooks proposes the margins as a site of possibility: "I want to note that I am not trying to romantically reinscribe the notion of that space of marginality where the oppressed live apart from their oppressors as 'pure.' I want to say that these margins have been both sites of repression and sites of resistance" (21). In this location on the margins, hooks distinguishes between imposition and choice: "I make a definite distinction between that marginality which is imposed by oppressive structures and that marginality one chooses as site of resistance—as location of radical openness and possibility. This site of resistance is continually formed in that segregated culture of opposition that is our critical response to domination" (23). hooks also highlights struggle as a necessary means to achieve such resistance and a space of freedom: "we come to this space through suffering and pain, through struggle ... we are transformed, individually, collectively, as we make radical creative space which affirms and sustains our subjectivity, which gives us a new location from which to articulate our sense of the world" (23). For Anjum, this new location is the graveyard, which becomes her new home and a site of resistance. Anjum "owns" the space. She welcomes or rejects guests to Jannat Guest House. When it becomes a funeral parlor, Anjum also decides whom to bury and how: "The one clear criterion was that Jannat Funeral Services would only bury those whom the graveyards and imams of the Duniya had rejected" (80). In this sense, Anjum snubs the duniya and its traditions. She frees herself from the constraints and violence of the duniya by establishing her own world in which she functions as the decision-maker. Her resistance becomes a tool for overcoming her pain—both physical and metaphorical—as a hijra. Anjum has found a space of her own in the graveyard.

CONCLUSION

In this chapter, I have analyzed representations of Anjum as a hijra in Arundhati Roy's 2017 novel, *The Ministry of Utmost Happiness*. Born Aftab and becoming Anjum during her formative years, Anjum finds a home in the Khwabgah, the House of Dreams for a community of hijras in Delhi. Despite feeling at home among themselves, the hijras are constantly marginalized in society as they feel that they do not belong in public spaces in Delhi. Contemporary neoliberal India does not include queer identities. It relegates them to the margins, in a life of begging, performing, being outcast, and being feared. I have explored how the novel situates the so-called third gender at the intersections of space and gender. Roy's novel presents Anjum's queer identity as an integral part of the spatial interrelations in the contemporary Indian city. I read *The Ministry of Utmost Happiness* as carving out a recognizable space for Anjum's queerness as a non-binary individual. It is after an incident during the religiously motivated riots in Gujarat in 2002 that Anjum is traumatized, decides to leave the Khwabgah, and ultimately finds a new home in her marginalized existence in the graveyard. Using Teresa Caldeira's (2017) theory of peripheral urbanization in the context of the social dimension and construction of space, I argue that the graveyard becomes Anjum's queer home. It represents an example of peripheral urbanization as it becomes a metaphorical space on the margins that allows Anjum a dignified existence where she is in control and able to help other marginalized people in Delhi. Even though the cityscapes of Delhi in the novel are not built to include queer individuals, Anjum manages to subvert this negligence and create a space for herself. This heterotopic space of the graveyard presents a queer home and a site of resistance (hooks 1989) as it questions heteronormativity and spatial production in neoliberal India.

REFERENCES

Aitkenhead, Decca. 2017. "'Fiction Takes Its Time': Arundhati Roy on Why It Took 20 Years to Write Her Second Novel." *The Guardian*, May 27, 2017. www.theguardian.com/books/2017/may/27/arundhati-roy-fiction-takes-time-second-novel-ministry-utmost-happiness

Bannerji, Himani. 2016. "Patriarchy in the Era of Neoliberalism: The Case of India." *Social Scientist* 44, no. 3–4 (March–April): 3–27. www.jstor.org/stable/24890241?seq=1#metadata_info_tab_contents

Caldeira, Teresa PR. 2017. "Peripheral Urbanization: Autoconstruction, Transversal Logics, and Politics in Cities of the Global South." *Environment and Planning D: Society and Space* 35, no. 1 (July): 3–20. journals.sagepub.com/doi/10.1177/0263775816658479

Chakrabarty, Anup Shekar. 2020. "Negotiating the Queer and the Politics of Sexualities in Urban Spaces: Sanitized Spaces, Vocality, Display and Visibility in Kolkata City." In *Urban Spaces and Gender in Asia*, edited by Divya Upadhyaya Joshi and Caroline Brassard, 109–129. Cham, Switzerland: Springer.

Das, Raju J. 2015. "Critical Observations on Neo-liberalism and India's New Economic Policy." *Journal of Contemporary Asia* 45, no. 4: 715–726. content.csbs.utah.edu/~mli/Economies%205430–6430/Das-Neoliberalism%20and%20India_s%20New%20Economic%20Policy.pdf

Datta, Anindita. 2021. *Gender, Space and Agency in India: Exploring Regional Genderscapes*. New York: Routledge.

Dutta, Aniruddha, and Raina Roy. 2014. "Decolonizing Transgender in India: Some Reflections." *TSQ: Transgender Studies Quarterly* 1, no. 3 (August): 320–337. read.dukeupress.edu/tsq/article-abstract/1/3/320/24718/Decolonizing-Transgender-in-IndiaSome-Reflections?redirectedFrom=fulltext

Gopinath, Swapna. 2020. "Gendered Spaces Captured in Cultural Representations: Conceptualising the Indian Experience in Arundhati Roy's *The Ministry of Utmost Happiness*." *Humanities* 9, no. 1 (December): 2. www.mdpi.com/2076-0787/9/1/2

Gurarani, Shubhra, and Lorraine Kennedy. 2021. "The Co-Production of Space, Politics and Subjectivities in India's Urban Peripheries." *SAMAJ: South Asia Multidisciplinary Academic Journal* 26. journals.openedition.org/samaj/7365

hooks, bell. 1989. "Choosing the Margin as a Space of Radical Openness." *Framework: The Journal of Cinema and Media* 36: 15–23. www.jstor.org/stable/44111660?seq=1#metadata_info_tab_contents

Lertlaksanaporn, Tanrada. 2020. "Transgender People's Deterritorialization in Arundhati Roy's *The Ministry of Utmost Happiness* and Trace Peterson's '*After Before and After*.'" *Manusya* 23, no. 1 (March): 116–126. brill.com/view/journals/mnya/23/1/article-p116_116.xml?language=en

Massey, Doreen. 2005. *For Space*. London, UK: SAGE.

Mendes, Ana Cristina, and Lisa Lau. 2020. "The Precarious Lives of India's Others: The Creativity of Precarity in Arundhati Roy's *The Ministry of Utmost Happiness*." *Journal of Postcolonial Writing* 56, no. 1 (December): 70–82. www.tandfonline.com/doi/full/10.1080/17449855.2019.1683758

Nair, Sonya J. 2022. "Introduction: Transgender to Transperson: An Overview of Indian Histories of Self, Sex, and Society." In *Transgender India: Understanding Third Gender Identities and Experiences*, edited by Douglas A. Vakoch, 1–16. Cham, Switzerland: Springer.

Narrain, Arvind. 2004. "The Articulation of Rights around Sexuality and Health: Subaltern Queer Cultures in India in the Era of Hindutva." *Health and Human Rights* 7, no. 2: 142–164. www.jstor.org/stable/pdf/4065351.pdf

Raju, Saraswati, and Tanusree Paul. 2016–2017. "Public Spaces and Places: Gendered Intersectionalities in Indian Cities." *IIC Quarterly* 43, no. 3–4 (January): 128–138. www.researchgate.net/publication/316877267_Public_Spaces_and_Places_Gendered_Intersectionalities_in_Indian_Cities

Roy, Arundhati. 2008. *The God of Small Things*. 1997. New York: Random House.

Roy, Arundhati. 2017. *The Ministry of Utmost Happiness*. New York: Knopf.

Shah, Svati P. 2015. "Queering Critiques of Neoliberalism in India: Urbanism and Inequality in the Era of Transnational 'LGBTQ' Rights." *Antipode: A Radical Journal of Geography* 47, no. 3 (August): 635–651. onlinelibrary.wiley.com/doi/full/10.1111/anti.12112

Tickell, Alex. 2018. "Writing in the Necropolis: Arundhati Roy's *The Ministry of Utmost Happiness*." *Moving Worlds: A Journal of Transcultural Studies* 18, no. 1: 100–112. oro.open.ac.uk/56045/

UN Habitat. 2018. "SDG Indicator 11.7.1 Training Module: Public Space. United Nations Human Settlement Programme." unhabitat.org/sites/default/files/2020/07/indicator_11.7.1_training_module_public_space.pdf

Ung Loh, Jennifer. 2018. "Transgender Identity, Sexual versus Gender 'Rights' and the Tools of the Indian State." *Feminist Review* 119, no. 1 (July): 39–55. journals.sagepub.com/doi/abs/10.1057/s41305-018-0124-9

Wilson, Kalpana, Jennifer Ung Loh, and Navtej Purewal. 2018. "Gender, Violence and the Neoliberal State in India." *Feminist Review* 119, no. 1 (July): 1–6. journals.sagepub.com/doi/10.1057/s41305-018-0109-8?icid=int.sj-abstract.similar-articles.2

Chapter 3

Mirrors of Reality

Toxic Masculinity, Traveling Women, and the Representation of Acid Attack Victim-Survivors in Priya's Mirror

Nidhi Shrivastava

The prominence of the #MeToo movement resulted in the conviction of Harvey Weinstein in March 2020. Referring to the Weinstein case in America, the popular Indian actress Nandita Das (2017) claimed that the culture of silence reinforces and perpetuates the culture of fear. India's current climate does *not* encourage rape survivors to express themselves. Undeniably, the atmosphere for women's safety is also a concern *within* Indian public spaces. While there are many forms of gender-based violence, one of the most heinous and atrocious kinds of violence is acid attack. In this vicious crime, the perpetrator violates and injures the acid attack victim-survivor who is usually on the move; the attack occurs mostly as a punishment if a woman rejects the advances of a man.

Although acid attacks happen worldwide, they are prevalent in the South-Asian sub-continent, including India, Pakistan, Bangladesh, and Cambodia (Gill and Dias 2016). Section 326A of the Indian Penal Code classifies acid attack "as a distinct, specific offence, carrying a penalty of imprisonment for a minimum of 10 years and a maximum of life" (Gill and Dias 2016). Harsimran Gill and Karen Dias (2016) report that even though there have been laws established since February 2013 that are designed to curb acid attacks, crime rates are continuing to increase. According to the National Crime Records Bureau, the acid attack crimes between 2014 and 2018, there were an estimated 1,483 acid attack cases in India (Roy 2020). With that said, Gill and Dias also observe that such rates have been called inaccurate by acid attack campaign groups, who suggest that many cases go unreported; especially where the victim is male because male victim-survivors often feel shamed and emasculated if they make their attack visible to the public.

Acid attack victim-survivors arguably experience a social death. This may be better understood with the help of Veena Das's "Language and Body: Transactions in the Construction of Pain" (1996) in which she observes that women who were raped and abducted during the 1947 partition of India were condemned to social death. In other words, Das elaborates "the classic ritualistic solution [,] in this case [,] *is for the social body to cut itself completely off from the polluted individual.* This is objectified and made present by the performance of symbolic mourning for the 'dead' person, by such ritualistic devices as the breaking of a pot that comes to stand for the person who has socially died but is physically alive" (Das 1996, 79; emphasis added). Indeed, acid attack victims experience an even more severe form of social death because their bodies are not only considered polluted but are often seen as damaged goods (as a conservative society problematically assumes they will never be able to marry or become independent). Ram Devineni, the creator of the *Priya's Shakti* series, also correlates with the lives of victims of sexual assault and acid attacks, which I will discuss in the next section. In the recent past although *Chhapaak* (2020), a Hindi film from Bollywood, tells the story of a real-life acid-attack victim-survivor, Laxmi Agarwal, her character was portrayed by the glamorous Deepika Padukone. Such a portrayal can be considered controversial and problematic because acid-attack survivors are *not* being given the platform of mainstream media to make their presence and stories known. Moreover, the narratives of acid attack victim-survivors demonstrate that women's spaces continue to be regulated by misogynistic and patriarchal attitudes, as discussed by feminist academic scholars, which I will explore later in this chapter.

PRIYA'S MIRROR AND THE FUTURE OF STORYTELLING

In contrast to filmic depictions as in *Chhapaak*, as a comic book, *Priya's Mirror* re-casts shame and understands the ostracization of acid attack victim-survivors as a form of toxic masculinity while underscoring women's lack of safety in public spaces in India. Indeed, its story encourages the acid attack victim-survivors to accept their wounds and embrace their public presence. In the story, the acid attack victim-survivors reclaim their identities and resist the systematic culture of oppression, which is often shaped by the misogynistic and patriarchal attitudes that create and allow conditions which make it acceptable for a man to throw acid on a woman in public spaces without any fear of consequence or punishment just because a woman has rejected him. *Priya's Mirror* is an effective and powerful tool to educate young children and teenagers, especially boys, who can engage in these difficult conversations from an early stage with their teachers in school or with their parents about gender rights and respect for women. Nonetheless, by reading and accessing *Priya's Mirror*, young children have an opportunity to engage with their family members about issues relating to women's vulnerability in Indian public spaces.

My chapter draws an analysis of *Priya's Mirror* as a cultural and analytical text and engages with the personal interviews I had with Monica Singh, Ram Devineni, and Paromita Vohra. I explore the themes of toxic masculinity and its complexities, shame, double standards of beauty and society's (lack of) acceptance of acid attack victim-survivors, mirror as a metaphor, and the dangers women face while they travel in public spaces. Unlike the Hindi film industry, in which filmmakers see it as a discomforting narrative rarely acknowledging or exploring real traumas, the authors of *Priya's Mirror* use the aid of augmented reality (AR) and incorporate the narratives of real-life acid attack victim-survivors to integrate a mask campaign and use—the mirror of love—to destabilize the toxic masculinity that surrounds the victims' lives. Thus, the creators of *Priya's Mirror* have a two-fold goal in this comic book. For one, to create an atmosphere of acceptance of acid attack victims. While society shuns them and paints them as villains, *Priya's Mirror* encourages their acceptance and asks us as readers to normalize their public presence so that they can have the lives they had imagined before the heinous attack occurred. Secondly, the comic book also seeks to complicate the misogynistic and patriarchal attitudes that allow conditions that create dangerous situations for traveling women in public spaces who are subject to rape and acid attacks.

Culturally and historically, these attacks have been viewed as an act of retaliation or revenge after the assailant experiences rejection from the acid attack victim-survivor. One of the powerful narratives embedded within the plot of *Priya's Mirror* is of the acid-attack victim-survivor Monica Singh. In June 2005, Singh was driving her car in Lucknow, the capital city of Northern India, when two men who were on bikes threw sulphuric acid on her (Hirschfield 2017). The heinous attack resulted in acid burns on 65 percent of her body. Her face was destroyed, and its reconstruction took nine years and 46 operations (Hirschfield 2017). Although the men were later convicted, it was revealed that they were hired by a man whose proposal she had rejected to elope with him because she wanted to pursue an education at the National Institute of Fashion Technology (Mukherjee 2020). Robert Hirschfield (2017) further reports that due to the vicious nature of her attack, "Singh was confined at first to a remote, cage-like structure that sealed her in from potential germ carriers, [sic] but made her feel like she was 'an animal in a zoo' or a woman in her coffin." Monica Singh's story gives us a lens into the complex cultural customs that exist for women who are faced with the prospect of acid attack violence. While the physical scars are debilitating, the psychological, social and emotional trauma accompanies the long-term effects of such a heinous crime. Since her attack, however, Singh continued to pursue her dream of becoming a fashion designer and ultimately, on International Woman's Day on March 8, 2016, she was also invited to speak on the United Nations Initiative "Planet 50–50 by 2030: Step It Up for Gender Equality." She is also the Youth Ambassador of UN Women and Speaker at the United Nations representing Face of Resilience from India & United States of America. Additionally, Singh is the founder of the Mahendra Singh Foundation, which provides medical treatment, counselling, and a platform for other acid attack survivors to shape their dreams. It is in 2016 when Ram Devineni and Monica Singh met that she gave a speech at the United Nations ("Comic Book Superheroine to Spotlight" 2016).

Monica's story, along with other acid attack survivors, including Lakshmi Agarwal, Sonia Choudhary, and Natalia Ponce inspired Ram Devineni's second installation called *Priya's Mirror* of the *Priya's Shakti* series. *Priya's Mirror*, a sequel to *Priya's Shakti* has been written by feminist filmmaker Paromita Vohra, illustrated by Dan Goldman and co-created by Ram Devineni. Due to the acid attack's strong correlation with rape, the team chose to work on acid attack as the next subject following the success of *Priya's Shakti*, which was based on the story of a rape survivor in the aftermath of the 2012 Delhi gang rape case. Her mission was to combat patriarchal and misogynistic attitudes and create empathy for victims of rape and sexual violence. *Priya's Shakti* received international success with over half a million downloads. Devineni mentioned in the interview with *DW*, "The main character, Priya, resonated with audiences and was written about in 400 news publications reaching nearly 20 million readers" ("Comic book Superheroine to Spotlight" 2016).

Indeed, this topic of gender-based violence and the treatment of women in public spaces is a common thread in *Priya's Shakti* series as can be seen with the third sequel, *Priya and The Lost Girls* (2019), which focuses on sex trafficking and was launched during the 16 Days of Activism Against Gender-Based Violence and the launch event took place in Agra at the Sheroes Hangout—a café entirely run by acid attack survivors (Shete 2019). As a graphic narrative, *Priya's Mirror* exemplifies these acid attack survivors like Singh reclaiming and re-asserting themselves within spaces in which they would otherwise be shunned to become inspirational role models despite the difficulties and challenges they have faced.

Priya's Mirror and the Questionable Safety of Traveling Women

The second chapter in the *Priya Shakti* series, *Priya's Mirror*, is part of a global campaign of the parent company, Rattapallax, a literary publishing company based in New York City and New Delhi India. The goal of these comic books is to create global awareness as part of the larger entertainment-education (EE) initiative (Devineni 2016). As I have mentioned elsewhere that by deploying new forms of media across class and location, Devineni and his creative partners reimagine the mythological characters that are inspired by the *Amar Chitra Katha* to see all cultural norms and sexuality as malleable rather than fixed, which opens up a new space in terms of how a rape culture may be changed and challenged (Shrivastava 2018).

In the first volume, Priya, a rape victim-survivor, finds the strength to survive her ordeal after the divine intervention that transforms her into a superhero and gives her the courage to face the society that shuns and shames her. *Priya's Shakti* was released in response to the heinous Delhi gang-rape case when Jyoti Singh was gang-raped in a moving bus in the late hours of December 2012. In *Priya's Shakti*, Priya, a lower-class girl from rural India is raped by the men in her village. Upon learning of her sexual assault, her family ostracizes and blames her for seducing the men and shames her. Ashamed, she escapes to the forest hoping to end her life. At this moment we see Goddess Parvati's divine intervention who sees her ordeal. As she enters Priya's body and confronts the men who raped her. Seeing her vulnerable, the men attempt to rape her again and are shocked to learn that they are facing an angered Goddess Parvati in her true form. Meanwhile, Parvati's husband, God Shiva wakes up from his slumber only to discover the ill-treatment of his wife and curses the men to become impotent. Unlike other superheroes we see in popular comic books that draw physical strength to combat evil villains, Priya, transforms into a superpower advocate and activist for women's rights who seeks to change Indian society by striving to end violence against women. In the second installation, we see Priya deploying her powers of advocacy to empower victims of acid attacks, who are trapped by the villain, Ahankaar (ego in Hindi).

Ram Devineni as he conceptualized the graphic works realized that both acts of violence—rape and acid attack—shared similar emotional, psychological, and socio-cultural effects on the victim-survivors. According to Katie Dupere (2016), Devineni met with acid attack survivors in New Delhi during his research trip in 2015. At this time, he listened to their personal experiences, which later led to the creation of *Priya's Mirror*. He made a crucial observation that he shared with me during a personal interview:

There is such a clear correlation between rape survivors and acid attack survivors, even though not all acid attacks are sexually based . . . I was looking at it from the survivor's point of view. *Lots of acid attack survivors literally face the same social stigmas that rape survivors did, but it was much more apparent because they were physically altered and had to deal with the physical trauma along with that.* After they were released, they were isolated, hidden in the houses, away from the rest of the world, and dealing with that, and going into [a] deep depression, not knowing what their lives were going to be like. So not only on an emotional level but also on a physical level. (Devineni 2019, emphasis added)

As we learn from his interview, the traumatic effect of the acid attack leads victims to often feel isolated and hidden from the world. His goal, along with Dan Goldman and Paromita Vohra, was to not only create awareness of the trauma that acid attack victim-survivors experienced, encourage acceptance of them in public spaces, and educate young children and teenagers to create empathy for them.

Priya's Mirror tells the stories of acid attack survivors, their internal struggles and fears, and how they cope with social death. Sharing her ordeal as a rape victim-survivor, Priya encourages and motivates the acid attack survivors who are trapped in the demon, Ahankaar's "sanctuary" (Devineni et al. 4)—a castle that is surrounded by a moat filled with acid released from Ahankaar's mouth. Priya meets Rafi, a villager who has fallen in love with Anjali, an acid attack victim-survivor who had been wounded by acid that a man who was stalking and harassing her had thrown on her. In due time, both Rafi and Anjali fall in love and decide to marry. Angry, Ahankaar refuses the prospect of Anjali's marriage and accuses Rafi of misleading Anjali with false hope demonstrating his tyrannical presence in the lives of acid attack victim-survivors. Subsequently, he throws Rafi into a dungeon, who manages to escape and informs Priya of his ordeal.

After listening to Rafi's account, Priya decides to act against Ahankaar. With the help of her tiger, Sahas (courage in Hindi), Priya flies inside the castle and overhears Ahankaar convincing the women that they will not be loved by anyone else but him and are only safe from the outside world with him. Priya seeks guidance from Goddess Parvati, who shares Ahankaar's background that led him to become a demon-king. We learn that Ahankaar's real name was Prem. In his life as Prem, he meets and falls in love with a girl named Kusum. Kusum also shares his sentiments and feelings and accepts the poems that Prem had dedicated to her. Things turn for the worse when her brothers discover his love notes and force him to drink acid and accuse him of harassing Kusum. Kusum prays to God Shiva for Prem's safety. While Shiva saves Prem by giving him a boon, he also observes that the effects of the acid will haunt him and leaves it to Prem/Ahankaar to choose his actions. As he wakes up, Ahankaar burns Kusum by spewing acid on her. When confronting Priya, he reminds the acid attack victim-survivors that they should believe Priya at their own peril as the "world is evil and cannot change."

In the story's climax, Priya offers the acid attack victim-survivors the "mirror of love." While others resist and accuse Priya of cruelty for encouraging them to look at the mirror, Anjali volunteers. After looking at the mirror, the women begin to feel empowered and start seeing beauty in themselves. After escaping from Ahankaar's castle, they initially feel restricted in the moat. But, as they take a step forward, the moat's acid turns into water upon their contact. As they leave, Ahankaar rises from the castle—larger and stronger. Just then, Priya shows him the mirror of love, which breaks the spell, and he returns to his former self as Prem. Priya, then, tells him to find strength, not in control of others but in true courage. Kusum remains with him.

In the epilogue, we see that a year has passed. Anjali and the other women have built their café where they have found strength in numbers. Not only did they win a case where acid was made illegal for distribution in India, but they have become independent, empowered women who have accepted themselves. Although the banning of acid attack is an attempt to protect women, it is *not* a sufficient step in protecting women in public spaces. We need texts such as *Priya's Mirror* to educate young boys and men to respect women's rights to safety in public spaces.

MIRROR, SHAME, AND THE PLIGHT OF ACID ATTACK VICTIM-SURVIVORS

Feminist geographers and academics, both in India and globally, have studied extensively how women are viewed within public spaces. The field of feminist geography emerged in the 1980s. Gerda R. Wekerle (1985), for example, argues that there is an inherent and conventional bias reflected in urban development in North American cities that relegates women as homemakers while men as breadwinners of independent nuclear families (11–12). As she emphasizes, "cities are still planned for men by men" (Wekerle 1985, 11). As a result, women are left vulnerable because public spaces are male-dominated. Often, the cities lack policies that protect women from violent crimes. Feminist Geographer Gill Valentine (1989) uses the case study of Deborah Linsey who was stabbed to death in 1988 to demonstrate that women are concerned about instances of male violence. Due to the fear of male violence in the forms of rape and sexual assault, women are dependent on men (whom they are familiar with) to enter and use these spaces. Valentine suggests that "women's inhibited use and occupation of public space is, therefore, a spatial expression of patriarchy" (1989, 389). Further extending on Valentine's argument, sociologist Elizabeth A. Stanko (1995), thus, contends that due to this fear of physical harm and violence, "women police themselves by restricting their activities in public spaces . . . " (51). Moreover, Valentine and Stanko also demonstrate it is also the women who are blamed for the crimes that take place upon their bodies. In *The Sphinx of the City: Urban Life, the Control of Disorder, and Women,* Elizabeth Wilson (1992) surveys the politics of women's movement within cities in Europe and America. For Wilson, the sophisticated urban consciousness was equivalent to male consciousness that was predominant in Europe but also extends to the United States. She observes that "the city offers untrammelled sexual experience; in the city the forbidden—what is most feared and desired—becomes possible. [The] woman is present in cities as [a] temptress, as whore, as [a] fallen woman, as lesbian, but *also as virtuous womanhood in danger*, as heroic womanhood who triumphs over temptation and tribulation" (Wilson 1995, 6; emphasis added). Although this scholarship dates back to the 1980s and 1990s, Leslie Kern (2020)'s scholarship suggests that these issues highlighted decades ago continue to remain relevant today when it comes to women's safety in urban and public spaces. In *Feminist City: Claiming A Space In A Man-Made World*, she notes that during the time of her research for her monograph, the #MeToo movement had exploded.

> Their [the stories of the rape victim-survivors] resonate with the vast literature on women's fear in cities. The constant, low-grade threat of violence mixed with daily harassment shapes women's urban lives in countless conscious and unconscious ways. Just as workplace harassment chases women out of positions of power and erases their contributions to science, politics, art, and culture, the spectre of urban violence limits women's choices, power, and economic opportunities.

Gendered violence is a universal and global issue. More specifically, India continues to deal with the issue of safety for women in public spaces. Scholars have pointed out that female sexuality has always been a major concern in Indian society (Chatterjee 1994; Niranjana 2001; and Chakravarti 2006). Tanushree Paul (2011) also points out, "[i]t is important to mention at this juncture that sexuality, physical vulnerability, and reproductive role of women have been typically held responsible for legitimising their confinement within private space since time immemorial" (252). In a recent article, journalist Vartika Rastogi (2021) observes that in contemporary times, public safety issue in India is complex and nuanced. Rastogi argues that "it is not

Mirrors of Reality 59

uncommon for police personnel in India to blame and shame women for their choices [w]hen women approach [the police] regarding issues like harassment and advising them to take 'precautions' like dressing a certain way or not frequenting certain places at certain hours" ("Can Indian Cities Be Better Designed" 2021).

Figure 3.1. The Women Facing the Mirror
Source: Reproduced by the kind permission of Ram Devineni.

In keeping with the problem of women's vulnerability in public spaces, although the ending of *Priya's Mirror* is a hopeful one, acid attacks continue to remain prevalent in India. Unfortunately, this malaise in Indian has some of the highest rates in the world. While statistics may not be wholly reliable as many of these attacks go unreported, there were 182 acid attacks that were reported in 2020 (Statista). According to Vidhik Kumar (2021), at least "60% of the cases are never reported," because "victims are reluctant to report because they feel shame and stigma, and resources are not available to deal with the crime in rural areas" (2). He further adds that the crime is perceived as an act of violence against women because women are victimized in "more than 80% of the cases" and in most cases, 84 percent of the perpetrators are men (Kumar 2). Furthermore, the organization Acid Survivors Trust International (ASTI) has found in its research that "in most cases (76%) the attack is committed by someone who is known to the victim" (ASTI "A Worldwide Problem"). Recent news reports as early as January 2022 suggest that women's safety as they travel or are in public spaces remains a concern in India. As I write this, there is also a rise in acid attacks in India. In January 2022, a woman was attacked in the Jaunpur district of Uttar Pradesh for simply filing a First Information Report (FIR) with the police over a land dispute. She was attacked with acid and died two months later from the burns. She was a mother of two children. As Devineni had pointed out, these attacks do not have to be sexual in their nature. In another case, an acid attack occurred in the Chatra district of Jharkhand, Bihar. On August 4, 2022, a seventeen-year-old battled for her life as her classmate (and her stalker) who had been harassing her threw acid that burned 30 percent of her body (Angad 2022, "Teen Attacked with Acid"). These recent cases underscore the value and importance of stories such as those told in *Priya's Mirror* so that we not only recognize the trauma that these women face but also that these attacks continue to happen and now with even younger perpetrators, as can be seen from the most recent case.

The women who face acid attack violence are subjected to a similar shame and isolation that rape victim-survivors face. However, the physicality of their trauma is one that is hard to overlook. In the film, *Chhapaak*, we see Malti Agarwal (Deepika Padukone) not only let out a harrowing and haunting scream when she faces the mirror, but we also see her constantly shrouded in public spaces (almost as if she is intentionally making herself invisible) within the world. These scenes are not only shown in the movie but are also present in the trailer of the film itself to draw audiences to the lived experiences of acid attack victim-survivors. Films and documentaries that are based on their experiences are also difficult to see and can be triggering for many. Therefore, many of their stories fall into the cracks placing them further into the margins of our society.

For the acid attack victim-survivors, however, their lives are permanently changed due to damage to their bodies, face, and eyes. Mridula Bandyopadhyay and Mahmuda Rahman Khan (2013) write that the intention of the acid attack is to "destroy a woman's potential for marriage and to ensure that no one else would want her" (68). They also suggest that acid attacks are different from other burns because "acid burn causes disfigurement, long term disability, and pain. Severe disfiguration forces women into isolation. Sometimes due to continued threats from the perpetrators, the victims might also lose shelter. Trauma, depression, anxiety, isolation, and disturbed conjugal life" (68). One such case reported in 2010 was of Anu, who was nineteen years old at this time and was training to become a nurse in Chandigarh, India. According to Sally (2011), Anu was the eldest child of her family and was working to contribute financially to support her family and help her mother raise her siblings. On January 28, she was returning home with her friends when a man, unfamiliar to Anu, threw acid on her. This untimely attack resulted in 70 percent burns on her face, neck, and arms. Her friend also suffered burns. The perpetrator remains at large with no sign of him receiving any punishment for his crime. For Anu, the attack resulted in her withdrawing from her studies as "she stopped going to college soon after the incident and now spends her time behind closed doors, conscious and scared of the people's stares" (Sally 2011). Moreover, her case further reveals the complexities and nuances of the trauma that the acid attack victim-survivors face daily. For instance, Anu's mother took her to the hospital but the doctors informed them that it was a "sensitive case" for the surgery, which was going to be expensive for the family. According to Ankita Raj (2022), these surgeries for rehabilitating acid attack victims are becoming greatly unaffordable in India. One acid attack survivor, Haseena Hussein shares in an interview with Priyali Sur (2014), her experience of having 35 surgeries over the course of fifteen years:

> Surgeries cost almost Rs. 2 million (US$32,400). My entire face is reconstructed—nose, lips, eyelids, everything. My parents sold off everything they had to pay for my surgeries—our house, my mother's jewelry. After 35 long and painful surgeries, I realized that the surgeries were not making much difference to my face. So I decided to stop the surgeries and concentrate on my life.

Unlike Haseena's parents who made sacrifices to support their daughter's countless surgeries, Anu's family is compelled to rely on extended family for financial support. However, such dependency leaves them in a precarious position within society. When *Times of India* approached the District police, his response is indicative of how difficult it is for acid attack victim-survivors to seek justice: "I am not aware of this matter as nobody from the victim's family has approached me yet. I will now put my best efforts to solve this case" (Sally 2011). Stories such as these left an impression on Devineni, who observed in an interview:

> What I discovered after talking with them is that they faced the same cultural stigmas and reactions from [the] society that rape survivors had to endure. How society treated them intensified the problem and their recovery. How they were treated by their family, neighbours and society determined what they did next. Often, they were treated like villains and the blame was put on them. Our comic book focuses on this and tries to change people's perceptions of these heroic women. (Devineni 2019)

Indeed, *Priya's Mirror* represents the narratives of real acid attack victim survivors including Monica Singh and Natalie Ponce who are portrayed as heroes.

As mentioned before, Monica Singh's empowering story embodies her resilience after surviving the acid attack. In an interview with *Logical Indian*, Singh informs, "When I see my 'mirror of reality,' like Priya's 'mirror of love,' I see healed scars. The mirror shows you the reflection you want to see. I see potential and so much happiness in having the strength to change my life" (Chaudhuri 2017). The mirror functions as a powerful force to empower the strength within. In a recent interview with me, she shared how she used to look in the mirror every day to gain strength. For her, the mirror is emblematic of acceptance of herself because she said that for acid victim-survivors: "It is not only physical harm, but also the mental and psychological harm as well, and to get out of this thing is near to impossible for many cases. What happens is that you need to have that willpower to keep surviving and living and accepting the fact that 'ok shit this happened and now you have to move on . . . you have to accept yourself and stop measuring yourself with other people because now reality has changed so you need to deal in such a way that it doesn't affect your future" (Singh 2019). Therefore, Singh's powerful story reframes the mirror as a tool of empowerment and the very truth that indeed our beauty lies within us and in our strengths to overcome trials and tribulations.

The creators of *Priya's Mirror* approached the issue of representing acid attack survivors in an ethical manner by humanizing them. In an interview with *Mashable*, Ram Devineni shares that it was essential that the survivors play a role in vetting their own representations (Dupere 2016). The comic book also shares the stories of other prominent acid attack survivors and activists, including Lakshmi Agarwal, the founder of the Stop Sale Acid Campaign, acid attack survivors Sonia Choudhary and Natalia Ponce de Leon. Natalia, who is Colombian, also had a liter of acid thrown at her body and face by a man she was unfamiliar with. Ponce started her own campaign titled "The Last Mask Campaign" in which she sent out physical masks to politicians, celebrities, soap opera actors, and sports stars in her country. All of them wore masks to draw attention to the issue of acid attacks. Her campaign garnered national media attention. Her campaign was an effort to change laws to punish the attackers in her country. Inspired by her campaign, readers of *Priya's Mirror* put on a digital mask using AR and then share their photos on social media to show solidarity and support for the victims.

PERPETRATORS OF VIOLENCE, LAWS, AND TOXIC MASCULINITY

In the aftermath of the 2012 Delhi gang rape case, international newspapers such as *Forbes* rated India as the ninth most dangerous country for women travelers (Bloom 2019). Although these statistics are horrifying, they indicate the dangers that women face in public spaces because of the patriarchal and misogynistic attitudes toward women that continue to shape Indian society and play a role in discriminating cultural practices against girls and women. Indian Lawyer Indira Jaising (1995) points out that female infanticide has been a practice for centuries. Even though it was criminalized in 1994 when the Indian government enacted the Pre-Natal Diagnostic Techniques (PNDT) Act that prohibits sex selection, it remains an issue. As I have mentioned elsewhere, British filmmaker Leslee Udwin who was the producer of the documentary, *India's Daughter* (2015), observed in an interview with me that the Indian culture devalues women and that rapists and perpetrators of acid attacks are "product of patriarchy" (Shrivastava 2021). She further adds, "anytime he [a boy/man] sees a girl being born, there are no sweets being distributed, and there are commiserations. Anytime a meal is being had by a family, the girl eats last. You know, why would he question that? Of course, he is certain that girls are worthless because we tell him that they are" (Shrivastava 2021). Indeed, society and culture play a key role in shaping the attitudes that perpetrators have toward women. Educated, vocal, and independent women, much like Singh, are reduced to sexual and reproductive beings in the eyes of their perpetrators.

The ill-treatment of acid attack survivors is not only an example of the systematic culture of oppression, but the laws that are in place continue to remain insufficient to protect women from becoming victims of acid attacks. Although there have been laws implemented since 2013, they have been inadequate and insufficient to rehabilitate the lives of acid attack survivors or prevent these attacks from happening. In 2013, Section 326A of the Indian Penal Code was implemented and was designed to punish the perpetrators for a minimum of ten years or a maximum of a life sentence (Hameed and Bhattacharya 2022). Section 357A also calls for the State government to make a payment of a fine to the victim under section 326A or section 376D of the Indian Penal Code. Nehaluddin Ahmad (2012)'s research also points out that not only do the acid attack victim-survivors receive inadequate funds for reconstructive surgeries and medical expenses, but their pay is "erratic" (64). In a case in Maharashtra, for instance, the state ordered the husband to pay Rs. 2000 for the attack on his wife (64). As Shaheema Hameed and Bhupal Bhattacharya (2022) argue through their research, "despite legislative amendments in the Indian judiciary, it is obvious by the rising number of acid attacks that much more needs to be done to operationalize data on rehabilitation measures, NGO initiatives, and other support systems available to acid attack survivors."

Referring to the case of the seventeen-year-old girl who was victimized by a boy of the same age and is currently fighting for her life in 2022, it is evident that acid is now available much more freely in India. Ahmad (2011), for example, notes, "Hydrochloric and sulphuric acids are very easily available in medical and other stores. Acid is also a very inexpensive weapon to procure, as a liter can be obtained for as little as INR 25 (half a US dollar) at most locations" (Ahmad 64). This recent attack also demonstrates the fact that the perpetrators who procure acid are getting younger and younger, thus endangering more lives of women who are in public spaces. It is, therefore, crucial that we need to have these conversations with young boys and teenagers from an early age to shift their attitudes toward women and help them gain respect for girls and women.

Comic books such as *Priya's Mirror* further explore these patriarchal and misogynistic attitudes toward these acid attack victim-survivors through the representation of Ahankaar. According to Priti Salian (2017), the World Bank was also involved in the efforts and had partnered with Devineni and his co-creators for the second installation of the Priya Shakti series. World Bank's WEvolve campaign that deals with world-wide gender-based violence played a role in not only funding *Priya's Mirror* but also was excited about the organization's "edutainment" approach to address the social norms that, in their view, is the root of these attitudes (Saitan 2017). Maria Correa, the founder of WEvolve, noted that "We need to turn our attention to the behaviours of the perpetrators and ask what is driving them to use this violence . . . there is a dire need to introspect why so many men use violence against women, even in their own family, why is it so commonplace across the world and how institutions, peers, and women themselves perpetuate this practice" (Saitan 2017). The World Bank, therefore, not only funded but also played an important role in the creation of *Priya's Mirror*.

At the core of its story, we see that the acid attack victims are trapped with the villain—Ahankaar's moat—which is surrounded by acid. The victims are afraid of returning to public spaces due to the prolonged shame and judgement

Mirrors of Reality 65

Figure 3.2. Ahankaar in His Castle
Source: Reproduced by the kind permission of Ram Devineni.

that they fear they will face. Devineni remarks that "teenage boys are the *true* audience they're targeting. Young boys are the next generation of potential aggressors, and they're essential in the fight to shift a culture that normalizes all forms [of] gendered violence" (Dupere 2016; emphasis added). Devineni and Vohra reimagined the traditional comic book villain making him multifaceted and nuanced. During the interview with me, Devineni elaborated on this decision:

> Ahankaar is complex for sure. I think he represents what toxic masculinity can transform you into. Even the innocent man gets corrupted [because] he keeps his castle to protect the acid attack survivor women from society, but in reality, he

is imprisoning them in their own fears. Often in India, I would hear statements from male police officers or authority figures or parents about "protecting" their daughters—statements like "women should not be allowed to go out at night because it is dangerous." And similar statements. In reality, this is a form of "control" over women—limiting their choices. (Devineni 2019)

Devineni sees toxic masculinity as a form of control that is evident in the society that seeks to silence victims of gender-based violence, whether it be acid attacks or sexual violence. In fact, in another interview, Monica Singh calls for highlighting the problematic ways society treats the perpetrators while shunning the victim. Although she had the support of her father to continue with her education and pursue her dreams to have a career in the industry, traditionally women who undergo this trauma are held inside and responsible for their attacks as if they were the ones who had committed the crime. In Monica's case, two of the accused men were acquitted for the attack on her for mere Rs. 25, 000 (US$334). Singh writes poignantly, "That's the cost of my life, my identity" (Mukherjee 2020).

In my interview with her, Vohra points out that "*Priya's Mirror* is, in fact, the tragedy of the villain. It is not the tragedy of the person. It is a tragedy that he is not able to leave and liberate himself. [The] women liberate themselves finally. Priya helps the women to see the mirror to see themselves differently and to see themselves with the eyes of love" (Vohra 2019). Vohra also pointed out that the villain, named aptly as Ahaankar, is trapped on the island where he had initially convinced the acid attack survivors that no one would accept them because he has swallowed the acid as well. After the acid attack survivors are rescued with Priya's help, he is still stuck on this island. Ahankaar is a testament to toxic masculinity and patriarchy that traps people from moving on and onto acceptance of gender-based violence survivors. In the comic book, the acid alludes to the toxicity of patriarchy and masculinity that only moves society from transcending and breaking away from the archaic social norms that continue to leave many on this metaphorical island:

> In the case of Ahankaar . . . the villain figure . . . the antagonist of *Priya's Mirror*, even though the women tell him and leave the mirror for him, and a woman is left with him who knew him and loved him because she knew him before . . . but Ahankaar is stuck to the wound and now that he does not have the power to hate and make people fear through his hate, he is nothing because he has not allowed himself to become another person . . . Patriarchy traps all of us . . . In the case of *Priya's Mirror*, patriarchy traps men and doesn't let them liberate themselves and doesn't liberate women. It doesn't allow them to say to women that they should go forward. When the women liberate themselves, he is still stuck in his patriarchal framework. (Vohra 2019)

Through Vohra's insights about Ahankaar's characterization, we see that the patriarchal and misogynistic conditional thinking not only cages societies but leads them to not accept victim-survivors of acid attacks. With that said, I would argue that the comic book inadvertently also makes a revolutionary move by highlighting those men and other gendered identities can also be victims of acid attacks, although that is not well-known. By making Ahankaar a villain painted with complexities and nuances, we see that the chains of patriarchal and misogynistic thought keep us from accepting victim-survivors of acid attacks so much so that as a society often we do not see them as being part of our everyday lives.

CONCLUSION

Although there has been a rise in acid attacks in India as is evident from the recent cases discussed in this chapter, it is also important to acknowledge the efforts being made by the creators of the *Priya's Shakti* series who are calling attention to the safety of women in public spaces as well as encouraging acceptances of women who are victim-survivors of brutal acid attacks that take away their agency as well as their futures. Through both *Priya's Shakti* and *Priya's Mirror*, the creators seek to use the technique of edutainment and comic books to give tools to parents and family members to engage in these topics with their children, especially their sons and teenage boys, to discuss these issues and challenge the patriarchal and misogynistic attitudes. Although patriarchal and misogynistic attitudes remain entrenched in the society, these efforts demonstrate a move to target younger boys and teenage men to create a change in attitude within the society in the long-term rather than only punishment as a short-term solution.

Moreover, through the efforts of Ram Devineni, Paromita Vohra, and Monica Singh, the issue of acid attacks is reframed to make it accessible not just to children who would read the comic book, but to anyone who comes across their work. *Priya's Mirror*, therefore, is an important contribution to this conversation to not only criminalize acid attacks but also to normalize and encourage acceptance of acid attack survivors and also to make public spaces friendlier to women.

REFERENCES

Acid Survivors Trust International (ASTI). n.d. "A World Wide Problem." Accessed September 15, 2022. www.asti.org.uk/a-worldwide-problem.html

Ahmad, Nehaluddin. 2011. "Acid Attacks on Women: An Appraisal of the Indian Legal Response." *Asia-Pacific Journal on Human Rights and Law* 2: 55–72.

Angad, Abhishek. "Jharkhand: Teen Attacked with Acid Serious, Set for Surgery Today." *Indian Express.* Last Modified September 1, 2022. indianexpress.com/article/india/teen-attacked-with-acid-serious-set-for-surgery-8123957/

Bandyopadhyay, Mridula and Mahmuda Rahman Khan. 2003. "Loss of Face: Violence against Women in South Asia." In *Violence against Women in Asian Societies*, edited by Linda Rae Bennett and Lenore Manderson. London: Routledge.

Bloom, Laura Begley. "20 Most Dangerous Places for Women Travelers." Forbes. Last modified July 26, 2019. www.forbes.com/sites/laurabegleybloom/2019/07/26/20-most-dangerous-places-for-women-travelers/?sh=5ae52890c2f4

Chakravarti, Uma. 2006. *Everyday Lives, Everyday Histories: Beyond the Kings and Brahmans of "Ancient" India.* New Delhi: Tulika Books.

Chatterjee, Partha. 1994. *The Nation and its Fragments: Colonial and Post-Colonial Histories.* Delhi: Oxford University Press.

Chaudhuri, Pooja. 2017. "The Story of a Superhero Who Fights to Save Acid-Attack Survivors." Logical India. Last modified on December 25, 2017. thelogicalindian.com/exclusive/monica-singh-acid-attack

Das, Nandita. 2017. "Culture of Silence Isis Manifestation of Culture of Fear: Nandita Das." YouTube video, Mumbai Collective, 15:18, December 20, 2017, www.youtube.com/watch?v=4iAs3dBSH8A&t=36s

Das, Veena. 1996. "Language and Body: Transactions in the Construction of Pain." *Daedalus* 125, no. 1: 67–91.

Devineni, Ram. 2019. Interview by author. Zoom, August 12.

Dupere, Katie. 2016. "New Augmented Reality Comic Book Shows the Resilience of Acid Attack Survivors." Mashable. Last modified October 2, 2016. mashable.com/article/priyas-mirror-acid-attacks-india

DW. "Comic-Book Superheroine to Spotlight India's Acid-Attack Menace." Last modified October 24, 2016. amp.dw.com/en/comic-book-superheroine-to-spotlight-indias-acid-attack-menace/a-36141976

Gill, Harsimran and Karen Dias. 2016. "Indian Acid Attack Victims Share Their Stories." *Al Jazeera.* Last modified March 10, 2016. www.aljazeera.com/features/2016/3/10/indian-acid-attack-victims-share-their-stories

Gulzar, Meghna, dir. 2020. *Chhapaak.* India: Fox Star Studios, 2020. DVD.

Hameed, Shaheema and Bhupal Bhattacharya. 2022. "Scarred for Life: Thoughts on Legal Perspectives of Acid Attacks in Selected Countries with a Focus on India." *Journal of International Women's Studies* 23, no. 1: 1–9.

Hirschfield, Robert. 2017. "Monica Singh: Acid Attack Survivor, Gender Rights Warrior." *International Examiner.* iexaminer.org/monica-singh-acid-attack-survivor-gender-rights-warrior/

Kern, Leslie. 2020. *Feminist City: Claiming Space in a Man-Made World.* New York: Verso.

Kumar, Vidhik. 2021. "Acid Attacks in India: A Socio-Legal Report." *Dignity: A Journal of Analysis of Exploitation and Violence* 6, no. 1, Article 5. doi.org/10.23860/dignity.2021.06.01.05

Mukherjee, Nairita. "Acid Survivor Monica Singh: The Accused Were Let Off for Rs 25k. That Is the Cost of My Life." India Today. Last updated February 25, 2020. www.indiatoday.in/lifestyle/people/story/acid-survivor-monica-singh-the-accused-were-let-off-for-rs-25k-that-is-the-cost-of-my-life-1649541-2020-02-25

Niranjana, Seemanthini. *Gender and Space: Femininity, Sexualization and the Female Body.* New Delhi: Sage Publications, 2001.

Pandey, Ajay. 2022. "Hindi: Acid Attack Woman Suffered and Died Due to Acid Attack in Jaunpur." *Tv9 Hindi*. Last modified March 30, 2022. www.tv9hindi.com/state/uttar-pradesh/acid-attack-victim-dies-in-jaunpur-1144443.html

Paul, Tanushree. 2011. "Public Spaces and Everyday Lives: Gendered Encounters in the Metro City of Kolkata." In *Doing Gender, Doing Geography*, edited by Saraswathi Raju and Kuntala Lahiri-Dutt, 250–270. London: Routledge.

Raj, Ankita. "Why Does India Have Such High Numbers of Acid Attacks." *Feminism India*. Last modified May 12, 2022. feminisminindia.com/2022/05/12/why-does-india-have-such-high-numbers-of-acid-attacks/

Rastogi, Vartika. 2021. "Can Indian Cities Be Better Designed for Women?" *Feminism India*. Last modified February 9, 2021. feminisminindia.com/2021/02/09/indian-cities-can-be-better-for-womens-safety/

Roy, Pulaha. 2020. "India Saw almost 1,500 Acid Attacks in Five Years." *India Today*. Last modified January 12, 2020. www.indiatoday.in/diu/story/india-saw-almost-1-500-acid-attacks-in-five-years-1636109-2020-01-12

Sailan, Priti. 2017. "How the World Bank Got Involved with a Comic Book Series on Crimes against Women." *Scroll.In*. Last modified February 26, 2017. scroll.in/article/830288/how-the-world-bank-got-involved-with-a-comic-book-series-on-crimes-against-women

Sally, Gourav. 2011. "Acid Attack still Waiting for Justice." *Times of India*. Last modified July 17, 2011. timesofindia.indiatimes.com/city/chandigarh/acid-attack-victims-still-waiting-for-justice/articleshow/9253988.cms

Shete, Yugandra. "'Priya and the Lost Girls' Comic Pays an Ode to the Female Superheroes in India." *Animation Xpress.* Last modified December 16, 2019. www.animationxpress.com/latest-news/priya-and-the-lost-girls-comic-pays-an-ode-to-the-female-superheroes-in-india/

Shrivastava, Nidhi. 2018. "The Representation of Gender and Sexuality in *Priya's Shakti* (2012)." *South Asian Review* 39, no. 1–2: 212–226. doi.org/10.1080/02759527.2018.1509553.

Shrivastava, Nidhi. 2021. "Leslee Udwin's India's Daughter (2015), the Power of Storytelling and Question of Social Change in the #MeToo Era." *Journal of Applied Journalism & Media Studies* 10, no. 2: 183–198. doi.org/10.1386/ajms_00056_1

Singh, Monica. Interview by author, phone. August 19, 2019.

Stanko, Elizabeth A. "Women, Crime, and Fear." *Annals of the American Academy of Political and Social Science* 539, Reactions to Crime and Violence (May 1995): 46–58. www.jstor.org/stable/1048395

Sur, Priyali. "Indian Government Fails Acid Attack Survivors, Activists Say." *Women's Media Center*. Last modified August 8, 2014. womensmediacenter.com/women-under-siege/indian-government-fails-acid-attack-survivors-activists-say

Valentine, Gill. 1989. "The Geography of Women's Fear." *Area* 21, no. 4: 385–290. The Royal Geographical Society (with the Institute of British Geographers).

Vohra, Paromita. Interview by author, September 26, 2019.

Wekerle, R. Gerda. 1985. "A Woman's Place in the City." *Antipode: A Radical Journal of Geography* 6, no. 5: 11–20.

Wilson, Elizabeth. 1992. *The Sphinx of the City: Urban Life, the Control of Disorder, and Women*. Berkeley: University of California Press.

PART II

Bollywood's Traveling Women (I)

*Misogyny, Roads, and
Female Vulnerability*

Chapter 4

Stepping Out

Global Bollywood, Gendered Landscape, and Undercurrents of Neoliberal Pleasures

Madhuja Mukherjee

ONCE UPON A TIME IN THE CINEMATIC-CITY

This chapter revisits gendered urban spaces, in the context of neoliberalism and the swelling megacities in India, as reflected in contemporary Bollywood films. I, however, take a long route and examine a number of Hindi popular films which are set in the post-partition era, as well as certain early Bollywood films, in an attempt to understand the altering role of women vis-à-vis economic and social transformations, and analyze the ways in which a woman, and a wanderer, arrive at and gain access to evolving cities. I evoke the figuration of the iconic *"flaneur"*—an (male) urban-explorer and a quintessential figure of the modern world—as theorized by Walter Benjamin in his landmark and influential writing on Paris, to inquire: how does female *flanerie* (the act of streetwalking) materialize in recent filmic texts, marked by global travels of people, technologies, cultures, media and finance? The seminal readings of the "invisible *flaneuse*" by Janet Wolff (1985), subsequently, by Pollock Griselda (1988), followed by crucial rethinking of the feminine and feminist modes of *flanerie* by Elizabeth Wilson (1992), and more recent work by Deborah Parsons (2003), compel us to ask: is strolling by an observant woman possible in recent Bollywood films that offer pleasures of global travel? Can *she* walk around purposelessly, listening to the narratives of the cities? What are consequences of *her* transgressions? How do we locate this elusive persona of female *flaneur/flaneuse* in popular films and in the rapidly globalizing Indian cities?[1]

Let us, therefore, begin with a story. Consider a solitary woman, back to camera, walking down a city street during the night. The camera follows her, and a screeching sound engulfs the scene. This, as we are aware, is a typical scenario of unease—resulting in multiple orders of violence—which has been constructed over the years via numerous Hindi popular films, produced from Bombay (now Mumbai), India. Nevertheless, let us consider an unusual instance from the film *Aaram* (Dir. D. D. Kashyap, 1951), which opens with a night shot of an empty street. A woman (donning a fashionable sari and large a purse) enters the frame; later, we see her more closely. As she begins to speak, initially it appears that she is speaking to herself, however, a man enters the frame shortly, and it is apparent that she is addressing him. She says: "Why I am travelling through the empty streets at the depth of the night? Shall I tell you?" At the outset, we hear a heavy voice, the man says: "I don't need to know all this"; thereafter, he enters the frame and adds: "You are following me unnecessarily. Where do you want to go?" Captured in a composite shot, with slanted light illuminating only half their faces, the woman (Madhubala) laughs and hints that she doesn't know where she would like to go, and further stresses that she neither has an address nor is there any journey's end. Indeed, her destination would be the place where she would retire, following this wearisome journey. The man (Dev Anand) replies in a caustic tone and indicates that his house should not become her destination, since he is both poor and unmarried, and then, quickly exists the scene. After he leaves, dark clouds and thunder begin to cover the night sky; and the scene cuts to a close shot of the woman, who runs her fingers through her hair. Afterward, she looks up, smiling—into the sky—and gets drenched in the rain.

While eventually she takes refuge at the man's house, this image of a woman soaking up in the rain, in the middle of the night, is worth our deliberations as the character appears to be an imaginary, yet, a "visible" *flaneuse*.[2] Gayatri Chatterjee writes:

> She sleeps in his bedroom, while he spreads a mat on the kitchen floor. He finds her name is Leela; but does not question why she is out at night alone.
>
> Clearly nothing happens between them that night; . . .
>
> The figure of the lone woman out in the streets and then spending the night in a stranger's house is thus fully normalized. . . .
>
> But we ask: who is this Leela? This new woman in the city is not a bad-woman. She is not punished for her transgressions. She fulfils her many desires: to be free, to fall in love and pursue some goal. She becomes the partner of a hero

similarly footloose and fancy- free. Actually, she might be new to the Indian urban scenario, but not to Indian literature . . .

pari is a free agent flying in the sky. She is intelligent, wise and able to perform miracles. She resides in some zone between the heavens and the earth called paristan or the land of the pari. . . . Films borrow the pari figure to create female characters in contemporary settings. (2010, 52–53)

Indeed, a similar situation involving a "free agent"—a *flaneuse* perhaps—transpires in the film *Solva Saal* (Dir. Raj Khosla, 1958), which opens with shots of young women walking down the street. Gradually the group becomes larger and as the women take a bus, and the sprawling city of 1950s Bombay unfolds via their gaze.[3] Later, a picnic scene, and a song performed during the episode, introduces the heroine, Laaj (Waheeda Rahman), and her boyfriend, Shyam (Jagdev), to the audience. In the course of events, Laaj (now dressed in T-shirt and trousers) and Shyam decide to elope since her father is against the match. Subsequently, late in the night, after overcoming her dilemma, Laaj leaves her parental home with an expensive pearl necklace and meets her partner at a railway station. As Laaj and Shyam board the train (toward Bombay central) they are tailed by two men, who find their conversations suspicious. In time, one of the men (Dev Anand) hums the popular song "*Hain apna dil toh awara*" ("My heart is footloose and fancy-free"), much to Laaj's annoyance. As the events progress, Shyam escapes with the necklace leaving Laaj stranded (alone) at the main station. Consequently, the mysterious person/singer—a journalist named Pran (Dev Anand)—who has been following them, accompanies Laaj in order to help her find the man with the stolen necklace. In pursuit of the lover turned crook, they arrive at a taxi drivers' "*adda*" or a place of gathering, and the driver(s) become curious about this woman who traveling across the city during the night, and therefore, they inquire about her identity. Pran immediately breaks into a song and describe her as a "pari," and as the quintessential feminine figure for whom lovers over generations have risked their lives and have wandered places. Once again, Gayatri Chatterjee reminds us that:

The men have certainly read and heard such stories—and so have members of the audience. They all know it is perfectly normal for a pari to wander alone in a city, get friendly with a man and share an adventure. This beautiful girl could be a winged creature, [who has] come down on earth to carry out some good deeds; and so there is nothing wrong here. . . . These films seem to bear the promise that . . . [i]t is possible for a city-girl to share a night with a man, and team up with him in the pursuit of adventure and romance—or in order to carry out some task. Such a woman is one who a man can marry when the job is done. (2010, 54–55)

Alternately, the woman on the street, walking without anxiety during the night, could be a streetwalker, as in case of *Pyaasa* (Dir. Guru Dutt, 1957), or she could be dressed as a man, as evident in *Taxi Driver* (Dir. Chetan Anand, 1954). Likewise, in films of the 1970s, women playing thieves and outlaws, as in the case of *Parvarish* (Dir. Manmohan Desai, 1977), could traverse the city streets with relative freedom. In addition, a superstar like Sridevi, replaying the Seeta/Geeta trope (as presented in *Seeta Aur Geeta* [Dir. Ramesh Sippy, 1972]) as Anju/Manju, in the film *ChaaBaaz* (Dir. Pankaj Parashar, 1989), possesses the autonomy to be somewhat tipsy, and sing and dance with strangers during the night, and hum "*kisi ke haat na aayegi yeh ladki*" (No one can touch this girl, at 39:01 on the timeline), and also get drenched in the rain. The film introduces the characters—the twin sisters, Anju (the good but meek one) and Manju (the deviant and feisty one), as well as their prospective partners—in succession; preceding the song, Manju meets Suraj (Sunny Deol) in a bar, and later, she gets drunk after gulping down several bottles of beer. Her drunkenness, the company of an unknown man, the rain and the thunderstorm, however, do not appear as any potential threat. Rather, as the song and dance sequence continues, the men dancing around her ask: "*Yeh ladki bheegi bhaagi si, kya ghar se bhaag ke aayi hai?*" (implying—"This drenched and absconding girl, has she escaped from home?"); and, consequently, quote the popular Madhubala-Kishore Kumar song "*Yeh ladki bheegi bhaagi si*" (this drenched runaway girl) from the film *Chalti Ka Naam Gaadi* (Dir. Sayen Bose, 1958). To this Manju (Sridevi) replies: "*Yeh ladki nahin hain, nagin hain, jo neend se jaag ke aayi hain*" (She isn't a girl, she is a serpent who has been awakened from her slumber). Set in an urban and mediated location (made conspicuous by the setting of a video store, screens, neon lights, and the presence of a musical band), the song induces a series of audio-visual quotations as Sridevi brings back a dancing gesture from her own blockbuster hit *Nagina* (Dir. Harmesh Malhortra, 1986), and then swings around by holding a car tire, which reminds us of the *Solva Saal* song discussed earlier (except that, in the previous version it was Dev Anand who was swinging), just as, the setting and properties prompt us to recall songs like "*Pyaar huya, ikraar huya*" ("We are in love . . . "), from the film *Shree 420* (Dir. Raj Kapoor, 1954). Nonetheless, it is clear from the above discussion that, either the "pari" (fairy), or a (super) star, or creatures, and streetwalkers and petty thieves, seemingly have the choice to traverse the beguiling city streets—the stage on which the drama of modernity unfolds—and participate in the pulsating nightlife that the modern worlds introduced to us. Subsequently, following feminist re-imagination of the *flaneur*, we inquire: can we locate the "flaneuse" in contemporary films, produced in the context of post liberalization and in a post-global scenario? We further question: is the so-called female *flaneur* invisible? And, what are consequences of her visibility on the streets?[4]

MEGACITIES, GLOBAL TRAVELS, AND BOLLYWOOD

The city-cinema-modernity dynamic is perhaps one of the most pertinent debates within cinema studies and urban histories.[5] Besides, among others, cities such as Mumbai and Kolkata have figured as iconic settings, and have become the locus of multiple narratives about late and post-colonial urban India, and about stories of arrival, the restive youth, subjects of unemployment, migration, housing problems, issues of (under) development, alongside conditions of lawlessness, crime, despite projecting the enticement of a new world, spaces of entertainment, engagements and personal achievements.[6] As pointed out by Madhava Prasad, the city as social space is a "pre-eminent space of representation(s)"; in addition, the city is a place where the "anonymous "citizen'" witnesses the play of modernity "on behalf of the Big Other, The Nation" (2002, 73, 75). To draw attention to the contemporary issues of globalizing Indian cities and the question of gender, I borrow from Arjun Appadurai to underline that the "new global cultural economy" needs to be understood as a set of "complex, overlapping, disjunctive order, which cannot any longer be understood in terms of existing centre-periphery models" (1990, 296). In an attempt to address global cultural flows, Appadurai emphasizes five dimensions of the phenomenon and explains them as follows: "ethoscapes" (or a landscape of people comprising tourists, visitors, immigrants, laborers, and other travelers), "technoscapes" (or global configuration of technologies, which are both high and low as well as includes both mechanical devices and information technology), "financscapes" (or global flow of capital), "mediascapes" (the production and dissemination of information both by the state and publics) and "ideoscapes."[7]

I am, however, also considering the structural and architectural transformations of the cities and its fluid and transforming limits, which have transpired following global imaginaries.[8] Moreover, in the context of this chapter, the socio-spatial restructuring of Delhi becomes crucial, particularly with regard to India's liberalization, the opening up to the global economy, and the emergence of the upwardly mobile neomiddle classes, and the remaking of the Indian metropolises into global cities.[9] Venonique Dupont reminds us how "national urban strategy that was then [1980s] adopted hinged on the concepts of "decentralization, deregulation and privatization," and adds that:

> [e]conomic liberalization and political decentralization reforms are also the product of the pressures exerted by international donor agencies (the World

Bank and the International Monetary Fund) on India. Therefore, there is a dialectic relationship between neoliberalization and globalization in Indian cities; the global has strongly influenced the 1990s reforms and the setting of the new urban scene, and, in return, the implementation of a neoliberal agenda in Indian cities favoured the incorporation of the biggest metropolises into the larger global movement. (2011, 536–537)

Basically, the post-partition planned city of (New) Delhi has swelled in all directions, but, especially toward Noida and Ghaziabad (in Uttar Pradesh) as well as toward Gurgaon (now Gurugram) and Faridabad (in Haryana), and has developed into a sprawling mega-city—the largest in the world.[10] "Global" cities effectively imply certain specific structural changes in the existing cityscape and its maps; and, they are flagged by rapid growth of the high-rises, shopping malls, multiplexes, business centers, gargantuan gated housing complexes, hotels, hospitals, serpentine freeway flyovers, widening of roads, expansion of highways, various commercial and wellness facilities, as well as growth of (media) communication. Nonetheless, the swift makeover of consumption habits of the middle-classes, and the altering city landscape, does not mean that the working classes and the underprivileged have the basic amenities, such as year-long jobs, effective health care system, access to (higher) education, housing, electricity and water.[11]

It is in light of such conditions that I examine a set of recent Bollywood movies, which have been produced following *two* crucial (social and cinematic) conditions (discussed later). First, I draw attention to the advancement of "Global Bollywood" during the 1990s, following economic liberalization and cultural globalization. Formation of Bollywood not only caused changes in the production-distribution-exhibition networks of Bombay cinema, but it also corporatized film (making) cultures by integrating a range of media and cultural industries, including lifestyle products, fashion, travel, tourism, music, and so on. Therefore, "Bollywoodization" implies "corporatization" of Bombay cinema, which efficiently re-integrated finance, production, and distribution, and cinema's industrial networks with other media industries (including television, music industry, and online platforms).[12] The formation of what I described as "Brand Bollywood" and its ramifications, thus, become critical in the present context.[13] Additionally, Madhava Prasad alerts us that, "successful commodification of Indian cinema as Bollywood in the International market is based on the idea of an unchanging essence that distinguishes it from Hollywood" (2008, 49).

Discussions on the corporatization of Bombay cinema (or "Bollywood"), over the last two decades, have generated a wealth of readings, and I reiterate a few key points to emphasize the moot point of this chapter.[14] For instance, Daya Kishan Thussu in his essay titled "The Globalization of

"Bollywood" examined how Indian films traveled across Global North and superseded Hollywood productions. Bollywood films of the period were not only released across the globe and were hits, these regularly presented travel motifs and addressed the Indian Diaspora as well as a global imaginary of the Indians back home. Note, the stupendous successes of Hindi popular cinema, produced from Bombay, across the Global North was premised on the branding of a certain kind of aesthetics, visual designs, themes, which easily translated into lifestyle products and sites—for example, into T-shirts, caps, bags, coffee mugs, upholstery, cafes, restaurants, night clubs and so on.[15] Likewise, writing about the "scenic interiors" of Bollywood films, Ranjani Mazumdar suggested that, these were scenes "of pleasure, desire, anxiety, and eroticism" while a "surface culture" materializes through them; moreover, the "[s]urface here refers to the expressive forms of architecture, advertising, print, television, film, and fashion . . . The new sensorium of urban life" (2007, 115).

I have examined elsewhere ("Mustard Fields, Exotic Tropes, and Travels" 2012) the significance of the travel motif, and journeys that the (female) protagonists undertake in Bollywood films. Such narrative explorations, although not new, is renewed in the era of global consumerism, as evident in films such as *Dilwale Dulhaniya Le Jayenge*/DDLJ (Dir. Aditya Chopra, 1995), *Jab We Met* (Dir. Imitiaz Ali, 2007), *Love Aaj Kal* (Dir. Imtiaz Ali, 2009), among others, and in the now cult film *Queen* (Dir. Vikas Bahl, 2013). I argue that such "travel and living" prototypes and trips, in quest of forbidden joys and pleasures (for instance, sex, adventure, money, freedom, pleasure), are gendered and, in the present circumstances, intimidating. With regard to the early Bollywood films, Rachel Dwyer suggests that while romance is part of a contemporary consumerist culture,[16] it is connected with travel, going out, exchange of gifts, etc., and thus becomes "essential components of courtship" (2002, 164). Dwyer further writes that:

> travel is one of many ways in which Hindi films depict space and place, in particular places suitable for love and romance, and the idea of transnational Indian.
>
> In addition to movement of media (mediascapes) and other flows, we also see the actual movement of people. To be part of a transnational family is almost hallmark of being middle class in India . . . [and that] [t]ravel and romance have been linked in Western culture as consumerist activities. This is also seen in Hindi films, where travel is associated with consumerism, ranging from shopping in duty-free shops, eating and drinking out. (2002, 164–165)

Indeed, a range of Bollywood films, including *Dil Toh Pagal Hai* (Dir. Yash Chopra, 1997), *Dil Chahta Hai* (Dir. Farhaan Akhtar, 2001), *Salaam Namaste* (Dir. Siddharth Anand, 2005), and particularly *Zindagi Na Milegi Dobara*

(Zoya Akhtar, 2011), which was supported by Spain's tourism arm, became a means of foregrounding present-day consumer products and cultures, and the enchantments of (international) travel. So, "[a]ir travel, car travel, leisure, art, discos, music fashion, style attitude, grace, love, . . . a combination of all these" (Ranjani Mazumdar 2007, 192), and more (activities like sports), is perfected via a variety of Bollywood films. In a manner of speaking, I propose that Bollywood flags its (diasporic) market; produced by the migration to the Global North following Second World War, through own its narratives.

Furthermore, I have analyzed ("Mustard Fields, Exotic Tropes, and Travels" 2012) in what way DDLJ tackles the crises of Diaspora, migration, displacement, and issues of labor, through the character of Baldev (Amrish Puri). Baldev's daughter Simran (Kajol), is a happy-go-lucky young woman, who is also a poet, and in fact, seemingly embodies the so-called Diaspora dilemma of being "Western outside/Indian inside." Therefore, she seeks her father's consent to travel and experience life (actually Europe) before she is married off to a person of her father's choice. What follows thereafter is a tour across Europe in the famed Euro-rail (and in cars and buses), which explore the idea of adventure and anticipation, and present contemporary notions of lifestyle, friendship, courtship, love, travel, independence, and marriage. On the said trip Simran meets the hero—Raj (Shah Rukh Khan)—and they travel across Switzerland, Germany, so on and so forth; practically, enjoying a life of high consumerism and desire. In one of the pivotal sequences of the film, nevertheless, Simran and Raj spend a night together as they miss their train to Zurich. Following the popular song *"Zara sa jhoom lu main . . . aa tujhe choom lu main"* ("Let me sway a little, let me kiss you"), and a night of heady merrymaking, in which Simran (under the influence of alcohol) expresses her spontaneity and exuberance, next morning, upon waking up in Raj's shirt, Simran is petrified imagining that she might have had a sexual liaison. Contrarily, Raj, after making some flirtatious comments, assures her that he appreciates the value of *izzat* (honor) of an Indian woman, and hence, they would never transgress the (existing pre-capitalist) moral codes.[17] Unlike *ChaalBaaz*, in which Manju (a street-performer) enjoys some drinks and the company of men without sensing any probable physical threat, in case of DDLJ—despite the film's focus on travel and tourism—Simran's drinking is presented as an aberration of sorts, and stir up an apprehension (even if casually) regarding the loss of a woman's *izzat* following exhilarating night-outs.

Besides, I contend that, this travel trope has evolved to generate multiple ramifications. For instance, a definitive Bollywood hit, *Kuch Kuch Hota Hai* (Dir. Karan Johar, 1998), shows how the binaries of "West-East," "Outside-Inside," "World-Home" are increasingly becoming fuzzy.[18] So, *Kuch Kuch Hota Hai* offers the good life of the West, without actually going to the West; instead, it creates a virtual West within India, through the construction of its characters, setting, costumes, color, locations, and music as well as by placing a variety of life style products within the scene. Moreover, in the last two decades, besides the allure of foreign locales, the middle-class and multiplex audiences of the global (Indian) cities as well as of the "second-tier cities" and towns,[19] have *also* experienced (the seemingly exotic and) culture specific Indian locations via a range of recent Bollywood films (for instance, in *Bunty aur Babli* [Dir. Shaad Ali, 2005], *Ishqiya* [Dir. Vishal Bhardwaj, 2010], *Gangs of Wasseypur* I & II [Dir. Anurag Kashyap, 2012], *Shuddh Desi Romance* [Dir. Maneesh Sharma, 2013], *Bareilly ki Barfi* [Dir. Ashwiny Iyer Towari, 2017], and so on).

More to the point, a number of films set in Mumbai and Delhi (for instance, *No Smoking* Dir. Anurag Kashyap, 2007], *Delhi 6* [Dir. Rakeysh Omprakash Mehra, 2009], *Dhobi Ghaat* [Dir. Kiran Rao, 2010], *Delhi Belly* [Dir. Abhinay Deo, 2011], *Ugly* [Dir. Anurag Kashyap, 2013] and *Gully Boy* [Dir. Zoya Akhtar, 2019]) explore the big cities, highlight the unseen underbelly and the presence of multiple cities within *the* city, and focus on the disunions on lines of class, caste, community, and gender.[20] These films foreground a deeply fragmented and potentially precarious cityscape—as in case of *Dhobi Ghaat* in which the young bride from a B-tier town arrives at Mumbai, experiences the city through her camera, and eventually kills herself by suicide, as well as in case of *Ugly* in which the little girl is dumped in a vehicle trunk and is left to die—which are laced by the unease and perils of neoliberal advancements.[21]

Current Bollywood films or "new" Bollywood, thus, lead us to our *second* point of contestation. In this chapter, I argue that, as portrayed in certain recent films, the global cities and their unplanned extended "peripheries" create fear, apprehension, quandary, regarding the marginal quarters and the city underbelly—inhabited by immigrants and laborers—those that remain in dark, and have limited accessibility to economic growth. I am particularly considering the alarm generated among middle-classes (and media) following the gruesome Delhi gang rape and murder case of Jyoti Singh (Nirbhaya) in 2012. While liberalization offers urban expansion, high-end consumer products, growth of media and related industries, as well as gender empowerment and media democracy, I suggest that the 2012 Delhi rape and murder case (and its aftermath including nationwide protests and media coverage) provoked unforeseen anxieties about the flow of capital, media, technologies, cultures, and particularly the people, where travel for women are concerned. I reiterate Tupur Chatterjee's point to inquire:

> What is the relationship between these films and the multiplex viewer? As mentioned above, the multiplex seeks to eliminate all outside "dirt," "disorder," and potential class miscegenation to create a "safe" and sanitized environment for

film viewing. All psychogeographic uneasiness is transferred to the space/site of the screen—the multiplex film. (2017, 15)

I, therefore, propose that, a range of contemporary Bollywood films, including *Pink* (Dir. Aniruddha Roy Chowdhury, 2016), and *NH 10* (Dir. Navdeep Singh, 2015), address the growing disenchantments with neoliberal gratifications, and specifically deal with the crises of the frenzied urban growth vis-à-vis women's mobility in and around Delhi (toward Noida and Gurgaon), and confront the problems of arising from neoliberal prospects.[22]

Within this framework, I particularly examine films such as *Pink*, and *NH 10*, as well as *Highway* (Dir. Imtiaz Ali, 2014), which are set in Delhi-Gurgaon and beyond, and explore the possible threats mushrooming along the (old) National Highway number 10. In a manner of speaking, *N H 10* and *Highway* mirror each other, even when the points of departure are similar. For instance, while both Veera (Alia Bhatt) from *Highway* and Meera (Anushka Sharma) from *NH10* have comparable privileged backgrounds; however, on the one hand, Veera's journey into the formidable unknown territory becomes a means of her freedom; on the other, Meera's weekend trip to some villa, beyond Gurgaon, opens up a can of worms and reveals the murky underbelly of neoliberal development, and the complexity of (unaddressed and unequal) development and gender inequities. I reason that, films like *Pink*, *NH10* (and *Highway*) raise crucial questions with regard to women's safety within the expanding urban spaces, and highlight her susceptibility—as well as her vigor—and spotlight the various stages of underdevelopment in urban, peri-urban and rural sectors, despite the planned "growth" of Delhi. Mixing multiple generic elements (like thriller, action, courtroom drama, road movie, even elements of slasher), and disparate visual and sonic tropes, as well as thematic such as rape, violence, murder, blood, gore, suffering, resistance, these films follow women's journey from a cushioned life to liberty and autonomy.[23] Woman's function and agency in this history of multiple and fragmented phases of under/development therefore, become decisive, as they inform us about the undercurrents of neoliberal flows.

AN EXPLORATION INTO ENGENDERED LANDSCAPE

One hears voices, on a black screen, of what sounds like young men and women partying and enjoying themselves. A female voice insists that she wants to "call it a night," however, a male voice asserts that she should have "one for the road." Afterward, the opening sequence presents a wounded man and his friends driving in a car by the night, hastily. They wonder, agitatedly, whether they are going to get entangled in a police case. Cut to another car speeding by on empty streets; three women are seated inside it. The sequence, thereafter, intercuts between the men in the car, and the women in another one. We realize that the characters are caught in an unwarranted situation since the men vouch that they shall take revenge. Next, as the men enter a hospital, alternately, we are welcomed to the city of Delhi, and the audience are informed that an "incident" has taken place at Surajkund (near Faridabad, Haryana). Following this, the women enter a residential colony in South Delhi; seemingly they are home, although, they are anxious. Falak (Kirti Kulkarni), introduced earlier, says that she had sought to leave early; Andrea (Andrea Tariang) contemplates, "what if something happens" to them. Later, Minal (Taapsee Pannu) wipes off the blood from her neck and arms. That's how *Pink* begins, presenting us the hazardous (night) life of the working girls in Delhi, and their perilous sojourns (beyond Gurgaon) into the risky urban highlife (involving rock concerts in night clubs, parties at villas, and so on).

While latter half of the film focuses on the court case that transpires following the altercation between Minal and friends and Rajveer (Angad Bedi) and company, at the onset the film constructs a sensorial picture of Delhi neighborhoods, comprising neon lights, shops, parks, streets, houses, peering neighbors, which are laced with the lurking fear molestation and assault, and a sense alienation of the young women, who have arrived at the megacity for work. So, (in another scene) even when they force themselves to laugh, the situation intensifies without their knowledge. Eventually, Vishwajyoti (Tushar Pandey), a common friend of Rajveer and Falak, advises them to make a truce, and apologize to Rajveer; however, before such an action may be taken, Minal files a case with the police. At home, as Falak tries to convince Minal to apologize, she states: "Why are we here? . . . We are here to do our jobs, we are here for work, we are here to lead a normal life" (0:32:00 to 0:33:00 on timeline).

Here it is worth noting that "Employment trends in India" (Indrani Mazumdar, Neetha N., 2011) shows that the Female Work Participation Rates (FWPR) have actually dropped steadily in the last few decades. Mazumdar and Neetha N. mention that "[i]n urban areas too, FWPR has fallen substantially from 13.5 per cent in 2004–05 to below 12 per cent in the case of UPS [usual employment status] employment and from close to 17 per cent to below 14 per cent in UPSS [usual principal subsidiary status]" (2011, 2). Mazumdar and Neetha N. further add that, "[t]he 2007–08 survey shows a worrisome fall in both PWPR as well as standard WPR for urban women, underlining the fact that the most distinctive period of corporate led high growth in the country yielded negative results for even urban women's employment" (2011, 15). And, in conclusion they (Mazumdar and Neetha N.) suggest the following:

> At a more general level, it is worthy of note that with all the hype regarding expanding opportunities for women's employment that has become a kind of common sense among particularly the educated classes, the shocking reality is that if one removes unpaid labour from the work participation count, in 2007–08, only 15 per cent of the female population in the country received wage/income for their labour in comparison to 51 per cent of the males. In other words, 85 per cent of the female population was completely economically/financially dependent and without any employment/ income when GDP growth rates had reached an all time high. (2011, 25)

In the present scenario of shrinking and gendered workspaces, despite the growing number of educated women, I, therefore, inquire what do films like *Pink* and *NH10* put in the picture? Consider for instance, the first sequence of *NH10*, which opens with night shots of Gurgaon, as viewed from a car window, and thereafter, focuses on Delhi-Gurgaon Metro, petrol pumps, high-rises, rows and rows of cars, until the characters arrive at the destination. Initially the audience is introduced to the romantic couple, Meera (Anushka Sharma) and Arjun (Neil Bhoopalam), which is followed by a party scene, which involves banter about other cities like Bangalore (described as "nice and cool" by Meera, and as place where "bars are closed before midnight" by Meera's acquaintance (06:11 to 06:18 on timeline). However, a fearsome and threatening midnight situation in Gurgaon unfolds in the next scene as Meera heads back to office, to attend the requirements of her high-paying, high on productivity, corporate job.

The film prepares us for the hazardous nightlife in a global city, and its shifting margins, as Meera walks alone to the car. Thereafter, it produces a mise-en-scene (or a setting) of dread as we see a lonesome woman, speeding through the wintry night, while two men riding a bike chase her and break the windshield of her car. Next morning, at the police station, the officer suggests that Gurgaon is like a "developing child . . . it will bounce around, [then to Arjun] but, why do let her travel alone during the night?" (10:30 to 10:35 on timeline). Highlighting the problems of overgrowth coupled with a long history of under development, the Police too—seemingly—fear the condition and hence, advise her to get a gun. Consequently, between drinks, romantic chitchats, swimming, as well as late night work and business presentations, Meera and Arjun manage to acquire a gun and take a weekend break on the occasion of her birth anniversary. However, as they head out of Gurgaon, and drive toward (old) National Highway number 10, the impending violence begins to unfold, gradually. A person at the Toll Plaza, for instance, informs them that four armed men had gunned down one of his colleagues a few moments earlier. Moreover, I wish to underscore that, the film also explores the barren landscape at the "periphery" and stresses the troubles of a burgeoning megacity. Sumit Vij, Vishal Narain, Timothy Karpouzoglou, and Pratik Mishra (2018), for example, prompt us to note the economic, social and ecological disasters involved with such (un)planned growth. Vij et al. write:

> the urban agglomeration of Gurgaon has been made possible by the acquisition of private agriculture and common lands from periurban areas (Das, 2017). This re-presents an implicit bias in urban planning. . . . This has created a periurban landscape, characterized by a duality in which modern high rise buildings and gated communities co-exist with village settlement areas (Vij and Narain, 2016). There have been efforts at augmenting urban infrastructure. This includes efforts at connecting the city with other cities in the National Capital Region [Delhi] through a modern tollway built under a PPP (public-private partnership) model and a Metrorail; however, connecting the city with peripheral villages, that maintain close links with the city for sustaining their livelihoods, has been given scant attention by planners and policy makers (Thornton, 2008; Narain, 2017) . . . this same bias is re-enforced in the acquisition of land and water resources from the periurban spaces to meet the needs of the growing city. (2018, 36)

Such massive underdevelopment, and destruction of traditional economy and the eco-system, I contend, erupts violently in *NH10* and other related texts. Therefore, as Arjun (driving) takes one wrong turn, they head toward an inevitable tragedy, and encounter a series of vicious acts—honor killing (of Pinky and Mukesh), followed by an accidental killing, and yet another murder in self-defense (by Arjun-Meera), and eventually, Arjun's death due to his fatal wound and profuse bleeding. In one of sequences, after Arjun is attacked and injured by the Pinky's family (her brother Satbir and others), Meera begins to run alone—for assistance. During her flight, she first encounters a vehicle crowded with elderly villagers (men) who wonder why a woman is wandering around alone during the night. Thereafter, Meera, finally, finds a Police station. At the Police station, the officer sends her off because they are not in a position to prosecute the persons who are entangled in the honor killing case. Yet, Meera, exhausted, emotionally charged and edgy, finds a bicycle (at the station) and continues to look for support. On her way, she is apparently rescued by another Police officer. On their way (to save Arjun), nonetheless, he requests Meera not to complain about the man at the station; he says: "Madam, Police don't dangle in the thin air. They live in the village, with the community. He would have been ostracized. He has three sons, who would marry their daughters to them? In any case we don't have enough girls here."[24] Then, after a pause, the officer asks Meera about her caste. Meera says, "Singh. I am Puri after marriage." While the man comments on her "inter-caste" marriage, he continues to enquire: "Singh-Puri are surnames Madam. Caste? [What's your caste?] For instance, Brahmin, Baniya, Jaat, Gujjar, . . . that's the difference between you and us, Madam. Ask a twelve-year-old kid in the village, he will know his caste . . . and even that of his neighbors!" "You must have read Manu [Manusmriti]," and, the officer continues to explain the complications of the so-called inter and intra-caste marriages, and asserts that: "In Gurgaon democracy and constitution come to an end at the point where the last [shopping] mall is located. We don't have electricity and water here; what do we know of the constitution? . . . Thankfully we have the caste-system . . . or else there would be chaos" (1:03:38 to 1:05:38 on timeline). In actuality, the officer leads Meera directly to the murderers (Satbir); although, Meera has the grits and the vigor to overpower him, and escape with the car. The car—a potent symbol of the modern world—and Meera's ability to drive it with boundless proficiency, in fact, becomes her shield and her weapon.

Nadeem Hasnain reminds us that

ROLE OF TRADITIONAL PANCHAYATS AND VAGARIES OF THE ROAD

[t]hough such violence, stretching to killings, is reported from throughout India except perhaps the tribal regions, the largest number of reports come from Punjab, Haryana, Rajasthan and Western Uttar Pradesh. Many such killings go unreported largely because of its consent from the entire village community." (2014, 16–19)

Numerous studies have shown that the traditional panchayats are still playing a strong and important role as a tool of social control in the village societies despite the establishment of statutory panchayats under Panchayat Raj. Of all such traditional panchayats, the Khap Panchayats of Harayana have grabbed the biggest attention because of its highly questionable role. Thus, through the night, Meera is chased by the murderers, and as she drives feverishly from one place to the other, she keeps walking the bloody trail until she reaches a deserted village. Soon she realizes that the villagers have gathered for a night of festivity and performance. In the course of events Meera finds out about the village head (Sarpanch, played the veteran actress Deepti Naval), yet, after she reaches what was supposed to be a space of legality—the house of the Sarpanch—she realizes that it was Amma ji who had masterminded the killing of her daughter (Pinky) to save the "honor" of the family. While in the climax Meera turns into what Lalitha Gopalan (1997) had described as "avenging" woman, subjects of a deeply patriarchal social system, gender and caste discriminations, lack of basic amenities (electricity, water, transport), lawlessness, and the persistence of a feudal structure amid the formation of global cities at a distance, produce the density of the text.

Furthermore, I draw from Adrija Dey and Bev Orton to emphasize how:

[t]he Nirbhaya case demonstrated a very peculiar case of intersectionality. . . . In this context Kabeer (5th March 2015) comments that the Nirbhaya case has brought out in front of the world the effect of the widening inequality in a modernising and globalising economy. She says, "this was violence perpetrated by men from the underclass of Delhi, men who will never share in the benefits of 'shining' India, against a woman who symbolised the country that India hopes to become" . . . (Kabeer, 5th March 2015).

Middle class people across the country could relate to Nirbhaya and her story. . . . She was educated, belonged to the urban middle class, . . . Everything about the circumstances was extraordinarily ordinary. . . . Geography also played an important role as the case happened in the heart of the capital city of Delhi. (2016, 99–100)

One may, therefore, ask again: What more do such fictive stories and films communicate about present-day India? I argue that the disquiet produced by uncontrolled overgrowth, and the complications generated by the (peripheral) underdevelopment, threaten the calm at the "center." The fear of fatality, violence, destruction (of property), and the unforeseen threat of unexplored (exotic) territories and volatile "peripheries," is palpable in such texts; moreover, in the course of action they layout a visceral image of neoliberal growth. Additionally, the ideological tussle between the new patriarchy (for instance, Deepak Sehgal [Amitabh Bachchan] in *Pink*) and the old patriarchy (performed by Rajveer and Satbir in *Pink* and *NH10*, respectively) are evident in such films.[25] On the one hand, such films bring the woman back on the streets, and debate about working women's participation in neoliberal enjoyments; on the other, they negotiate the disappointments regarding global flows, and the abhorrence toward the what may be described as social "surplus and residue" that is piling up at (pristine) peri-urban sectors.

CONCLUSION

In conclusion, I discuss *Highway,* to illustrate the manner in which the film builds a similar situation *only to reverse it in the end*, and in the process, underlines the fact that a higher rate of sexual violence takes place within familial and familiar spaces.[26] For example, *Highway* opens with the pre-wedding "videos" of Veera (Alia Bhatt);[27] however, in the course of events, at the middle of the night, she coaxes her fiancé to take her to the

"Highway" so that she can get some fresh air. At the highway Petrol pump (gas station), however, Veera is kidnapped by Mahavir (Ranadeep Hooda), an outlaw and an "outcaste," whose mother had suffered upper caste/upper class exploitation and long drawn sexual assault. Nonetheless, despite the potential crisis situation, Veera enjoys—even if momentarily—a life of mobility, freedom and joy (albeit following initial brutality), as they travel across Northern India, unto the foothills of Himalayas. At the end of it, while Mahabir is betrayed and brutally killed by the police (and men in power) and Veera is forced to revisit home, upon her return she exposes the person (Uncle) who had sexually abused her at the time she was a child, and thereafter, returns to the hills to start her own business. *Highway* in effect, spotlights the sharp increase of women's self-employment in the current economic situation,[28] and, provokes us to rethink beyond the dichotomies of center-periphery, and review the glitches of the evolving global cities.

As discussed in this chapter, reflections on the disparate phases of modern India, Bombay cinema and Bollywood films show a transforming urban landscape in relation to women—from possible and imagined sojourns carried out by the "new" women, and streetwalking and wandering by the night, to promised global travels following neoliberal policies of India, we arrive at a disquieting and unsettling "here and now," in which unequal growth seem leave a stain and a scar on the globalizing megacities. I contend that, research shows in what ways statistics and data on women's work and risky urban life inform such narratives of *"flaneuse"* of the post-colonial cities, those which have been reinvented in the context of megacities, and thereby, illustrate the perilous pathways of the "midnight's" daughters and focus on the shifting history of the present.

REFERENCES

Appadurai, Arjun. 1990. "Disjuncture and Difference in the Global Cultural Economy." *Theory, Culture & Society* 7, no. 2–3: 295–310.

Athique, Adrian Mabbott, and Douglas Hill. 2007. "Multiplex Cinemas and Urban Redevelopment in India." *Media International Australia* 124, no. 1 (August): 108–118.

Benjamin, Walter. 2002. The Arcades Project. Cambridge MA: Belknap Press.

Chatterjee, Gayatri. 2010. "Writing History for Cinema: Archives, Archaeological Sites and Homes." *Journal of the Moving Image* 9: 47–60.

Chatterjee, Tupur. 2019. "Rape Culture, Misogyny, and Urban Anxiety in *NH10* and *Pink*." *Feminist Media Studies* 19, no. 1 (August): 130–146.

Desai, Jigna. 2004. *Beyond Bollywood: The Cultural Politics of South Asian Diasporic Film*. New York an: Routledge.

Dey, Adrija and Bev Orton. 2016. "Gender and Caste Intersectionality in India: An Analysis of the Nirbhaya Case, 16 December 2012." In *Gender and Race Matter: Global Perspectives on Being a Woman*, edited by Shaminder Takhar, 87–105. Bingley: Emerald Group Publishing Limited.

Dupont, Véronique. 2000. "Spatial and Demographic Growth of Delhi since 1947 and the Main Migration Flows." In *Delhi: Urban Space and Human Destinies*, edited by Véronique Dupont, Emma Tarlo and Denis Vidal, 229–239. New Delhi: Manohar Publishers.

———. 2011. "The Dream of Delhi as a Global City." *International Journal of Urban and Regional Research* 35, no. 3 (February): 533–554.

Dwyer, Rachel. 2002. *Yash Chopra: Fifty Years in Indian Cinema*. London: British Film Institute.

Fernandes, Leela. 2004. "The Politics of Forgetting: Class Politics, State Power and the Restructuring of Urban Space in India." *Urban Studies* 41, no. 12 (July): 2415–2430.

Gopalan, Lalitha. 1997. "Avenging Women in Indian Cinema." *Screen* 38, no. 1 (March): 42–59.

Gopal, Sangita. 2011. *Conjugations: Marriage and Form in New Bollywood Cinema*. Chicago: University of Chicago Press.

———. 2021. "Lethal Acts: Bollywood's New Woman and the Nirbhaya Effect." In *Bollywood's New Woman: Liberalization, Liberation, and Contested Bodies*, edited by Megha Anwer and Anupana Arora, 40–53. New Brunswick, NJ: Rutgers University Press.

Harvey, David. 2006. *Spaces of Global Capitalism*. London: Verso.

Hasnain, Nadeem. 2014. "Gender, Patriarchy and "Honour Killing' in India." *Anthropological Bulletin* 3, no. 2: 16–19.

Kaarsholm, Preben. 2007. *City Flicks: Indian Cinema and the Urban Experience*. London: Seagull Books.

Kaur, Raminder and Ajay Sinha eds. 2005. *Bollyworld, Popular Indian Cinema through a Transnational Lens*. New Delhi: Sage.

Malik Surbhi. 2021. "The Provincial Flâneuse: Reimagining Provincial Space and Narratives of Womanhood in Bollywood." *South Asian Popular Culture* 19, no. 1 (February): 33–45. 10.1080/14746689.2021.1880859

Mazumdar, Ranjani. 2007. *Bombay Cinema: An Archive of the City*. Minneapolis: University of Minnesota Press.

Mazumdar, Indrani and Neetha N. 2011. *Gender Dimensions: Employment Trends in India, 1993–2010 (Occasional Paper No. 56)*. New Delhi: Centre for Women's Development Studies.

Misra, Anil Kumar. 2010. "A River about to Die: Yamuna." *Journal of Water Resource and Protection* 2, no. 5: 489.

Mukherjee, Madhuja. 2009. "Photoshop landscapes: Digital mediation and Bollywood cities." *Journal of Moving Images* 8: 52–72.

———. 2012. "Mustard Fields, Exotic Tropes, and Travels through Meandering Pathways: Reframing the Yash Raj Trajectory." In *Travels of Bollywood Cinema,*

From Bombay to LA, edited by Anjali Gera Roy and Chua Beng Huat, 35–53. New Delhi: Oxford University Press.

———. 2012. "South City Mall and Solace: The City in Cinema, and Cinemas in the City." In *Persistence of Vision: Pasts and Futures of Indian Cinema*, edited by Ashish Rajadhyaksha, 255–272. Shanghai: Shanghai People's Publishing House.

———. 2013. "Flaneuse, Viewership, Cinematic Spaces: The Site/Sight of Theatres, Engendered Structures and Alternative Art Projects." *Media Fields Journal* 7, (December). mediafieldsjournal.squarespace.com/flaneuse-viewership-cinematic/

———. 2014. "Hindi Popular Cinema and its Peripheries: Of Female Singers, Performances, and the Presence/Absence of Suraiya." In *Bollywood and Its Other(s), Towards New Configurations*, edited by Vikrant Kishore, Amit Sarwal and Parichay Patra, 67–85. Hampshire: Palgrave Macmillan.

———. 2017. "Mediated Narrations: Contemporary Bollywood films and the Digital Interface." In *Following Forkhead Paths: Discussions on the Narrative*, edited by Debashree Dattaray, Epsita Halder, Sudip Bhattacharya, 263–298. Kolkata: Setu Prakashani.

———. 2017. "Sounding Dystopia: Anurag Kashyap's films and relocation of popular tropes." In *Behind the Scenes: Contemporary Bollywood Directors and Their Cinema*, edited by Aysha Iqbal Viswamohan and Vimal Mohan John, 185–214. New Delhi: Sage.

Nandy, Ashis. 2007. *An Ambiguous Journey to the City: The Village and Other Odd Ruins of the Self in the Indian Imagination*. New Delhi: Oxford University Press.

Parsons, Deborah L. 2003. *Streetwalking the Metropolis: Women, the City, and Modernity*. Oxford: Oxford University Press.

Pollock, Griselda. 1988. "Modernity and the Spaces of Femininity." In *Vision and Difference: Femininity, Feminism and the Histories of Art*, edited by G. Pollock, 50–90. London: Routledge.

Prakash, Gyan, ed. 2010. 2010. *Mumbai Fables*. Princeton: Princeton University Press.

———. *Noir Urbanisms: Dystopic Images of the Modern City*. Princeton: Princeton University Press.

Prasad, M. Madhava. 1998. *The Ideology of the Hindi Film, A Historical Construction*. Delhi: Oxford University Press.

———. 2002. "Realism and Fantasy in Representations of Metropolitan Life in Indian Cinema." In *City Flicks: Cinema, Urban Worlds and Modernities in India and Beyond (Occasional Paper no. 22)*, edited by Preben Kaarsholm, 71–83. Roskilde University, Denmark.

———. 2008. "Surviving Bollywood." In *Global Bollywood*, edited by Anandam P. Kavoori and Aswin Punathambekar, 41–51. New Delhi, Oxford University Press.

Rajadhyaksha, Ashish. 2003. "The 'Bollywoodization' of the Indian Cinema: Cultural Nationalism in a Global Arena." *Inter-Asia Cultural Studies* 4, no. 1: 25–39.

———. 2009. *Indian Cinema in the Time of Celluloid, From Bollywood to the Emergency*. New Delhi: Tulika Books.

Roy, Manas and Madhuja Mukherjee. 2002. "Bollywood in Diaspora: In the Tracks of a Twice—Displaced Community." *City Flicks: Cinema, Urban Worlds and*

Modernities in India and Beyond (Occasional Paper no. 22), edited by Preben Kaarsholm, 113–146. Roskilde University, Denmark.
Sudhira, H. S., T. V. Ramachandra, and M. H. Bala Subrahmanya. 2007. "Bangalore." *Cities* 24, no. 5: 379–390.
Thussu, Daya Kishan. 2008. "The Globalization of "Bollywood." In *Global Bollywood*, edited by Anandam P. Kavoori and Aswin Punathambekar, 97–113. New Delhi: Oxford University Press.
Vij, Sumit et al. 2018. "From the Core to the Periphery: Conflicts and Cooperation over Land and Water in Periurban Gurgaon, India." *Land Use Policy* 76 (July): 382–390.
Wilson, Elizabeth. 1992. "The Invisible *Flâneur*." *New Left Review* 191 (February): 90–110.
Wolff, Janet. 1985. "The Invisible Flâneuse. Women and the Literature of Modernity." *Theory, Culture & Society* 2, no. 3: 37–46.

NOTES

1. Also see Malik "The provincial *Flâneuse.*"
2. Also see Mukherjee, "Hindi Popular Cinema and Its Peripheries."
3. Also see Prakash, *Mumbai Fables*.
4. See Mukherjee, "Flaneuse, Viewership, Cinematic Spaces."
5. See Kaarsholm, *City Flicks*.
6. Also see Nandy, *An Ambiguous Journey to the City*.
7. See Ramachandra, and Subrahmanya. "Bangalore."
8. Also see Mukherjee, "South City Mall and Solace."
9. See Fernandes "The Politics of Forgetting."
10. See Dupont, "Spatial and Demographic Growth of Delhi since 1947 and the Main Migration Flows." Also see Misra, "A River about to Die."
11. Also see Harvey, *Spaces of Global Capitalism*.
12. See Rajadhyaksha, "The 'Bollywoodization' of the Indian Cinema."
13. See Mukherjee "Photoshop Landscapes."
14. See Kavoori and Punathambekar edited *Global Bollywood*, Kaur and Sinha edited *Bollyworld*, and Desai, *Beyond Bollywood*.
15. Also see Rajadhyaksha, *Indian Cinema in the Time of Celluloid*.
16. See Gopal, *Conjugations*.
17. See Prasad, *Ideology of Hindi Film*.
18. See Roy and Mukherjee, "Bollywood in Diaspora."
19. See Athique, and Hill, "Multiplex Cinemas and Urban Redevelopment in India."
20. See Mukherjee "Mediated Narrations."
21. See Mukherjee, "Sounding Dystopia."
22. Also see *Kill Dil* (Dir. Shaad Ali, 2014), and Netflix series such as *Delhi Crime* (2019) and *Paatal Lok* (2020).
23. Especially see Sangita Gopal, "Lethal Acts."

24. The male–female sex ratio in India shows that, in states such as Mahrashtra, Haryana, Jammu and Kashmir, the male percentage is significantly higher than the female figures.

25. Also see *Drishyam* (Dir. Nishikant Kamat, 2015).

26. Also see *Sandeep Aur Pinly Faraar* (Dir. Dibakar Banerjee, 2021) released on Amazon Prime.

27. Note, "wedding" has been a pivotal aspect of Bollywood films, as reflected in DDLJ, *Band Baaja Baaraat* (Dir. Maneesh Sharma, 2010), *Hasee Toh Phasee* (Dir. Vinil Mathew, 2014), *2 States* (Dir. Abhishek Verman, 2014), etc.

28. See Mazumdar and Neetha "Gender Dimensions."

Chapter 5

Celluloid Women Rewriting Rules of Travel in Contemporary Hindi Cinema

Rima Bhattacharya

In a highly patriarchal society such as India's, men are seen as breadwinners, while the role of women is restricted to being a good homemaker and a good mother. However, with the advent of modernization and globalization, the role of women in society has changed dramatically. The contribution of films in portraying women in their varied shifting roles has received much less attention. Over the past decades, women's appearance in Indian cinema has undergone a significant transformation. With the advent of satellite television in the 1980s, narrative cinema began to view the image of women from a historical or social perspective. Gradually women's struggle for an egalitarian society brought Indian women from the margins to the center of the cinematic world, which then, for a change, began to focus on female subjectivity. Some filmmakers such as Aparna Sen, Vijaya Mehta and Aruna Raje have shown portraits of women protagonists highlighting their social and sexual identity. The Indian feminist writer Urvashi Butalia stated that one of the most powerful mediums of communication in Indian society is commercial Indian cinema. Butalia argues that although many directors in the past few years have produced films about women's social issues such as marriage, widowhood, dowry and rape, not many have managed to portray women as human beings in their own right. Despite dealing with the social issues related to women, such movies continue to portray the heroism of men rescuing women from such issues. Therefore, according to Butalia, such movies "show a superficial concern with 'women issues'" (1984, 108). Further, since its early days, the Hindi film industry has restricted the free movement of women protagonists.

For ages, the Hindi movie heroines have been portrayed as homely, content to stay happily confined within the limits of their homes. To justify their restricted access to the roads and the public world, Hindi movies have, time and again, portrayed women as timid and helpless. One would find such women characters avoiding the road and venturing out, only in the presence of a male support. Stereotypically, it could be a girl who requires the protective presence of her father or brother to go to her college, or a married woman who is scared to leave her husband's side, or a harassed mother who patiently waits for her male children to grow up and avenge her. Unfortunately, most commercial films continue to portray women as sex objects and unequal partners. It is high time that Indian cinema avoid the same stereotypes while negotiating women's image.

Films have a massive impact on society. Popular Hindi cinema is a vivacious and lively medium for bringing about communal change, a guidebook for the public and private materialization of human conduct and a reflection of dominant ideologies. Therefore, it is essential to appreciate movies that portray women from a humanistic and rational point of view for the betterment of society. In the contemporary world, the audience is no longer interested in viewing films where women are only seen and not heard. They look forward to seeing strong and powerful female protagonists who can rise beyond their conformist roles of wifehood and motherhood. However, this change in the mentality of the Indian audience did not happen overnight. The emergence of strong androgynous female protagonists in Hindi cinema has a long history. Indeed, studies reveal that Hindi cinema in the 1970s portrayed women in different working roles such as a singer, a doctor, general manager of a company, and even a driver. In these movies women ventured out of their domestic realm to pursue their career and carve out an identity of their own. They took their own separate roads to success, though they were not always highly educated. Quite unexpectedly, by the 1990s, images of working women had vanished from the silver screen, once again relegating them to the confines of their home. Hindi movies of that era popularized the stereotypical portrayal of women with no importance given to their points of view. Instead, women's role was mostly governed by myth, custom, and ritual within the Indian society. Significantly, posing as a victim or what one might also call a victimization syndrome was also another major component of women's image portrayed in the Hindi cinema of the 1980s and the 1990s. Victimizing women simultaneously allowed male protagonists to act as saviors and thereby control and limit women's subjectivity and sexuality as per the norms of society. It is only in the Hindi films of the post-millennial period that one gets to see some realistic portrayals of women going out to work, spending time with friends, traveling long distance alone, and returning home late-night from work or party. Thankfully, over the last decade, things have changed for the better and women in contemporary Hindi movies have been granted the power to face the outside world alone and even defend themselves when in danger. My aim is to study two such contemporary movies, *Mardaani 2* (2019) and *Chhapaak* (2020), to understand whether such cinematic representations of economically and emotionally independent women in films are merely superficial in nature or do they really facilitate social change in the treatment of women in the highly patriarchal Indian society.

THE SOCIAL CONTROL OF WOMEN'S MOVEMENT

Early films often depicted vulnerable women characters enduring social and familial oppression, unlike the male hero, whose glorious life-story constituted the center of attraction. Women in these early films had to stick to their domestic and motherly roles and could not step out on the road without depending on the male hero who was responsible for protecting her. Such films repeatedly magnified sexual violence against women in public spaces to highlight their sexual vulnerability on the road. Thus, various forms of sexual violence, such as eve-teasing and rape were depicted as price paid by modernized women who dared to step out in public without male support. Their public exposure permitted the repeated depiction and even glorification of such acts of violence.

Within the domain of Indian cinema, the notions of the male gaze and spectatorship have, for ages, contributed to the passive display of female bodies in both private and public spaces. Therefore, even films that celebrate women's so-called independence, in terms of their mobility and other aspects, eventually reduce them to passive sex objects. The passive display of the female body in public also promotes stalking, which is the first step the hero of a film takes to make the woman fall in love with him. Explaining the connection between the female body and visual pleasure, Laura Mulvey states that "in a world ordered by sexual imbalances, pleasure in looking [or *scopophilia*] has been split between active/male and passive/female. . . . In their traditional exhibitionist role women are simultaneously looked at and displayed, with their appearance coded for strong visual and erotic impact" (1989, 19). Significantly, most mainstream film narratives always subject the women characters venturing into public spaces to voyeurism for the sake of the audiences' visual pleasure. Further, practices such as fetishism and voyeurism, often associated with men's sadomasochistic fantasies, have led to the successful subordination of women to the male gaze, even when they appear to be confident in public spaces. Summarizing how the concept of male gaze is used as a technique of classical filmmaking, Budd Boetticher states, "What counts is what the heroine provokes . . . She is the one, or rather the love or fear she inspires in the hero, or else the concern he feels for her, who makes him act the way he does. In herself the woman has not the slightest importance" (qtd. in Mulvey 1989, 19). Therefore, often sexual violence toward women in public spaces and on roads is assumed to be a consequence of their provocation.

The existing socio-cultural realities of women and their real-life roles as mothers, daughters and wives conditioned the roles that they received in films. In India, where women and their actions are considered epitomes of family honor and social respectability, their need to preserve honor is expressed in Hindi cinema through their willingness to exist within the confines of domestic spaces, following codified behavioral patterns and remaining dependent on their husbands. Therefore, having inherited specific social and cultural roles, women characters always are typecast or stereotyped. Female characters are stereotypically portrayed as ideal wives and mothers or vamps in the mainstream film industry. The vamp flouts tradition and imitates Western women. Therefore, modernity and westernization are often equated with being imperfect. In other words, women are either pure wives, self-sacrificing mothers, sisters, or immoral prostitutes, cabaret dancers, strippers and vamps. These are very clear-cut categories in films. However, in neither case did the women characters have the power to choose their roles for themselves. This constitutes a vicious cycle in which the stereotypically traditional or sexually-charged portrayal of women characters reinforces pre-existing socio-cultural stereotypes.

In keeping with the socially acceptable stereotypical roles of women, the Hindi film industry has for several decades promoted the traditional ambience of patriarchy which is wary of a woman's outgoing nature and demands a subjugation of her desires by confining her within the limits of home. Therefore, quite naturally, women who are comfortable in public spaces and bold enough to wear modernized attire in public are deemed uncultured and arrogant. Significantly, such perspectives demonstrate that public spaces are highly masculinized and heterosexually dominated. Indeed, several sociologists, historians, geographers and space theorists have argued that every place has a gendered identity and practically there are no politically neutral spaces. However, with many women joining the film industry as directors or producers and with many lead actresses performing influential roles, there has been a transition in the representation of women's movement in the films of recent decades. Women both in real and reel life are now challenging norms of confinement and breaking masculine and feminine stereotypes by traveling freely on their own. Thus, the destabilization of gender categories expressed through the unrestricted movement of the female protagonist in movies such as *Kahaani, Queen, Tamasha, Highway, Chennai Express, Jab We Met,* and *English Vinglish* is reminiscent of Virginia Woolf's notion of androgyny that provides men and women a chance to express themselves, in both public and private spaces, without being conscious of their gendered identity. In her most famous work, *A Room of One's Own*, Virginia Woolf describes the most ordinary and comfortable state of a human being as a condition in which both the male and female aspects of the personality can "live in harmony together, spiritually co-operating" (1998, 128). The notion of androgyny can also refer to an individual's freedom and right, irrespective of being a man or a woman, to flourish in public life, regardless of such opportunities culturally deemed as exclusively feminine or exclusively masculine. Further, as Judith Butler claims, if gender is "performative," where each individual can perform roles of the alternate gender, then one might say that the celluloid women who appear as solo-travelers in the films of recent decades have been performing several roles not conventionally aligned to their gender (1990, 275). Refuting the age-old notions of "damsel in distress," "angel in the house" and so on, the female protagonists of modern Hindi cinema have chosen alternative, transgressive, and ultimately liberatory ways to express their freedom and self-dependence through movement in public spaces. Further, in *Gender and Agency*, Lois McNay (2000) discusses how the notion of agency redefines gender identity and exposes the dichotomy between male domination and female subordination. The reconceptualization of agency brought about by the female protagonist's decision to travel alone in some contemporary Hindi movies affirms that gender identity is not immutable and can be challenged.

THE EMERGENCE OF ANDROGYNOUS WOMEN TRAVELERS IN HINDI CINEMA

A look at the history of Hindi cinema reveals the changing patterns and trends in the depiction of women beginning with the traditional and mythological roles attributed to them in early Hindi cinema to their emergence as strong, independent individuals with an identity of their own, in the contemporary cinematic world. Whereas the early Hindi cinema of the 1950s and 1960s followed the Indian epics, *Ramayana* and *Mahabharata*, in modelling the female protagonists after pious female mythological characters such as Sita-Sati-Savitri, those of the 1970s had women characters playing supporting roles to the male superstars. Significantly, the changing socio-political environment of the 1970s gave birth to the title "angry young man," represented mainly by the superstar Amitabh Bachchan, but there was no sign of the emergence of an "angry young woman" (Manzar and Aravind 2019, 2). Images of women subjected to domestic and sexual violence dominated the films of the 1980s. However, the 1990s witnessed a change in the portrayal of female characters with the commodification and objectification of their body. If such representations gave women the freedom to express their sexuality and the right to display their bodies, it also invited male spectators to indulge in scopophilia and voyeurism. However, the rising debates on spectatorship did not stop women characters from expressing their sexual desires even in the movies made after the new millennium. These films marked the beginning of a new era and a new genre of Hindi noir cinema that sought to break the previous stereotypes and showcase women as strong figures existing without male support. Films made post-2010 began to portray women characters who could speak out against male dominance and were strong enough to openly confront oppressive social conditions that confined them to domestic households in the name of family and marriage. Thus, the new Indian woman emerged, who was not the epitome of feminine virtues deriving lasting fulfillment from the domestic roles of motherhood and wifehood, but an androgynous character physically, emotionally and psychologically equipped to face the outside world. Strikingly different from the earlier meek and docile version, these women considered themselves no less than men and demanded equal respect and opportunity in public spaces.

Although the act of solo-traveling is conventionally associated with a man due to qualities such as physical strength and courage, the emergence of the new Indian woman in contemporary movies such as *Mardaani 2* and *Chhapaak* reflect the multiplicity within the seemingly homogeneous notion of confined Indian femininity projected by filmmakers for ages. Jack Halberstam in *Female Masculinity* has questioned the societal norm of constructing powerless static female figures by arguing that the "female masculinities are framed as the rejected scraps of dominant masculinity in order that male masculinity may appear to be the real thing" (1998, 1). Significantly, female masculinity is a trait of any woman who challenges the male monopoly on adventure and freedom by expressing emotions and executing rights associated only with men. The expression of female masculinity in Hindi cinema has come a long way after passing through several stages of evolution. The early expressions of female masculinity began with Hindi movies of the 1950s and 1960s, where female protagonists indulged in cross–dressing to disguise themselves as males or protect themselves from rapes or sexual harassment in public spaces. Female protagonists undertook these disguises not always to demand gender parity but to opt for a third space where the notion of identity remained ambiguous. Although the masquerade did not empower women characters adequately, it played a significant role in dismantling male hegemony and exposing the hypocrisy of the patriarchal society that could not protect its women. Maithili Rao argues that such women are "lady avengers," and their actions "reflect the cultural schizophrenia in our society" (1988, 24). Rao further disapproves of such films depicting "lady avengers" for being "hostile to female sexuality" and claims that, in reality, they depict nothing more than "victimization masquerading as female power" (1988, 24–26). Although Rao is perhaps correct in pointing out the superficial nature of these early movies on women empowerment, she ignores that these were the first steppingstones to the evolution of authentic androgynous women solo-travelers in contemporary Hindi cinema. These early films paved the path for women-centric movies of the later ages where women travelled on their own, practiced self-defense and fought against the injustices of the patriarchal world to create a public space where they could be treated as equal to men. Questioning gendered categories became more realistic in the movies of the 1990s in which the male attire was no longer a means of disguise but something that gave more power to women and reflected qualities like strength and courage. These women characters did not need to renounce their identity to subvert their power equation with the opposite sex. The post-2000 Hindi movies introduced strong, self–reliant and independent female characters who, like their male counterparts, had dreams of their own and took to the road to achieve something in life. Shivani and Malti in the films I examine here are two such androgynous characters who break free from the shackles of ideological confinement and depict that public spaces are not meant only for men.

Hero, the central figure in any Hindi cinema, always represents the masculine spirit of adventure. A man possessing heroism is always perceived to have the power to safeguard his woman in public spaces. Ursula K. Le Guin in *Earthsea Revisioned* explains how "heroism has been gendered" and claims that "The Hero is a man. Women may be good or brave, but with rare exceptions . . . women are not heroes" (1991, 5). Constrained by her gender role, the heroine is expected to be a fragile character who can do nothing but call for help and wait for the hero, a macho man, to rescue her from a life and honor-threatening situation on road. Though similar to the term "hero'" the term "heroine" is fraught with inherent contradictions as, unlike a hero, the heroine is incapable of protecting herself due to her own shortcomings. Interrogating the biological determinism that disassociates women from the notion of heroism and the act of solitary travel, women characters in recent movies like *Mardaani 2* and *Chhaapak* perform heroic deeds that bring about a change in their fate and the society around them. These heroines do not merely work like a man in public spaces but embrace both masculinity and femininity traits while in public, despite being female-bodied. Thus they transform themselves into an entirely different kind of hero, i.e., a female hero. Moving away from victimhood and functioning as active agents, these women epitomize Butler's theory of gender performativity by switching over to opposing gender roles as per their requirements of travel and work. While some film critics have argued that such movies on women solo-travelers have emerged in response to the demands of an audience that was tired of viewing typical male adventure films, the actresses enjoyed playing such powerful roles of unlimited freedom not always because they believed in them but took it as a welcome break from the stereotypical roles of confined and submissive wives or mothers. Operating beyond the realm of the strict restrictions due to their biological vulnerability, the heroines of these movies prove with their courage and fearlessness that solo-traveling need not be an authentic expression of masculinity or be exclusive associated with males. The movie's title, *Mardaani 2*, implicates and connotes a patriarchal arena where previously ideal women could not venture. However, contrary to the norm, the movie's entire plot revolves around the female lead, Shivani Sivaji Roy, who, despite being attractive, feminine and heterosexually appealing to the male gaze, has the personality and physical strength of a man that permits her to move fearlessly in public spaces.

MARDAANI 2: AVENGING WOMEN TRAVELERS

The title of the movie *Mardaani 2*, directed by Gopi Puthran, is highly significant. The Hindi word "mard" stands for man. The word "mardaani" is an adjective, which means "like a man" or "manly," but can also be used occasionally as a noun to mean "a brave lady." Since the adjective is associated with a woman in this movie, the title is paradoxical and provokes a debate on gender discourses. The word "mardaani" became popular after the Hindi Poet Subhadra Kumari Chauhan used it in her poetry to describe Lakshmibai, the Rani of Jhansi (1828–1858). The queen of the Maratha-ruled Jhansi State was one of the central figures to have participated in the First War of Indian Independence in 1857. The queen who joined the uprising against the British colonial power by organizing her own troops and fighting fearlessly to prevent the seize of Jhansi soon became a symbol of resistance and extraordinary strength. After her demise, Sir Hugh Rose, the commander of the British forces, described Rani Lakshimibai as "the most dangerous of all Indian leaders" despite being a woman. The poet uses the word "mardaani" for the queen because she fought like any man when it was unthinkable for women to venture out of their homes, leave alone fight in wars. Akin to the historical figure, Shivani Shivaji Roy, the protagonist of *Mardaani 2*, takes up the role of a hero and successfully deconstructs the stereotypical assumption that only males are apt for the job of a cop. A truly androgynous figure, Shivani is a brilliant and dutiful policewoman who has been posted in Kota, Rajasthan. She is soon assigned to capture a criminal who rapes young women in a fit of rage before cruelly murdering them.

Mardaani 2 belongs to a group of films that deal with the rising debates on women's safety with regard to rape and sexual abuse. Instances of sexual violence against women occur in a more significant number in male-dominated societies such as India. Therefore, Sexual harassment has become a topic of concern and discussion in Hindi films of recent decades. Using the word "sex" or discussing it in public is forbidden in many parts of Asia, including India. Since talking openly about sex in India is generally considered embarrassing, often instances of sexual assault or violence remain unreported and unexpressed. Despite victims not opening up about it, a heinous crime like sexual harassment or assault is an everyday fear and, in some unfortunate cases, a reality for Indian women. Significantly, sexual violence is used as a trope or a universal discourse in films showcasing the struggles of women in their attempts to be independent and assert their choices in married and domestic life without the interference of patriarchal hegemony. A persistent trend in the world of Hindi cinema has been to depict women targeted and subjected to sexual violence due to the assumption that they are weaker and powerless than men. Carrie N. Baker, in her book *The Women's Movement against Sexual Harassment*, describes sexual harassment as "a form of violence against women that reflected and reinforced women's subordinate status in the society" (2008, 44). She further argues that most of the victims of violence are those women who appear to pose "threats to the masculinity, power, or economic status" of men (Baker 2008, 44). However, rather than reinforcing the social outlook that decrees women to be compliant and meek and expects them to tolerate all sorts of torment, contemporary Hindi films like *Mardaani 2* depict women protagonists shedding their vulnerability to resist and even seek revenge for acts of sexual aggression committed by men.

Unfortunately, the depiction of sexual violence in Hindi cinema is mostly scripted. Significantly, a recurring and well-defined script determines the pre-conditions, nature, and repercussions of a sexual assault. According to such a script, young unmarried men are seen to be assaulting young women who flout traditional gender roles. Significantly, female victims are often depicted as being responsible for the occurrence of sexual assault due to their seemingly inappropriate actions such as stepping out of the home at night, wearing revealing clothes and being overambitious. Often working women who follow a dress code and are forced to work in office till late night do not have much of a choice in such matters and are targeted for their self-dependence. Explaining how movement and communication across public spaces is largely determined by gender, Doreen Massey states, "The degree to which we can move between countries, or walk about the streets at night, or take public transport, or venture out of hotels in foreign cities, is not influenced simply by 'capital,' but also by ethnicity and gender" (1993, 63). Such narratives of assault used in Hindi films may reflect socially and culturally embedded beliefs about sexuality and, therefore, can influence the sexual socialization of young Indians. The act of assault itself is depicted gruesomely, with the perpetrator combining physical and verbal aggression to torture the female. Despite actively resisting the assault, the female ultimately faces social defamation or succumbs to death. The perpetrator, in most cases, remains unprosecuted and unpunished. Although the film *Mardaani 2*, to some extent, perpetuates this stereotypical and dramatized depiction of sexual assault, it does not allow the perpetrator to escape without paying the price.

The plot of *Mardaani 2* begins with the depiction of a sexual assault. The monstrous rapist named Sunny is a true misogynist and finds particular pleasure in hunting down women who have self-respect or are proud of themselves. The first scene takes place in a Dussehra Mela (or a festive fair) where Sunny locates a young girl named Latika admonishing her boyfriend, Monty, for not picking up her calls and eventually leaving the fair without him in anger. Sunny directly addresses the audience and declares that targeting such arrogant girls is his specialty as he has done full-fledged research on them. He then follows Latika in a stolen car and traps her with a lie that her boyfriend has had an accident while returning home. Due to the scarcity of public transport during the night, Latika voluntarily hops into Sunny's car when he offers to take her immediately to the hospital, in which he claims her boyfriend is admitted. Following this, Sunny rapes, tortures, and murders Latika to punish her for being vocal, independent, and fearless. The next day Shivani Shivaji Roy, the police officer in charge, is seen examining the crime scene and the battered dead body of Latika lying in a pool of water. Being an efficient cop, Shivani quickly studies the evidence left-back by the perpetrator and mentally reconstructs the act of rape. Interestingly, apart from Shivani, the movie's protagonist, all other characters seem to act as mouthpieces of the society expressing cultural views on sexual violence and gender roles in India. Both the senior police officer, Brij Shekhawat and Latika's college teacher blames her directly or indirectly for her fate. Whereas Shekhawat questions the character of Latika by tagging her as a modern woman who cannot do without multiple boyfriends, Latika's college teacher finds fault with her straightforward nature, considering it to be provocative. Thus *Mardaani 2* shows how the cultural construction of sexual violence in India is based on a strong opinion on women's character and their adherence to traditionally prescribed gender roles. Women are expected to abide by traditional gender norms to be respected. Women transgressing social boundaries by stepping out of their home alone at night, refusing to be meek, and wearing non-conservative or western clothing are seen as deserving of such sexual violence and are even blamed for provoking it. Latika presence in the wrong place, at the wrong time determines her fate. According to the feminist geographer, Gillian Rose (1993), such violent attacks on women are often deliberately done to remind them that certain public spaces are not meant for them. "The ability to act in the public sphere," Rose claims, "is a privilege violently reserved for men"

(1993, 38). Thus, often city spaces are found to be divided into masculine and feminine areas depending on various security issues. Interestingly, the more women voluntarily restrict their mobility due to the fear of such violent attacks, the more male-dominated the public spaces become. *Mardaani 2* also shows that women adopting non-traditional gender roles like Latika are more vulnerable to sexual assault.

Though *Mardaani 2* stays clear of a dramatic and open depiction of the violent act of rape, the shrieks of Latika when inside Sunny's car and the discovery of her terribly battered body is enough to convey the dreadfulness of the crime. Like many other avenging women Hindi films, the rape scene and the tortured body of the victim is indispensable to the plot of *Mardaani 2*. The battered female body of Latika eroticizes the scene of violation and acts as a binding site of scopophilic pleasure for the audience. The visual representation of Latika's raped body instead of the act of rape is reminiscent of the authority of censorship. Nevertheless, the overlap between the representations of rape and rape itself encourages sadomasochistic identification with this scene. Moreover, unlike films of the masculine genre granting revenge-seeking male heroes unhindered access to power, *Mardaani 2* depicts the intervention of the figure of the State, in the form of the police officer, Shivani Shivaji Roy, from the very beginning of the movie. Being dead, the victim, Latika, does not get a scope to articulate her pain or avenge herself directly. Therefore, like other avenging women films, *Mardaani 2* also flaunts a rape scene as a substitute for violent sex and ultimately balances it with an equally horrific revenge scene at the end of the film to satisfy the audiences' sadistic demand for punishment. Significantly, the protagonist, Shivani, is allowed to seek revenge and assert her masculine power on screen momentarily by beating and torturing Sunny mercilessly at the end of the film only in exchange for Latika's rape and murder. Thus, the rape-revenge narrative used in the movie *Mardaani 2* is a recurrent feature in Hindi cinema, and all instances of female aggression depicted in such movies necessitate the presence of a horrific rape scene.

In a male-dominated industry like Bollywood, women are usually presented in weak or subordinate positions. Significantly, gender inequality in India is also reflected in women's invisibility and underrepresentation in the film industry. Gender stereotyping is a major hurdle that women in leadership positions have to overcome both in mainstream cinema and real life. In recent decades, with women contributing to the country's economy, their status has undergone some change, enabling talented women like Shivani to assume leadership roles within the workplace. Even a brave and committed female leader like Shivani is evaluated less favorably than her male counterparts and penalized for adopting masculine leadership styles. Her male co-worker, Brij Shekhawat, refuses to take orders from her and creates trouble for her at every step. Brij Shekhawat is also a typical misogynist who does not believe in granting freedom and independence to women. When Shivani refuses to permit a young but corrupt politician, Viplav Beniwal's rally, to avoid a traffic jam, Shekhawat argues that traffic jams in the city occur due to women driving their own cars. Shekhawat also uses his media connections to defame Shivani when Sunny kills a child witness placed under her care. Moreover, Shivani's senior male colleague frequently admonishes her for being emotional and outspoken. Showing his concern over the growing animosity between Shivani and Shekhawat, Shivani's superior reasons that when society allows a woman to be successful, people expect her to be meek, humble and polite in return. However, Shivani refuses to compromise and states that managing the egos of her male colleagues is not a part of her job. Although she is judged for her display of emotions, Shivani turns her emotional weakness into her strength and uses it to boost her determination to hunt down and punish the criminal, Sunny. Shivani shows that being a female police officer does not necessarily mean that a woman must discard her traditional caring and nurturing roles. She proudly uses her feminine attributes in her workplace but at the same time continues to demonstrate her ability to work professionally. Shivani does not step back from adopting masculine traits when necessary and even uses her physical strength to teach Sunny a lesson at the end of the film. Thus, Shivani is shown to have a mixture of feminine and masculine qualities that help her overcome gender stereotypes and deal with organized crime. Significantly, the film also shows how important it is for women to know self-defense techniques and be physically fit to handle a hostile or sexist situation in public spaces of India.

Sunny, a frightening criminal, is a cinematic representation of real-life threats that women face from men every day, in public places, offices, social circles and homes. The way he directly addresses the audience reminds one about the existence of such brutes amid us. Sunny, who has a shady past, comes from a misogynist family. On investigating, Shivani finds out that Sunny's father had killed his wife and was also a rapist and murderer like his son. Having inherited the misogyny directly from his father, Sunny detests any woman who raises her voice against patriarchal oppression and dreams of becoming equal to a man. When Sunny realizes that a female police officer is after him, he decides to teach Shivani a lesson just like his victims. Sunny is a new age criminal who is not afraid of being caught but wants to impress Shivani with his fearless antiques. Sunny takes up the false name, Bajrang, and starts working in a tea stall outside the police station to taunt Shivani and collect inside information about the investigation. Sunny continues to target many other women after Latika. When a girl called Tina slaps Sunny for secretly making a video of her chatting with her friends in a local Dhaba, he eventually gets hold of the girl and rapes her similarly. When Sunny fails to harm Shivani directly, he targets Sunanda Chaudhary, another accomplished woman who was planning to step into the world of politics. Sunny also kidnaps Priyanka, the grandchild of Panditji, the local goon who had hired him as a professional killer on her way back home from coaching classes. Thus, Sunny has no sense of loyalty and rampantly targets any woman who dares to step out of her home and dream big.

Contrary to one's expectations, no deviation in the victim's profile regarding her age, class, caste, marital status, or conservatism can safeguard her from a sexual assault. Further, *Mardaani 2* also shows that perpetrators mostly target women who venture out of their house alone to undertake a journey of independence, empowerment and self-development. Thus, the public space where the action of *Mardaani 2* takes place is equally life-threatening for the police officer, Shivani Shivaji Roy as it is for any other girl like Latika, Tina, and Sunanda. Shivani depicts how women can successfully overthrow even a frightening criminal like Sunny by using their brains along with their physical strength, to handle situations of crisis in public spaces. For instance, in one particular scene of the movie, despite knowing that Sunny who has entered her car disguised as Bajrang would surely attack her, Shivani remains calm instead of panicking and uses her physical skill to safeguard herself.

Significantly, one of the ways in which women can express the strength of their character and identity is by abandoning conservative and weaker forms of femininity in favor of adopting the masculine spirit of risk-taking adventure and travel. Women's ability to travel alone is often equated with their empowerment as it demonstrates their self-reliance, courage and determination to face situations alone. To be successful solo travelers, women must often achieve a fine balance between adopting the masculine discourse of adventure and following the feminine tradition of adjustment. One of the ways in which women are expected to negotiate the challenges of travel is by managing their emotions, such as fear and anger. The practice of remaining calm, happy, and humorous even in the face of adversities, including multiple forms of sexual harassment and bad behavior, is considered the key to women's fulfilling travel experience. Maintaining a positive outlook despite feeling angry, frightened or upset is an essential exercise that women are advised to carry out to get ahead in public and private life.

Significantly, every guidebook written on women's travel experience reiterates the discourses of emotional management and the maintenance of a positive attitude while traveling. However, such advice that "guide" women through their solo travel experiences are often contradictory. Such guidebooks encourage women to explore new places and take risks, despite reminding them to take care of their safety. Refusing to differentiate between individual travel experiences, these guidebooks, on the one hand, promote women empowerment by pushing women to overcome their fears, anxieties and doubts and assert their rights to access public spaces. On the other hand, they also reinforce the gender and emotional constraints enduring which women need to plan their travel to remain safe and protected. Although honest emotions such as anger toward injustice, fear of the unknown and resentment at being harassed are most common in women's travel literature, the guidebooks favor the use of control, intuition and common sense over such emotions. A special travel issue titled *More Women Travel: Adventures and advice from more than 60 countries* (1995) advises prospective female travelers to be enduring toward "all manner of comments" from strangers. It also warns women to avoid arguing with local men as it might lead to "ugly" situations. The book suggests that a woman can handle unpleasant situations by using her sense of humor (Davies and Jansz 1995, 370). Similarly, the *Handbook for Women Travellers* (1995) encourages women to use their humor and resilience to overcome and diffuse real feelings of anger and fear during independent travel. Further, the handbook states that losing one's temper may provoke "real hostility and make things worse rather than better" (Moss and Moss 1995, 243). These guidebooks fail to understand how negative emotions are produced naturally due to instances of harassment and how they give a clear and accurate picture of gendered interactions in public spaces. Thus, going by the discourses of such guidebooks, girls like Latika and Tina, who are not inhibited by their gender when in public spaces, invite trouble for themselves.

However, *Mardaani 2* shows that women can often be targeted in public spaces, even without any provocation. While giving an interview for the Swadesh TV in keeping with the journalist Amit Sharma's request, Shivani states, "The moment a woman steps into the public space, she becomes a public property" (Puthran 2019, 1:19:00 to 1:20:00 on timeline). Thus, Shivani reasserts the importance of women discovering their own "mardaani" and learning to defend themselves in public. Shivani extends the terrain of masculinity by defending herself and rescuing the other women captured by Sunny. She uses her physical strength and capability to take down Sunny and subject him to public torture by beating the hell of out him. In urging women to nurture their own "mardaani," Shivani does not imply that women must try to behave like men but develop within themselves traits such as self-confidence, self-reliance and valor usually associated with men. Reconfiguring the link between power and gender, Shivani explores the possibility of establishing the androgynous ideal within an individual gender category. The film illustrates that strong women like Shivani are not afraid of showing their tough side when in danger and can maintain their dignity and prove their leadership skills even in a male-dominated world full of threats and bent on degrading women.

Most acts of sexual violence or assault depicted in contemporary Hindi cinema emerges from a patriarchal perspective. Indian society expects young men to step into the outside world to provide for their families and protect them, while young women are instructed to stay inside their house and function as good wives and mothers. Such inequitable gender roles automatically grant men much more power than women and make their presence necessary for a woman's safety and survival in public spaces. Accordingly, film depictions propagate a set of beliefs about women inviting such assaults by stepping out alone of their house and typical misogynist men taking advantage of their vulnerability. Crime statistics in India indicate that women venturing out alone in public spaces are at a higher risk of being sexually assaulted. Interestingly, often films normalize acts of sexual harassment as a part of romantic love. Teasing, groping and coaxing are acceptable in romance even without the consent of the heroine. Therefore, naturally, unrequited love and humiliation often result in rapes and assaults. Significantly, the depiction of sexual harassment as a legitimate means of pursuing love can also shape cultural beliefs about sexual violence being an acceptable part of interpersonal and romantic relationships. In his study of selected Hindi films, Steve Derne (1999) depicts how violence and sexuality are often intertwined in films that legitimize men's use of physical aggression while seeking revenge for inter-caste conflict, family rivalry, and unrequited love (550).

CHHAPAAK: A VOICE AGAINST ACID ATTACKS

A film that aptly depicts a similar violent outcome of unrequited love is Meghna Gulzar's *Chhapaak*. The film offers a worthy female role model, Malti, who, in the process of fighting for her cause, becomes a symbol of strength and inspiration for many women. The movie narrates the story of a real-life acid attack survivor, Laxmi Agarwal. The movie begins with a public protest scene for the Nirbhaya rape case in Delhi. The public is deeply agitated by the increasing number of rapes taking place in and around Delhi, with victims being brutally tortured and murdered. However, none seems to care about or even be aware of the survivors of acid attack, a crime no less horrific than rape. Acid attacks on women have become quite common in different parts of India due to many reasons, such as disputes over property, dowry, and declined marriage proposals. However, the most commonly identified reason for such attacks is unrequited love or refusal of a proposal. The thwarted male lovers track down these women and attack them with acid, disfiguring them for life. Acid attack, which is a premeditated form of violence involving the throwing of a corrosive chemical such as sulphuric, nitric or hydrochloric acid on another human being's body, is considered by many as "one of the worst crimes that a person can commit" ("Living in the Shadows" 2003, 1). As the attack disfigures the victims for life rather than killing them, it also leads to the infringement of fundamental human rights. Most acid attack survivors fail to seek employment due to visual and physical impairment. Moreover, social ostracization and ruined marriage prospects do not allow such survivors to reinstate themselves into mainstream society. The crime of acid attack is committed following a specific gender dimension in India. Acid, being readily available compared to guns, knives or bombs, is used as a cheap weapon against women who refuse romantic or sexual advances. Acid attack is a gender-based crime committed chiefly against women with an aim to silence and control them. Feminist geographers such as Rachel H. Pain and Gill Valentine have shown how "all men benefit from the social control of women," emerging from fear of violence in public spaces (Pain 1997, 231). According to Gill Valentine, "the association of male violence with certain environmental contexts has a profound effect on many women's use of space" (1989, 385). Thus, women's fear of public spaces automatically reduces their confidence on road and makes them an easy prey for violent attacks.

The movie's central character, Malti, is a young teenage high school girl with big dreams. She wants to become a well-known singer by participating in the Indian Idol competition and thus takes her music training seriously. Like most teenagers, Malti has just stepped into adulthood and is keen to explore the world of romance with a boyfriend, Rajesh, from the same school. However, a family friend named Basheer Khan, aka Babbu, is in love with Malti and wishes to marry her someday. Basheer, who works as a tailor in a boutique, is thirty-six years old and much senior to Malti. Not being able to tolerate the growing closeness between Malti and Rajesh, Basheer tries his best to break their bond out of jealousy. When his threats fail to separate them, Basheer starts proposing to Malti over the phone and even stalking her. Malti, who thinks of Basheer as a brother and even addresses him so, can do nothing but avoid meeting him in public and delete his messages. However, Basheer, who feels dishonored and humiliated, plans an acid attack on Malti. Just the night before the attack, Basheer calls Malti and taunts her declaring that he would teach her a lesson for having big dreams and trying to make her parents proud. Basheer and his aide, Parveen Shaikh, attacks Malti in broad daylight on the streets of Delhi. Thus, Malti has to pay a high price for not paying heed to Basheer's threats and enjoying a continuous access to public spaces. Malti's fate is reminiscent of June Jordan's argument that there is "a universal experience for women, which is that physical mobility is circumscribed by our gender and by the enemies of our gender . . . This holds throughout the world for women and literally we are not to move about in the world freely. If we do then we have to understand that we may have to pay for it with our bodies. That is the threat" (qtd. in Rose 1999, 363). Linda McDowell also argues that such common experiences of women around the world allow them to connect on a global scale and create among themselves not just an "international sisterhood," but a "cartography of struggle" that maps their shared predicaments (1999, 214).

Acid attack is one of the many crimes committed in the name of honor. Once lost, honor can be reclaimed and reinstated through the transgressor's apology or the victim's erasure. Spurned lovers often choose to throw acid as a distorted means of reclaiming honor. The victim is publicly marked and punished for daring to refuse a man's proposal or deviating from the patriarchy's path into extra-marital relationships. Contemporary honor crimes like acid attacks are based on outdated codes of social conduct that place several restrictions on female behavior while simultaneously legitimizing male violence against women. Thus, if the motivation for acid throwing is to punish a woman for rejecting proposals of sex or marriage, then the woman herself is held liable for her loss of reputation. This is because the act of rejection that gives a woman agentic power to refuse a man indicates an insult of patriarchy. In other words, a man's experience of being turned down becomes more significant than a woman's power to choose. The feminist geographer, Daphne Spain points out how "men's experiences and concerns often are privileged over women's," due to what he calls "the universality of patriarchy" (1992, 137–138). Spain claims, "Women's position within society, whether measured as power, prestige, economic position, or social rank, is related to spatial segregation" (1992, 137). Thus, Malti, a woman, who shows the courage to reject Basheer's proposal is deliberately attacked with an intention to disfigure her and thereby prevent her from accessing public spaces. Cutting her off from public spaces was one of the ways in which she could be rendered helpless and reminded of her lower status.

The acid thrown at Malti by Parveen, a woman herself, disfigures her face and neck significantly. As per the patriarchal notion, women's social acceptance depends mainly on their physical beauty and their body. Thus, a violation of the body and its beauty through an acid attack is the ultimate means of retaliation chosen by rejected suitors. The victims often face physical challenges and suffer from a lifetime of psychological trauma even after bearing huge expenses of reconstructive surgery. Interestingly, despite several people witnessing the incident, none but only a Sardarji comes forward to help Malti and calls the police, who take her to the hospital. When police officers start investigating the case, they blame Malti for the incident and hints at her promiscuity on account of her cell phone carrying the phone numbers of several boys. However, what is inspiring and noteworthy is that despite having faced severe physical, psychological and social scarring, Malti, in the movie, appears to be a normal girl on a job hunt with no time for self-pity. She faces several rejections in the job market due to her scarred face. With the help of a well-wisher, Shiraz Jamshed, Malti undergoes many complicated surgeries to correct her physical scars and learns to overlook the emotional scars caused by the attack consciously.

Malti battles depression and manages to punish Basheer by winning against him in both the lower court and the High court, with the help of her efficient lawyer, Archana Bajaj. Although Malti has to give up her dream of being a singer, she does something meaningful with her life by working with an NGO for acid victims called "Chaya." With the support of a few friends and well-wishers such as Archana and her employer at the NGO, Amol Dwivedi, Malti succeeds in getting justice for herself and making the Supreme Court of India pass a law regulating the sale of acid by filing a PIL. Therefore, in this movie, like in *Mardaani 2*, the female protagonist, Malti, emerges as a winner because she does not let the tragedy of acid attack rule her entire life and at no point does she succumb to self-pity or the victimization syndrome. While demanding a ban on the open sale of acid, the lawyer Archana cites several acid attack cases as examples explaining to the jury members how perpetrators singled out and targeted girls who stepped out into public and wanted to achieve something in life through education and hard work. However, despite bringing Basheer Khan to justice, who is sentenced to ten years of imprisonment, the film does not end on a hopeful note. Depicting another incident of acid attack in December 2013, in which the victim succumbs to her injuries, the film laments the continuation of frequent acid attacks and the free marketing of acids, despite the implementation of new laws and sufficient media exposure of acid attack crimes.

CONCLUSION

Thus, Gopi Puthran's *Mardaani 2* and Meghna Gulzar's *Chhapaak* give us powerful female protagonists who use their determination and indomitable spirit to win their battle of life. Rather than offering idealistic solutions to women's problems, these contemporary films depict how women shed their submissive, fragile and helpless selves to evolve into strong and courageous individuals who can change their fate. Such films show a nuanced understanding of new Indian women of the twenty-first century who can achieve their goals without any male intervention. This is not to say that these women protagonists do not need men in their life. Rather men mostly play a supporting role in their life. Overall, maintaining a sense of distance from the various notions of patriarchal ideology allows them to explore their potential and achieve their dreams. Nevertheless, it is difficult to overlook the various instances of sexual violence such as rapes and acid attacks that continue to constrain women's progress and mobility even in this post-liberalized era. Popular Indian films play a significant role in educating the Indian public about the construction of sexuality because it is rarely discussed in other contexts. Therefore, motion pictures should be cautious about prescribing how men ought to behave with women in public spaces. For decades, Hindi films have depicted women's beauty and body as existing for men's pleasure and the use of force to express love toward women and develop relationships with them. Unfortunately, plotlines of even women-centric films such as *Mardaani 2* and *Chhapaak* both follows and deviates from the culturally embedded sexual assault script. Despite having women characters playing lead roles and protesting against sexual violence and gender inequality, such films show consistency with cultural expectations in portraying women being held responsible for their assault, victims facing social stigmatization, and perpetrators enjoying prolonged immunity due to the inefficiency of the Indian legal system. Significantly, both the films end with an indication of a continuation of rapes and acid attacks in India despite public awareness about such crimes. Thus, one can say that though the representation of women in Hindi cinema has changed in the past few years, a revolutionary narrative that would genuinely represent the changing dynamics of the modern society where women can safely compete with men and access public spaces is still awaited.

REFERENCES

Baker, Carrie N. 2008. *The Women's Movement against Sexual Harassment.* Cambridge: Cambridge University Press.

Butalia, Urvashi. 1984. "Woman in Indian Cinema." *Feminist Review* 17, no. 1 (November): 108–110.

Butler, Judith. 1990. "Performative Acts and Gender Constitution: An Essay in Phenomenology and Feminist Theory." In *Performing Feminisms: Feminist Critical Theory and Theatre*, edited by Sue-Ellen Case, 270–282. Baltimore, MD: Johns Hopkins University Press.

Derne, Steve. 1999. "Making Sex Violent: Love as Force in Recent Hindi Films." *Violence Against Women* 5, no. 5 (May): 548–575.

Gulzar, Meghna. 2020. *Chhapaak.* Fox Star Studios. 2hrs. www.imdb.com/title/tt9614460/.

Halberstam, Jack. 1998. *Female Masculinity.* Durham: Duke University Press.

Jansz, Natania, and Miranda Davies, eds. 1995. *More Women Travel: Adventures and Advice from More Than 60 Countries.* London: Rough Guides Limited.

Le Guin, Ursula K. 1991. *Earthsea Revisioned.* Bloomington: Indiana University Press.

LICADHO (Cambodian League for the Promotion and Defense of Human Rights). 2003. "Living in the Shadows: Acid Attacks in Cambodia." Accessed December 21, 2021. www.licadho-cambodia.org/reports.php?perm=41.

Manzar, Benazir, and Aju Aravind. 2019. "(Re) Thinking Women in Cinema: The Changing Narrative Structure in Bollywood." *South Asian Popular Culture* 1, no. 1 (April): 1–13.

Massey, Doreen. 1993. "Power-Geometry and a Progressive Sense of Place." In *Mapping the Futures: Local Cultures, Global Change*, edited by Jon Bird et al., 62–70. London: Routledge.

McDowell, Linda. 1999. *Gender, Identity and Place: Understanding Feminist Geographies*. Minneapolis: University of Minnesota Press.

McNay, Lois. 2000. *Gender and Agency: Reconfiguring the Subject in Feminist and Social Theory*. Cambridge: Polity Press.

Moss, Maggie, and Gemma Moss. 1995. *Handbook for Women Travellers*. London: Piatkus Books.

Mulvey, Laura. 1989. "Visual Pleasure and Narrative Cinema." In *Visual and Other Pleasures*, 14–28. New York: Palgrave.

Pain, Rachel H. 1997. "Social Geographies of Women's Fear of Crime." *Transactions of the Institute of British Geographers* 22, no. 2: 231–244.

Puthran, Gopi. 2019. *Mardaani 2*. Yash Raj Films. 1hr., 43min. www.imdb.com/title/tt5668770/.

Rao, Maithili. 1998. "Victims in Vigilante Clothing." In *Cinema in India*, October–December: 24–26.

Rose, Gillian. 1993. *Feminism and Geography: The Limits of Geographical Knowledge*. London: Polity Press.

Spain, Daphne. 1992. *Gendered Spaces*. Chapel Hill: University of North Carolina Press.

Valentine, Gill. "The Geography of Women's Fear." *Area* 21, no. 4 (December): 385–390.

Woolf, Virginia. 1998. *A Room of One's Own*. Oxford: Oxford University Press.

PART III

Bollywood's Traveling Women (II)
Vexed Dualities of Freedom and Fear

Chapter 6

The Conditional Promise of Empowerment and Pleasure

An Intersectional Analysis of Hindi Film Portrayals of Women Navigating Public Spaces in India

Uttara Manohar

The United Nations Global Settlements Program defines public spaces as "all places publicly owned or of public use, accessible and enjoyable by all for free" (UN-Habitat 2015, 6). However, Indian women continue to experience various forms of harassment and violence in public spaces, which creates a sense of fear and limits their ability to safely access streets, modes of public transportation, markets, and other public places (Roy & Bailey 2021, 2). Women's experiences are also shaped by hierarchies of caste, religion, geography, and class. For instance, gendered violence against Dalit women, religious minorities, rural women, and those who have a lower socio-economic status often gets normalized, ignored, or easily forgotten, whereas similar instances among Hindu, upper caste, urban and upper/middle class women get more attention from the media and the public (Dey 2019, 366). Phadke, Ranade, and Khan (2009) argue that urban women have higher economic and political participation and therefore have increased access to public spaces (186). However, they still do not have equal rights to enjoy the public spaces and engage in simple pleasures like loitering (Phadke, Ranade, & Khan 2009, 186), or walking on the streets anytime of the day without fear (Bharadwaj & Mahanta 2021, 3). Scholars argue that instances of sexual violence are often used to craft a narrative of cities as violent spaces that women should avoid for preserving their safety (Phadke 2013, 50). Overall, Indian women do not have equal rights to access and enjoy the public space.

In India, gendered norms exist about navigating public and private places. In addition to communication from parents, peers, and teachers, these norms are also reinforced through fictional and non-fictional media. Hindi films are very popular in India and can influence audience perceptions about gender, sexuality, and sexual violence (Manohar & Kline 2014, 235) as well as create aspirational ideas about travel and tourism (Nanjangud 2020, 132). This chapter examines how Hindi films represent neoliberal Indian women who are traveling or navigating various public places.[1] Using an intersectional lens that acknowledges women's realities anchored in the politics of religion, caste, geography, and class, I argue that Hindi films offer two contrasting cultural spaces for Indian women—one that promises freedom, adventure, and enjoyment to the privileged and the other—a site of violence and struggle for women with marginalized identities or those who subvert traditional gender roles. The chapter begins with a discussion of gendered norms regarding public behavior that are reinforced through various socialization factors. This is followed by a critical analysis of ten Hindi films to illustrate the two contrasting cultural spaces in Hindi films that vary based on women's socio-cultural identities, their adherence to traditional gender roles, and their overall orientation toward the public space.

GENDERED NORMS FOR NAVIGATING THE PUBLIC SPACE

Traditional socio-cultural norms in India prescribe a gendered dichotomy between public and private spaces, where women are expected to attend to the private spaces managing household chores whereas the outer/public space of material interests is dominated by men (Bhattacharyya 2015, 1344). Owing to these beliefs, women's presence in public spaces might be perceived as a disruption of traditional gender norms that can "invite" negative consequences. Women who venture into the public space must manage fears of molestation, acid attacks, and other forms of sexual and physical violence. Additionally, when navigating public places women and young girls are regularly subjected to the male gaze. For instance, a longitudinal ethnographic study of 45 young girls from Hyderabad (ages 6–8 years), found that from an early age, young girls understand and orient their bodies in gendered public spaces, where they are socialized to expect and resist various forms of harassment and violence (Aruldoss & Nolas 2019, 1603). Roy and Bailey's (2021) in-depth interviews and focus groups with young women (ages 24–35 years) in Kolkata also found that women learn to recognize and negotiate unsafe conditions in public spaces through avoidance, protection, and prevention (9). Social norms prescribe that to remain safe in the public space, women must enact "respectability" by illustrating linkages to familial structures and masculine protection (Phadke et al. 2009, 188). Additionally, norms of respectability also stipulate that when in public, women should wear conservative clothing, avoid traveling alone, and avoid being in the public space late at night.

Analyses of Hindi films have demonstrated how media representations can reinforce traditional Indian gender norms defining what constitutes appropriate and inappropriate behavior for Indian women and men. For instance, Khan and Taylor (2018) found that female protagonists in Bollywood films are rewarded when they uphold the traditional gender norms and experience negative consequences or punishments when they violate traditional gender norms (3651–3652). Banaji's (2002) analysis of the film *Raja Hindustani* and interviews with young audiences reveal how the film perpetuates a narrative of victim blaming by insisting that women who wear "modern" and skimpy clothing are responsible for inviting sexual harassment in public places as well as for corrupting the morality of young Indian men (185). Ramasubramanian and Oliver's (2003) analysis of sexual violence in Hindi films found that Hindi films often normalize public sexual harassment of women by depicting heroes who engage in eve-teasing as a way of getting the heroine's attention, professing their love, or engaging in lighthearted fun (334). Likewise, Manohar and Kline (2014) found that sexual violence is often depicted in Hindi films as a punishment for women who do not reciprocate a man's romantic interests, rebel against men, and violate traditional gender norms (240).

Hindi films that depict women's travels or their experiences in the public space constitute culturally embedded gender norms for navigating public spaces. Therefore, a critical content analysis is proposed here to examine Hindi film depictions of women's travel experiences. With the aforesaid critical debates in mind, this chapter has attempted a critical analysis of ten Hindi films released between 2012 and 2020 that portray neoliberal Indian women's experiences while traveling or navigating public spaces in India. This intersectional analysis examined how social hierarchies of caste, religion, geography, and class are represented in Hindi film depictions of women's experiences in public spaces. The analysis demonstrated the presence of two contrasting cultural spaces which are described based on three features about the women protagonists in public spaces: identity markers (caste, religion, geography, and socioeconomic status), traditional gender role conformity, and overall orientation to the public space.

PUBLIC SPACE: A SITE FOR FREEDOM, ADVENTURE, AND ENJOYMENT

The first cultural space depicted in Hindi films that this study has engaged with represents a space where women have the agency to be confident and assertive and can pursue a wide variety of goals including but not limited to: enjoyment seeking, adventure, self-discovery, personal growth as well as pursuit of instrumental goals pertaining to one's professional aspirations. The five films that represented this cultural space were: *Kahaani* (2012), *Yeh Jawaani Hai Deewani* (2013), *Highway* (2014), *Piku* (2015), *Qarib Qarib Singlle* (2017). This section begins with a brief description of each film followed by findings of a thematic analysis that describe the characteristics of this agency-affording and aspirational construction of the public space.

Case 1: Kahaani. Vidya Bagchi is a software engineer who travels to Kolkata to find her missing husband. While being pregnant and married, she manages to face various challenges, persuade people, and efficiently navigate several male-dominated public spaces to achieve her goal. The film ends by revealing that Vidya is not pregnant and is herself a secret agent who is on a mission to kill a man named Milan Damji.

Case 2: Yeh Jawaani Hai Deewani (YJHD). Naina Talwar is a medical student from a high socio-economic status who has led a largely sheltered life. On a whim, Naina joins her old school friends Aditi, Kabir (Bunny), and Avee on a hiking trip to Manali. The film focuses on how travel helps Naina, and her friends figure out their goals and relationships in life.

Case 3: Highway. Veera Tripathi, the daughter of a rich businessman is abducted and held for ransom by a criminal Mahavir Bhati. The film explores the relationship between the hostage victim and her captor, chronicling their journey on the road as they confide in each other about their childhood trauma and develop an unlikely connection.

Case 4: Piku. Piku Banerjee is an architect, a single a woman in her thirties who lives with her father Bhaskor Banerjee in Delhi. The film is a slice of life film that focuses on her relationship with her hypochondriac father who suffers from chronic constipation. A road trip with her father to her ancestral home in Kolkata allows her to rediscover her roots and reexamine her relationships.

Case 5: Qareeb Qareeb Singlle (QQS). Jaya Shashidharan is a 35-year-old middle/upper middle class working woman, who is a widow and lives by herself in the city. She meets Yogi Prajapati on an online dating website. The two embark on a trip to meet Yogi's ex-girlfriends in Dehradun, Jaipur, and Gangtok. The journey sparks self-reflection and chronicles the developing romance between the two protagonists.

In analyzing these film depictions of women's experiences with travel and/or navigating the public space, findings revealed that the women displayed similar characteristics in terms of identity markers, conformity to traditional gender norms, and their overall orientation toward the public space.

IDENTITY MARKERS AND WOMEN IN PUBLIC SPACES

The protagonists in all five films shared common identity factors pertaining to age, religion, caste, class, geography. All five women were in the 25–35-year age range. While none of the women were depicted as being religious, they were all upper-caste (*savarna*) Hindu women, as conveyed through their last names. All five women lived in urban Indian cities. Through markers such as depictions of their residences, workplaces, travel choices, spending habits, etc., the women appeared to belong to the middle or upper middle class and have a high socio-economic status in the society. Besides Veera from *Highway* whose education or profession isn't mentioned in the film, all the women were shown to have high educational qualifications, professional goals, and stable employment. Vidya from *Kahaani* is a software engineer/secret intelligence agent, Naina from *YJHD* is a medical student who eventually becomes a doctor, Piku is an architect, and Jaya is a corporate executive. All five women are depicted as bilingual and switch from Hindi/other regional Indian languages to English quite often in their daily conversations.

Traditional Gender Role Conformity

A unique characteristic in these representations is the depiction of the modern Indian woman who manages to balance traditional gender norms with non-traditional feminist ideas in terms of clothing, food, communication styles, and life philosophy. All women are seen embracing some aspects of traditional Indian femininity while also enjoying the freedom to make non-traditional choices in their lives. For instance, while Naina in *YJHD* is seen wearing shorts, traveling with friends, she is also seen wearing traditional Indian clothes at her friends' wedding. Adhering to the notion of traditional Indian femininity, she also expresses a desire to stay rooted in India, get married and bear children. While Vidya from *Kahaani* embodies the character of an independent and shrewd intelligence officer who is not afraid to question authority, she is also shown to have a keen interest in her husband's Bengali cultural heritage and displays a nurturing maternal side when interacting with kids. In *Piku*, the titular character is shown to be ambivalent about marriage, admits to having sexual needs, and has a friends-with-benefits arrangement with her colleague at work. However, she is also a caregiver to her aging father, who takes care of domestic chores, prays, and embraces religious traditions and rituals. Similarly, Jaya in *QQS* seeks companionship after being widowed for more than a decade, enjoys her own company, socializes with strangers but is also connected to her family, dresses in Indian clothes, and embraces Indian traditions. Veera's character in *Highway*, also demonstrates this duality as she follows the norms of politeness while interacting with her family, wears traditional as well as western clothes, enjoys English music but also has dreams of having a house in the hills where she can live a peaceful life away from the city.

All five women demonstrate family affiliations and are accompanied by men as they undertake travel or venture into public spaces. Vidya is married and pregnant and references her husband throughout the film. She is also accompanied by a male police officer throughout her journey. Veera is engaged to be married, and lives with her parents before she gets abducted, and her abuser turns into a savior who protects her from violence. Piku is single and dating but lives with her father and is connected to her extended family. She travels with her father, their male housekeeper, and Rana, the owner of the taxi service who drives them to Kolkata. Jaya is widowed, and dating, and is connected to her brother whom she video calls frequently. Naina is single, lives with her parents, and gets engaged at the end of the film. When traveling, she is accompanied by a group of young men and women.

Depictions of these women also subvert traditional gender norms and uphold neoliberal ideas of freedom and individuality. For instance, all women depicted in these films represent independent women who speak their mind and are not afraid to express and even assert their ideas and opinions. Whether they are talking to their family members, colleagues, or strangers in a public space, they communicate effectively to pursue their instrumental as well as identity goals. In demonstrating this, the portrayals often implicitly convey the negative connotations and social judgments about these women being "weird," "outspoken," "difficult to please" or "stubborn." For instance, Vidya is able to effectively persuade a police officer to break the law (*Kahaani*) in order to help find important evidence regarding her missing husband. Most of Vidya's interactions with men in public spaces are shaped by her identity as a married, pregnant, middle-class, educated, and English-speaking woman. Most men in their interactions with her use a consistent language of respect with her often referring to her as "madam," "Mrs. Bagchi" and even "your majesty." The police officers often refer to her as "the pregnant woman whose husband has left her," but they use this rhetoric in her absence, always resorting to norms of politeness when they are directly talking to her. Piku has a straightforward manner of communication and does not hesitate to give orders to the taxi drivers, the owner of the taxi service she uses, or her friend and business partner. Piku's father introduces her to a potential match at a party as "a financially and sexually independent woman, who is very moody, not a virgin and just looking for emotional companionship" (Sircar 2015, 00:34:06).[2]

In *QQS*, Jaya is constantly judged by her colleagues, friends, and even her brother for being weird and bossy. She is self-assured and confident while talking to the people in her life as well as complete strangers. In *Highway*, Veera, despite being abducted, is able to assert her wishes and opinions while talking to her kidnapper. Upon returning home, Veera also subverts the victim-blaming mentality regarding sexual abuse and confronts her abusive uncle and berates her family for silencing her. In both contexts, where she is expected to be submissive and silent, she manages to express her opinions, persuade others, and demand answers and explanations from abusive men.

The women in these films are depicted in public spaces enjoying the company of others as well as enjoying their own company. We see them driving, sitting in coffee shops, eating at restaurants, shopping in malls, and even watching movies in the theatre by themselves. When embarking on longer journeys and road trips, these women are depicted to have control over how they want to travel. For instance, except for Veera from *Highway* who gets abducted, all other women are in charge of their travel plans are capable of navigating all the challenges and hurdles whether that is dealing with unexpected flight changes, delays, or dealing with other people who prevent them from achieving their goals.

Safety as a Privilege for Women in Public Spaces

The travel experiences in these narratives are depicted with beautiful visuals of locations in rural and urban areas. In *YJHD* we see beautiful locations from Manali, Kashmir, and Udaipur as Naina embarks on challenging hikes, is seen singing and celebrating the festival of Holi in a crowded public space, and then eventually celebrating her friend's destination wedding at a beautiful heritage hotel in Udaipur. In *Piku*, we see the protagonist complete a road trip from Delhi to Kolkata with an overnight stop in Banaras. We see Piku clicking pictures of the scenic roads, shopping, and even enjoying some quiet time by the banks of the Ganga River. In *Kahaani*, while Vidya is on a mission, we see her hailing cabs, taking walks, and even partaking in Durga pooja celebrations in Kolkata. In *QQS*, Jaya travels to Dehradun, Jaipur, and Gangtok and is seen enjoying train rides, scenic destinations, a jungle safari, adventure sports, as well as mingling with fellow travelers on the journey.

As Veera travels on the roads in a truck with her kidnapper, the visuals of the roads help convey the gamut of emotions associated with the journey. The visuals of the roads are initially dark, gloomy, evoking a sense of fear about Veera's fate. However, as the narrative progresses and Veera finds freedom in her journey with her abductor, the truck travels through scenic rural routes surrounded by lush fields, green trees, and blue skies. On three separate occasions in the narrative, Veera refuses a chance to escape her kidnappers and chooses to continue the journey with them. On this unusual journey we see visuals of Veera running through the fields, dancing, climbing trees, sitting atop hills cogitating about her life and talking to herself out loud to process her emotions. At one point she says to her abductor Mahavir "I neither want to go back to the place from where you brought me, nor to the place where you are going to take me, but this road is very good, I don't want this road (journey) to end" (Ali 2014, 01:01:04).

In *YJHD*, *Piku*, *QQS*, the public space is seen as safe and enjoyable. It is a site for everyday tasks as well as travel and leisure where women have the right to explore, loiter, eat, roam, and have fun either by themselves or in the company of others. The public space in *Kahaani* is dangerous, but one that can be navigated through performing respectability by demonstrating one's marital status, traditional norms of femininity as well as establishing one's socio-economic status through manner of speech and dressing. In contrast with most popular Bollywood narratives about sexual violence, *Highway* casts the public space and the outdoors as a place for liberation while emphasizing the sexual violence women experience in their private spaces.

Overall, while these narratives create room for possibilities, freedom, and leisure for Indian women, it is important to note that these spaces are often reserved for upper caste (*savarna*), affluent and urban women, or women who are married and/or accompanied by men. These neoliberal narratives promise fun road-trips and adventures. *Highway* and *Kahaani,* acknowledge the physical and sexual threats faced by women. However, none of the five films foreground the reality that women who leave their homes must cope with the ubiquitous fear of sexual and physical harassment and violence.

Therefore, the women in this first cultural space have privileged identities that allow them to subvert traditional gender norms as they seek enjoyment, adventure and self-discovery while navigating the public space. The subversion of traditional gender norms is reprimanded with violent punishments or any negative consequences. These women rarely encounter physical and sexual harassment or violence in public places, and when they do, they can always avoid danger or protect themselves by enacting norms of respectability. Overall, the depiction of travel experiences in these narratives are utopian and promise freedom and pleasure without a fear of violence.

Public Space: A Site for Misogyny, Violence, and Resistance

The second and perhaps a more realistic cultural space depicted in Hindi films is where traveling and navigating a public space is not associated with women's pursuit of goals but focuses on their survival and safety while resisting misogyny and violence. The five films that depicted this cultural space were: *NH10* (2015), *Toilet Ek Prem Katha* (2017), *Pink* (2016), *Article 15* (2019), and *Chhapaak* (2020). Brief descriptions of the films are followed by a thematic analysis examining the features of this cultural space.

Case 1: NH10. This is a story about Meera and Arjun, an urban, upper middle class married couple from Gurgaon who witness an honor killing and get embroiled in a conflict with the perpetrators. While Arjun is killed, Meera fights to seek justice, engages in a physical combat, and eventually kills all the perpetrators.

Case 2: Pink. Minal Arora, Falak Ali, and Andrea Tariang are three working women who share a rented apartment in Delhi. The three women meet some men at rock show and join them for dinner and drinks. One of the men, Rajveer Singh (son of a powerful politician) tries to sexually force himself on Minal, which leads to her hitting him on the head with a beer bottle. While the women file a police complaint, the perpetrators continue to intimidate and harass them. What follows is an intense courtroom drama as the women seek justice with the help of a retired judge Deepak Sehgal, while the perpetrators try to falsely accuse the three women of prostitution and attempted murder.

Case 3: Toilet Ek Prem Katha (TEPK). This film revolves around the issue of open defecation in rural India. The protagonist of the film, Jaya, leaves her husband Keshav after discovering that his home does not have a toilet and that she must accompany local women to the fields to defecate. The film follows the conflict between Keshav and his religious father (who believes it is against his religion to have a toilet in the house) as well as Keshav's plea to the local government to build public toilets for women in the village.

Case 4: Article 15. This film follows the case of two minor Dalit girls who are raped and murdered by a group of upper caste men to teach them a lesson for rebelling and asking for a raise at work. The story is narrated through the eyes of an upper caste, urban, male police officer who tries to grapple with a rural socio-political landscape that is rooted in caste hierarchy.

Case 5: Chhapaak. This film is a story about an acid attack survivor, Malti Agarwal, a character that is modeled after a real-life acid-attack survivor Laxmi Agarwal. The film depicts the dual danger of public and private forms of violence whereby Malti's family friend is a scorned lover who throws acid on Malti's face in a public market. The story chronicles Malti's struggle as she copes with the attack, seeks legal justice, and advocates for legal reforms that would ban the sale of acid and mandate harsher punishments for perpetrators of acid attacks.

The five films that depict this cultural space represent the public space as a dangerous place where women must encounter and resist misogyny as well as physical and sexual forms of violence. The following paragraphs describe characteristics of the women represented in these film narratives.

Identity Markers and Women in Unsafe Public Spaces

The women in these films represent a wider variety of socio-cultural identities in terms of age, religion, caste, class, and geography. Meera from *NH10* is in the 25–35 age range, and is an urban, upper-middle class, upper-caste Hindu, married woman. Minal from *Pink* is also in the 25–30 age range and is an upper caste Hindu woman who is single, has parents and lives with two other single women. It should be noted that the other two women in *Pink* while also being single, and middle class, experience marginalization because of their religion and ethnicity. Falak Ali is Muslim, and Andrea is from Meghalaya and discriminated against as a northeastern girl in Delhi. Jaya from *TEPK* is also in the 25–35 age range and belongs to a Hindu upper caste but has a lower socio-economic status and lives in rural India. The two minor girls from *Article 15* live in rural India and are Dalit (lower caste) and belong to a lower class. Malti from *Chhapaak* is 16 years old Hindu upper caste and is from a lower socio-economic background.

Traditional Gender Role Conformity

In this category of films, the women tend to subvert traditional Indian gender roles and, in many ways, embody the so-called freedoms offered by neoliberal India. For instance, in *NH10*, Meera is a married woman but dresses in modern clothes, wears make-up, is financially independent, drives her own car, drinks socially, and smokes cigarettes. In *Pink*, Minal is a single, financially independent working woman who has late working hours, she lives with her roommates, drinks socially, and is not a virgin. In *TEPK*, Jaya seems to embody some non-traditional roles as she is focused on her education, fights back openly against eve-teasing men in the village, but is also quick to conform to traditional gender roles after she gets married. For instance, after marriage, she wears her "sari pallu" or loose end of the saree over her head as a symbol of decorum and becomes more submissive in her communication with her in-laws. In *Article 15*, we see very little visual representation of the two minor girls but are told that they worked as road construction workers, then demanded higher wages and took up jobs at a tannery after being denied the raise. In *Chhapaak*, while Malti wears traditional clothes and helps with domestic chores at home, she also has access to education and employment, has ambitions of becoming a famous singer, likes make-up and dancing, and has male friends.

In all five narratives, the subversion of traditional gender norms is depicted as the rationale for harassing women or inflicting physical and/or sexual violence upon them. For instance, in *Chhapaak*, Malti's scorned lover attacks her with acid because he thinks she deserves to be punished for rejecting his proposal and dating a guy of her own choice. In *Chhapaak*, we also see several victim-blaming sentiments from the police officers and the legal exchanges in the courtroom where Malti is accused of having a questionable character because she has phone numbers of several boys stored in her cellphone.

In *Pink*, Minal is seen as an easy target for sexual violence because she is single, dresses in a sexual manner, has had several boyfriends and male friends, drinks alcohol, goes partying, lives with her roommates, and returns home late in the night. In addition to that, when she doesn't pay heed to the perpetrator's verbal intimidation, his friend decides to abduct and molest her to 'teach her a lesson.' One of the perpetrators explains that by intimidating the outspoken women, he is simply following traditions. He says, "One needs to show women their place" (Chowdhury 2016, 00:34:42) and reiterates that he wants Minal to remember the assault as a lesson. Similarly, in *Article 15*, the two minor girls ask Anshu, their upper caste employer for a three-rupees raise in their salary and quit the job upon refusal. They take up a job at a tannery where they can earn three extra rupees. As a response, Anshu, along with two police officers, sexually assaults the two girls, murders them, and hangs their bodies on a tree visible for all villagers to see. He explicitly says that the assault and murders are meant to be a reminder for all the lower caste villagers to know their "*aukaad*" (their place in the society). In *NH10*, when Meera gets attacked on the highway, the police officer asks her husband why he lets her travel alone implying that women traveling by themselves are subverting the traditional norms and inviting harassment. Additionally, Meera also witnesses a rural woman and her husband being physically assaulted and murdered in the public space as punishment for marrying without their family's consent. In *TEPK*, Jaya is subjected to ridicule, harassment, and criticism from her in-laws as well as other villagers who find her demands of a toilet to be unreasonable and are quick to shun her from the village.

Another important aspect of these representations is the emphasis on the male-savior. In four out of the five narratives, women must directly or indirectly rely on men for their safety. For instance, *Article 15* there are two women who are depicted as having some access and agency in public spaces. Gaura, a villager, and local activist whose sister is the third girl who had accompanied the two victims and is missing. Gaura, who plays the love interest of the local Dalit leader Nishad, is always accompanied by other male activists and her lover. The other character is Malti Ram, a Dalit doctor who happens to create the post-mortem report for the two victims. The doctor is constantly pressurized and threatened by the perpetrators to not report/mention the sexual assault. Both women are seen as having some access to education but are constantly pressurized and silenced without the help of men. Gaura is supported by her boyfriend Nishad, while Malti is reassured by Ayan that he will take full responsibility for her safety if she helps to seek justice for the two girls.

While delivering a powerful message about sexual consent, *Pink* focuses on glorification of the male lawyer Deepak Sehgal, who represents the women in court and becomes their voice. In the courtroom exchanges between the lawyers and witnesses, Deepak Sehgal deduces a culturally embedded code for women's safety which reinforces that to retain their safety in public spaces, women should not go out with a guy alone, should not be friendly with the opposite sex, should not drink alcohol and should not be out in public spaces late at night. He argues that these behaviors by women are often interpreted as sexual consent and women exhibiting these behaviors are assumed to have a questionable character. In *NH10*, the police officer reminds Meera (and her husband) that she is not safe traveling late at night by herself or more specifically without her husband. He even suggests applying for a gun license to protect herself, which Meera gets. In one scene, Meera says that she doesn't need the gun when Arjun her husband is with her, implying that she can rely on him to protect her. In *TEPK*, while the problem of open defecation affects both men and women, the issue is framed as a matter of saving women's dignity and becomes the mission of the upper caste Brahmin man who is the savior who resolves to solve his wife's problem and becomes the face of socio-cultural progress in their village.

The exception to this male savior trope is *Chhapaak* where Malti doesn't rely on a male savior but independently pursues justice with the assistance of other women. She is financially independent and supports her family. She also challenges her male friend, Amol, when he tries to engage in virtue signaling by criticizing her for partying when the Indian Penal Code is amended to include a separate section for perpetrators of acid attacks. Malti also openly expresses her feelings for Amol and initiates a romantic relationship with him.

Orientation to the "Unsafe" Public Place

The public space as depicted in these films is a dark and dangerous space that evokes fear. In *Article 15*, we see a heavily male-dominated public space that has very little room for women's existence, let alone their safety or pleasure.

The intersection of caste and gender leaves very little agency for women. In *TEPK*, the public space also remains heavily male dominated where a young unmarried Jaya who is assertive and independent before marriage, turns into a docile traditional housewife who is forced to negotiate patriarchal religious beliefs to safeguard her health and dignity. *Chhapaak* showcases two facets of the public space, one where Malti is vulnerable and gets attacked in a busy market, and the other where we see Malti reclaiming the public space by traveling with her colleagues in a train or walking on the city streets without hiding her face. However, the film ends with a reminder about the grim reality that acid attacks remain common in India and highlights a few recent acid attack cases from the news. In *Pink*, the narrative about the public space is clear: While urban independent women have access to public spaces, the fear of sexual and physical violence is always present. Moreover, culturally mandated codes of respectability pertaining to clothing, drinking and time limits need to be followed to escape violence and harassment. Post the assault, the film is replete with visuals of dark and gloomy roads and the three women appearing scared and anxious with the background song that reinforces the vulnerability of women in the public. The song includes lines like "Why *is the light shackled?* Where is God while there are stones are hurled at butterflies? Where is God while knives gash silk robes?" (Chowdhury 2016, 00:34:42). In *NH10*, while emphasizing the increasing threats in urban as well as rural spaces, it is also made clear that women must resort to extreme violence and disregard the law to seek justice or retribution.

Overall, the representation of rural, *Dalit* (lower caste) women, religious minorities, those with a lower socioeconomic status, or women who subvert traditional gender norms, tend to focus on experiences of marginalization and violence in public spaces. Hindi films that acknowledge these intersectional identities represent the public space as a battlefield, a site of violence and struggle. Furthermore, the films that depict violence against women in the public space, often present solutions where women must rely on a male savior or subvert the law and resort to violence to seek justice. The constant association of marginal identities with stories of oppression and rebellion, can prevent audiences from seeing all women as fully human and deserving of safety as well as pleasure in public spaces.

CONCLUSION

Overall, this analysis argues that Hindi films construct two contrasting cultural spaces that represent two starkly different narratives about the public space. The first cultural space affords women the right to safety, pleasure, adventure, and exploration. Female protagonists represented in this cultural space are often urban Hindu women who belong to a higher caste and class. They either do not experience harassment and violence in public spaces or are depicted to possess characteristics that afford protection from and resistance to implicit misogyny as well as explicit forms of sexual and physical violence. This space is aspirational and portrays possibilities for increased agency and pleasure without the fear of violence. On the other hand, the second cultural space represented in Hindi films focuses on women's marginalized identities that are often subjected to discrimination, misogyny, and violence. Women depicted in these narratives are fighting for their basic human rights while being denied access to protection from physical and sexual violence, education, sanitation, health, and freedom of expression. This space is perilous and reinforces the dominant patriarchal framework that continues to constrain and police the mobility of female bodies in the public space. The dichotomies between romanticized road trips and violent subjugation in public spaces lack nuance in capturing Indian women's complex experiences in the public sphere that are shaped by the intersections of age, caste, class, religion, as well as their individual circumstances.

Future studies focusing on Indian media representations of travel can explore several other aspects that were not examined in this study. For instance, in addition to Hindi films, new web-series and streaming television series are becoming increasingly popular among Indian and global audiences. Shows like *Delhi Crime* on Netflix, or *Four More Shots* on Amazon Prime provide insightful narratives about Indian women's experiences while navigating the public space. It is also important to acknowledge other notable genres of Hindi films that were not included in this analysis. For instance, there are several films that depict women's travel outside India. While offering stories about female independence and celebrating female friendships these narratives sidestep conversations about women's agency and safety by erasing or sanitizing depictions of violence (e.g., *Queen, Veere di Wedding, Jab Harry Met Sejal, Dil Dhadakne Do*). Additionally, some recent films in the horror genre have flipped traditional narratives about women's safety in public spaces and represent poignant social commentaries about gendering of public and private spaces (e.g., *Stree, Bulbul*).

This chapter represents a first step in understanding how Hindi films depict Indian women's travel experiences and the potential impact of these representations in reinforcing gendered norms and expectations about navigating public spaces. Moreover, the findings demonstrate how Indian film representations replicate hierarchies of religion, caste, geography, and class in representing women's travel stories.

REFERENCES

Ali, Imtiaz. 2014. *Highway*. UTV Motion Pictures. 2 hr., 14 min. www.imdb.com/title/tt2980794/?ref_=nv_sr_srsg_8

Aruldoss, Vinnarasan, and Sevasti-Melissa Nolas. 2019. "Tracing Indian Girls' Embodied Orientations towards Public Life." *Gender, Place & Culture* 26, no. 11: 1588–1608. doi.org/10.1080/0966369X.2019.1586649

Banaji, Shakuntala. 2002. "Private Lives and Public Spaces: The Precarious Pleasures of Gender Discourse in Raja Hindustani." *Women: A Cultural Review* 13, no. 2: 179–194. doi.org/10.1080/09574040210148988

Bharadwaj, Gargi, and Upasana Mahanta. 2021. "Space, Time and the Female Body: New Delhi on Foot at Night." *Gender, Place & Culture* 29, no. 9 (May): 1–16. doi.org/10.1080/0966369X.2021.1916447

Bhattacharyya, Rituparna. 2013. "Criminal Law (Amendment) Act, 2013: Will It Ensure Women's Safety in Public Spaces?" *Journal Space and Culture, India*, 1(1): 13–26. Available at SSRN: ssrn.com/abstract=2399827

Bhattacharyya, Rituparna. 2015. "Understanding the Spatialities of Sexual Assault against Indian Women in India." *Gender, Place & Culture* 22, no. 9 (October): 1340–1356. dx.doi.org/10.1080/0966369X.2014.969684

Chandra, Tanuja. 2017. *Qarib Qarib Singlle*. Zee Studios. 2 hr., 5 min. www.imdb.com/title/tt7399470/?ref_=nv_sr_srsg_0

Dey, Adrija. 2019. "'Others' Within the 'Others': An Intersectional Analysis of Gender Violence in India." *Gender Issues* 36, no. 4: 357–373. doi.org/10.1007/s12147-019-09232-4

Ghosh, Sujoy. 2012. Kahaani. Viacom 18 Motion Pictures. 2 hr., 2 min. www.imdb.com/title/tt1821480/?ref_=nv_sr_srsg_0

Gulzar, Meghna. *Chhapaak*. Fox Star Studios 2 hr. www.imdb.com/title/tt10324144/?ref_=fn_al_tt_1

Harvey, David. 2007. *A Brief History of Neoliberalism*. New York: Oxford University Press.

Khan, Subuhi, and Laramie Taylor. 2018. "Gender Policing in Mainstream Hindi Cinema: A Decade of Central Female Characters in Top-Grossing Bollywood Movies." *International Journal of Communication* 12: 3641–3662. ijoc.org/index.php/ijoc/article/view/8701/2448

Manohar, Uttara, and Susan L. Kline. 2014. "Sexual Assault Portrayals in Hindi Cinema." *Sex Roles* 71, no. 5 (August): 233–245. doi.org/10.1007/s11199-014-0404-6

Mukherjee, Ayan. 2013. *Yeh Jawaani Hai Deewani*. Dharma Productions. 2 hr., 40 min. www.imdb.com/title/tt2178470/?ref_=nv_sr_srsg_0

Nanjangud, Apoorva. 2020. "Doing as Directed: Analysing Representations of Travel in Contemporary Bollywood Cinema." In *The Routledge Companion to Media and Tourism*, edited by Maria Mansson, Annae Buchmann, Cecilia Cassinger and Lena Eskilsson, 132–141. London: Routledge.

Phadke, Shilpa. 2013. "Unfriendly Bodies, Hostile Cities: Reflections on Loitering and Gendered Public Space." *Economic and Political Weekly* 48, no. 39 (September): 50–59. www.jstor.org/stable/23528480

Phadke, Shilpa, Shilpa Ranade and Sameera Khan. 2009. "Why Loiter? Radical Possibilities for Gendered Dissent." In *Dissent and Cultural Resistance in Asia's Cities*, edited by Melissa Butcher and Selvaraj Velayutham, 185–203. London: Routledge.

Ramasubramanian, Srividya, and Mary Beth Oliver. 2003. "Portrayals of Sexual Violence in Popular Hindi Films, 1997–99." *Sex Roles* 48, no. 7 (April): 327–336. doi.org/10.1023/A:1022938513819

Roy Chowdhury, Aniruddha. 2016. *Pink*. Rashmi Sharma Telefilms Limited. 2 hr., 16 min. www.imdb.com/title/tt5571734/

Roy, Sanghamitra, and Ajay Bailey. 2021. "Safe in the City? Negotiating Safety, Public Space and the Male Gaze in Kolkata, India." *Cities* 117 (October): 1–12. doi.org/10.1016/j.cities.2021.103321

Singh, Navdeep. 2015. *NH10*. Clean Slate Films and Phantom Films. 1 hr., 55 min. www.imdb.com/title/tt3742284/

Singh, Shree Narayan. 2017. *Toilet: A Love Story*. Viacom18 Motion Pictures. 2 hr., 35 min. www.imdb.com/title/tt5785170/?ref_=fn_al_tt_1

Sinha, Anubhav. 2019. *Article 15*. Zee Studios. 2 hr., 10 min. www.imdb.com/title/tt10324144/?ref_=fn_al_tt_1

Sircar, Shoojit. 2015. *Piku*. MSM Motion Pictures. 2 hr., 3 min. www.imdb.com/title/tt3767372/?ref_=fn_al_tt_1

UN-Habitat. 2015. *Global Public Space Toolkit: From Global Principal to Local Policies and Practice*. United National Settlements Program.

NOTES

1. Harvey defines neoliberalism as "a theory of political economic practices that proposes that human well-being can best be advanced by liberating individual entrepreneurial freedoms and skills within an institutional framework characterized by strong private property rights, free markets and free trade" (2007, 2).

2. All film dialogues referenced in the text are translated from Hindi to English by the author.

Chapter 7

Traveling Women and Their Male Companions

Framing Risks and Vulnerabilities in Indian Road Films

Pronoti Baglary

THE LONE WOMAN TRAVELER IN HINDI FILMS

Indeed, in India it is very rare to see women on the road, even in road and travel movies, bereft of a male figure whether as protector, chaperone, aggressor, or lover. With this truism in mind, in this essay I argue that very often filmic narratives of women's journeys on the road characteristically include a male companion, used mostly as a central driving tool to make the journey possible and palatable. This so-called safety is not just for the female characters themselves, but for the social structures that the films represent and recreate. The inclusion of the male companion also helps in playing out a politics of respectability to secure women travelers who are in turn drawn out or limited by the way the companion comes to regard them. These films interweave gender norms through the inclusion of the male road companion, on the one hand essentially exposing the inherent vulnerability of women on the road without men; and on the other, crafting roads as spaces which remain male dominated. I also examine the possibilities this trope offers through alternate means of viewing the dynamic between the traveling woman and her male-companion.

I further argue in this essay that the intersectionality of other identities with gender is central to the ways in which women and men on the road are represented, articulated, and perceived. While the politics of respectability still seems to play an important role in creating bodies on the road which inspire valuation or derision, one needs to account for the inclusion of ethnicity, race, and religion which categorically intersect with gender to determine what happens on the road and who the road belongs to. Therefore, the two central questions at the heart of this essay are: How do Hindi films, such as *Dil Se* (1998) and *Mr. and Mrs. Iyer* (2002) discussed here, address women on the road? And how do these films characterize men who become companions to these women on the road? While acknowledging the reality of community/caste-based and racial violence that distinguishes how upper-caste women's bodies are framed and treated versus those of women from minorities, I attempt to examine in this essay how bodies and their "being-ness" on the road are intractably linked with women's intersectional identities. Ultimately, in this essay I grapple with the question of how the Indian road-films offer limitless possibilities of encounters with the "other" and how these encounters unfold in the movies. I will, for my analysis, critically engage with two films: *Dil Se* (1998) written and directed by Mani Ratnam and *Mr. and Mrs. Iyer* (2002) written and directed by Aparna Sen, which are known for their compelling depictions of lone women travelers and their male companions.

THE *AKELI LADKI* ON THE ROAD: TRAVEL AND THE GEOGRAPHY OF WOMEN'S FEAR

The phrase *akeli ladki* can be translated as "lone girl" or "a girl by herself." In a patriarchal society like India, the figure of the *akeli ladki* stands as an anomalous occurrence. It features in everyday conversations on women's safety and intrinsic dangers of being an unaccompanied woman. This phrase has also been used in many Hindi films and songs to cast women as exotic and desirable with a strong subtext of the innate vulnerability of their positioning while making them objects of interest. The phrase can perhaps be traced back to Hindi films such as *Chalti Ka Naam Gaadi* (1958).

When wetry to examine the various ways in which lone women have been portrayed in cinema and specifically in road films, the concept is conspicuous by its absence. Because of the cultural framing of a woman being alone on the road as socially unacceptable or risky, a woman navigating public spaces alone at times and places deemed "unsafe" or "inappropriate," have been used in Indian films as a plot point to drive the story forward. This, however, has happened only in conjunction with a male companion. Thus, even in Indian road films that feature female leads prominently, it is but rare to view the female traveler alone on screen. In reality, women travel alone routinely. They do so sometimes for pleasure, sometimes out of necessity, and sometimes even as a mundane part of their daily life. Shilpa Phadke underscores how women's right to public spaces is embedded in the concept of "safety" and ensconced within the threat to her "respectability," and asserts:

> The insistence on sexual safety actively contributes to not just reducing women's access to public space but also to compromise their safety when they do access public space, by focusing more on women's capacity to produce respectability rather than on their safety. The discourse of safety then does not keep women safe in public; it effectively bars them from it. (Phadke 2007, 1512)

Such a protectionist view encourages women's "inhibited use and occupation of public space [and] is therefore a spatial expression of patriarchy" (Valentine 1989, 389). Gill Valentine in this regard claims that:

> This inability of women to enjoy independence and freedom to move safely in public space is therefore one of the pressures which encourages them to seek from one man's protection from all, initially through having a boyfriend and later through cohabitation. This dependence on a single man commonly limits women's career opportunities and general lifeworld. This in turn results in a restricted use of public space by women, especially at night, allowing men to appropriate it and hence making women feel unsafe to go out, reinforcing their comparative confinement in the home. Consequently, this cycle of fear becomes one subsystem by which male dominance, patriarchy, is maintained and perpetuated. (Valentine 1989, 389)

The persistent occurrence of a male companion with traveling women in Hindi films is an obvious reproduction of what feminist geographers have claimed. A scene in *Jab We Met*, directed by Imtiaz Ali, is a good example to elaborate this point. When the film was released in 2007, it was one of the most successful films of the year. Drawing from the road movie genre, *Jab We Met*, purportedly offered a fresh take on situating the modern Indian woman in a backdrop of a fast-paced economy and a diverse country. It promised, as critics claim:

> to dissolve the structures of traditional authority to fashion a new citizen and a new relation of conjugality predicated on mutuality and freedom of choice. This would suggest an ideological commitment to the empowerment of women, especially given that she is allowed an unprecedented mobility as the love story plays itself out in the public spaces of the road, the workplace and indeed, physical expanses of the nation itself. (Ghosh 2009, 58)

In a nail-biting sequence in the first half of the film, the heroine, Geet, played by Kareena Kapoor is stranded on a desolate railway platform in the middle of the night. The only other characters that appear in this sequence are all male: an auto-driver making lewd comments and a group of thugs who are visibly hostile to her. They stalk and verbally harass her as she makes her way to the station-master's office to ask for help. The station-master, a hapless old man who is seemingly uninterested in helping Geet or even shielding her from her harassers, tells her that she has no other choice but to wait for the next train. And then, to add insult to injury, he chastises Geet for her risky choices, urging her to remember that "Ek akeli ladki khuli tijori ki tarah hoti hai" (*Jab We Met*, 21:36:00) or "A solitary girl (or girl alone) is like an unlocked treasure chest" (translation mine).[1]

The implications of his words are clear: to be a woman alone on the road is like an invitation to be violated. The framing of this interchange in *Jab We Met* trudges a fine line between victim-blaming in the garb of ageless wisdom and a warning underlining the precarity of Geet's situation. Within the security of the comedic genre where the film is positioned, this line also serves the purpose of comedic relief: a wink-and-nudge at the audience which has the cultural cues to interpret, relate, and appreciate the wisdom; so useless in its timeliness and yet deemed so necessary. Perhaps one can even go further and read this moment of comedic relief as an attempt at dark humor that holds a mirror up to society: the moment where Bollywood shrugs and attempts to bridge the huge incongruence between the images of women it portrays on the screen and the reality of the statistics on crime committed on women unaccompanied or otherwise, at home or on the road, in India.

The words of the station master continue to echo throughout the rest of the first half of the film that unfolds in Ratlam, a northern suburb of India. Geet fumbles to secure safety while being stranded alone and stumbles into a man who mistakes her for a sex-worker, the only kind of woman who can seemingly be expected to occupy the streets at night. To Geet's (and the audience's) relief, she finally sees her estranged acquaintance (and the male lead of the film) Aditya, played by Shahid Kapoor and they are reunited. This moment of their reunion is played out slowly, and the upbeat tempo of the music that accompanies the scene provides the cue that the ordeal for Geet is over. The heroine and her male-companion are reunited and the plot can proceed without any more harrowing experiences.

In countless other films, too, the male-companion mediates the seeming incongruency between the screen and the reality. The addition of the male companion is one way to assuage "the genderscape of hate" (Dutta 2016, 178) while keeping the patriarchal core of the Indian society intact. On the one hand, the male companion softens any overt expression of autonomy or agency on the part of the women traveler, and makes her journeys palatable for the audience, while on the other hand, he tempers the real-life risks that such venturing might entail in a country teeming with grave violence against women every second, providing an apparently realizable fantasy. This trope of the "male companion" becomes a cinematic plot device which mediates between a fantastical celluloid world and one that remains responsive to the cultural, social, and sexual risks for women venturing on the road alone.

Shilpa Phadke has argued that "what women need in order to access the public spaces as citizens, is not so much the provision of safety as the right to take risks" (2007, 1510). It is this precise right to take risks which is diluted in road films through the male companions of the woman-traveler. As an addendum, the level of risks available to be taken in the public sphere are also determined by the intersections of other parallel identities that people have. How these intensectionalities are framed, in front of whom and to what extent, are also the crucial ingredients that determine the outcome of any such "risky" behavior. As mentioned earlier, the present essay examines how the lone female traveler and her male counterpart have been depicted in two popular Hindi films, *Dil Se* and *Mr. and Mrs. Iyer*, produced in neoliberal India.

PLOTLINES AND PROTAGONISTS IN *DIL SE* AND *MR. AND MRS. IYER*

Before engaging with issues of traveling women and their male companions, it is pertinent to have an overview of the complex and chaos driven plots of both *Dil Se* and *Mr. and Mrs. Iyer*. *Dil Se* (1998) completed Mani Ratnam's famed trilogy of the "political" vis-à-vis the "personal" films, with *Roja* (1992) and *Bombay* (1995). These films raised complex issues such as nationhood, ideology, and politics; and they were critically acclaimed for their acting, direction, and music. Arguably, *Dil Se* does not fully correspond to the road film category, but the first half of the film strongly adheres to elements from this genre. Much of the interaction between the two lead characters, Amar (played by Shah Rukh Khan) and Meghna (Manisha Koirala) happen on the road, against the backdrop of northern India, Assam and Ladakh. Not only that, in keeping with the tradition of the train song[2] in Bollywood, *Dil Se* also featured one of the most iconic "item song"[3] sequences filmed on a moving train with *Chaiyya Chaiyya*.

The narrative is about doomed love and obsession, framed against the issues of insurgency, regionalism, and nationhood. Amar is an All-India Radio host who is deployed in the politically disturbed state of Assam, which had been witnessing the rise of insurgent groups. There he comes across Meghna, a mysterious woman who he falls obsessively in love with. He tries everything he can in order to get to know her and win her over, while she remains aloof and wary of forming any kind of acquaintance. He ultimately follows her all the way from Silchar to Leh, where he succeeds in apparently making her succumb to his love, only for her to leave him once again, without any answers or information about where she is headed.

The second half of the film plays out in New Delhi, where Amar is originally from. We learn that he belongs to a family of a distinguished army veteran and is about to get married to a woman, Preeti (played by Preity Zinta). At this point, Meghna re-enters his life and the audience learn that unknown to Amar, Meghna belongs to a group of insurgents from Assam, who are on a suicide mission, with Meghna being the suicide bomber. She had ostensibly re-connected with him in order to use his contacts to further their terrorist plot. Amar finds out the truth about her identity and their plan just in time. He accosts her in an unpopulated place and ultimately foils the bombing mission. As Amar holds on to Meghna in a deathly embrace to prevent her from harming the Republic Day crowd, the bomb strapped to Meghna's body detonates and the film ends with both of them dying in the explosion.

The second film I discuss is *Mr. and Mrs. Iyer* (2002) by Aparna Sen. This film was crafted in the aftermath of the communal violence in Gujarat and the anti-Islamic violence post the 9/11 terror attacks in the United States. Both these incidents had a profound impact on Aparna Sen who set about making this film as a way to converse about sensitive issues such as religion and identity, while straddling within a world ripped apart by violence and hate. Meenakshi Iyer (played by Konkona Sen Sharma) is traveling with her toddler son from her parent's house to her in-laws' place, where she and her husband presumably live in a joint family. From the very beginning, it is clearly underlined that she is a Tamil Brahmin who is raised with strong traditional conditioning. At the bus-stop, she happens upon the friend of a mutual acquaintance of her parents, Raja Jehangir (played by Rahul Bose) who is a photographer. They form an acquaintance borne out of necessity as Raja helps her out on the bus when Meenakshi is overwhelmed with the task of caring for her upset toddler. As they form a slow acquaintance, the bus journey is impeded by violent communal riots. When the rioters force their way into their bus looking for any Muslim passengers to prey upon, Meenakshi saves Raja by handing over her infant son to him, and "giving" him her name, announcing themselves to the rioters as Mr. and Mrs. Iyer. The old Muslim couple on the bus are not so lucky as they are dragged out and killed by the blood-thirsty mob.

Raja and Meenakshi keep up this charade of being a Hindu couple and find shelter in an old forest bungalow, helped by a police officer who is impressed by Raja's profession and their appearance of domesticated respectability. Ultimately, Raja helps Meenakshi reach her husband but not before the two share moments and conversations that cement their intimacy and mutual affection. Before parting, Raja hands over the film-roll of photos he took of Meenakshi and her son, encapsulating the time they were once "Mr. and Mrs. Iyer."

Gendered Roads and Gendered Identities in *Dil Se* and *Mr. and Mrs. Iyer*

Dil Se opens with Amar Kant Verma (by Shahrukh Khan), a young All India Radio host making his way to a railway station in a taxi in Assam. The fact that the setting of the scene is in a disturbed area is conveyed by the nonchalance with which people around him talk about bombs, like they are everyday occurrences. Amar navigates the poorly run rail transport, displaying another systemic failure. He wants to light a cigarette and having run out of matches himself, tries to wake up the person sleeping on a bench nearby. The sleeping figure is fully covered by a blanket. As he harshens his tone to wake his neighbor, a gust of wind blows the blanket away, dramatically revealing that it is actually a woman: the female protagonist Meghna (by Manisha Koirala). This whole opening sequence is crucial to the framing of Meghna for the rest of the film. It is infused with the anomalous positioning of the *akeli ladki* or the lone female on the road at what could be termed as an inappropriate time. Likewise, it also subtly points out how a lone male traveler, here Amar, is safe and uninhibited even when he is navigating the most indifferent and isolated of terrains. The context of a youthful Meghna alone in the middle of the night is itself framed as part of her attraction, as what Amar says next would imply:

> Mujhe maaf kardijeyega. Maine aapko aadmi samajhkar aapse maachis maang li. Aap toh ladki hain aur wo bhi itni sundar. (*Dil Se*, 4:44:5)

> Forgive me. I mistook you for a man and asked you for a light. I'm really sorry. You're actually a girl and a beautiful one, at that.

Thus, Meghna is introduced to the audience from Amar's perspective. Her interpretation and representation are bound to the "male gaze" (Mulvey 1975). As Amar grows increasingly obsessed with wanting to win her over, and to de-mystify and possess her, we cannot but read these advances against the backdrop of the interaction between the idea of a mainstream India and it's encounters with Northeast India. Also, Meghna's portrayal as a minority woman from a fractured part of the country as well as her treatment in the film as the object of attention and obsession by the class and caste privileged male protagonist cannot be separated from the portrayal as well as treatment of minority women and their bodies by the mainstream narratives and representations. If the Northeast of India has been imagined as the "strangers in the mist" (Sanjoy Hazarika 1994), Meghna as "the stranger" or *ajnabee* referred to repeatedly through the title song composed by Amar, is almost a personification of this strange and estranged land, with the "stranger" continuing as a leitmotif throughout the film.

Mr. and Mrs. Iyer on the contrary, begins with the woman at the center, Meenakshi (by Konkona Sen Sharma) being constructed not as an *akeli ladki* (solitary girl) or a romanticized *ajnabee* (stranger), but rather as someone who could be defined as their anti-thesis: she is a wife and mother traveling with her baby. Her position in society as a mother, a daughter, and a daughter-in-law is soldered to her character from the very first scene of the film, where we hear from her father-in-law even before we get to hear her. On the other hand, Raja (by Rahul Bose) is a Muslim Bengali and a worldly photographer. He is also a distant acquaintance of Meenakshi, which makes his involvement with her as her friendly Samaritan seem innocent and without ulterior motives.

The bus itself has an assortment of motely side characters and parallel storylines: the young college students singing Bollywood songs, the judgmental older couple, the extended family traveling together, a mother with her son, and so on. It is interesting to note how all the women in the bus have their own versions of the "male companion." The two protagonists connect with each other despite the wide gulf in their worldview and the huge chasm of caste and religion separating them. Their experience of living through a terror filled journey and surviving, with each providing safety to the other and trying to understand each other's viewpoints, is what makes their encounter meaningful beyond the precarities that contextualize their journey. Ultimately their interactions on the road defy the stereotyped positioning of women and men on the road and this encounter provides a multi-layered juxtaposition against *Dil Se*.

Considering that both films can be located within the road film genre, the roads themselves are an integral part of the story. More specifically, in representing alien terrains, the roads in these films facilitate a clear depiction of gender norms wherein the male is predictably at an advantageous position compared to the female traveler. This is better understood with the help of Bennet Schaber's assertion that "[w]hat is at stake here is precisely 'the people.' And 'the road' is very much the locus of the revelation of these people" (Schaber 1997, 18). While the principal portion of the road scenes from the first part of *Dil Se* were shot in Assam and Leh, in case of *Mr. and Mrs. Iyer*, the director Aparna Sen chose not to have a clear geographical area marked as the location of her story. But the film was shot in West Bengal. Both the films convey a sense of periphery, not just via its principal characters but also through the roads and the locations themselves, providing a divergence from the mainstream notion of what the country looks like. In this way, these films also perform the task of "landscaping the nation" (Klinger 1997,179). They provide a visual topography of the extremities of India, not just through geography but also through the ways in which these geographies are encultured, while presenting settings which are visibly idyllic but with danger lingering underneath, representing religious and political anxieties of a fragmented country. And of course, through these terrains the gender norms of India find a nuanced articulation.

Both the male companions seem be distinctly acculturated and geographically unmoored, with them being accorded a freedom of spirit and mobility which is implied by their general attitude, clothing, and professions. Both the male companions in the two films are observers and wanderers by profession. While Amar is a journalist, Raja is a photographer. One is supposed to inquire and report, while the other is supposed to capture images and represent. And hence both the male companions are licensed to be men who, quite literally, gaze, explore, and wander. The women protagonists on the other hand are visually encultured and literally embody their cultural locations: Meghna's physical appearance is an integral part of her descriptor while Meenakshi's strong Tamil accent and clothing show her body as a vessel of her identity. Tellingly, both women's presence on the road is not defined by delight, a sense of wonder or exploration but rather as a task or even better, a mission.

Encounters with the "Other" on the road provides the ground for disengaged worlds to collide. Both *Dil Se* and *Mr. and Mrs. Iyer* present us with a blueprint of what happens when two separate entities, standing in for their social groups, collide with one-another, and how the exploration of the "other" unfolds cannot be but more different in both. Sharon Willis speaking on embodied experience on the road for minorities expresses the following:

> If the most conventional road movies follow a protagonist whose journey inscribes a deviation or a series of deviations from an imagined proper path, when socially "marginal" protagonists—any women at all, gays, and people of color—hit the road, they themselves come to embody the deviation that their travels also represent *sic*. That is, the central point and problem that define the journey reside in embodiment and visibility, as all meanings tend to be organized by race, gender, and sexuality. Shaped by the readings of the community that witnesses it, the meaning of the trip is inevitably understood through the meanings the witnesses assign to the bodies of the travelers. (Willis 1997, 287)

Meenakshi and Meghna's bodies are clear signifiers of their cultural locations: their physical being-ness conveying their place. Konkona Sen Sharma's Meenakshi wears a *bindi* (the red dot on her forehead), crisp sarees and coiffed hair, in contrast with Manisha Koirala's Meghna, with wild curly hair and varying outfits which changes from salwar kameez to traditional Ladakhi dress to westernized gowns. Meenakshi's sari, her *mangalsutra* (a necklace which is ceremonial for married women to wear) and most of all, a toddler wrapped in her arms convey her position as a married Hindu woman.

Meghna's social roles on the other hand is never pinned down, but it is done corporeally with respect to her ethnic belonginess to Assam (or the Northeast in general). Again, her traveling alone in the middle of the night unescorted, her mystery and the absence of protective male figures pointing to something atypical about her station in life.

In examining *Dil Se*, Sarah Berry claims that "Amar first encounters Meghna in a scene of unveiling, a familiar Orientalist trope from the 'Muslim social' genre, where a glimpse of the forbidden, veiled woman motivates the narrative" (Berry 2011, 309). Amar's gaze also veers on the fetishistic at times. On more than one occasion, Amar's monologic professions of love include molding her facial features into the dialogue, mentioning her "*chapti naak*" or flat nose and her "*choti aankhein*" or small eyes. Nose and eyes have always been the chief ways to mark race and in the dialogue, it underlines the facial features which are associated with the Mongoloid race. However, race itself remains absent in *Dil Se*, or any other mainstream film in India for that matter.

According to Rohini Rai, "'race' in India is a postcolonial- neoliberal construct, whereby colonial 'Mongoloid' is reconstructed into neoliberal 'Northeastern,' such that 'race' in India acts as a layered mode of constructing identity and difference" (Rai 2021, 1). Rai further explains how, "the 'Northeastern' category emerges as a result of exclusion from the 'Indian' category, which itself is racialized along Hinduised-Aryanised lines, such that racism is a product of a postcolonial center-periphery power-relation between India and its North-East" (Rai 2021, 1). Such issues can be better understood with the help of Sarah Berry's take on Mani Ratnam's male leads from the trilogy wherein she states that "Ratnam's male characters invariably call for a transcendent, multicultural nationalism but are confronted with the problematic aspects of that project and the intensity of resistance to it" (Berry 2011, 302). This stands true for Amar's portrayal of an imagined average Indian man. The fact that this model average that stands as the vantage point of the audience, is a Hindu Hindi-speaking man from Delhi, makes it clear who and what frames the notion of the "Other." If Amar then is full of agency, Meghna is compelled to find hers owing to the limitations of her ethnicity and her gender.

These problems are palpable again in the character of Meenakshi from *Mr. and Mrs. Iyer* who is an upper-caste Hindu woman. Here, the audience gets a window into both the characters' inner-lives. However, it is Meenakshi who becomes the vantage point through which the story is mostly told. Hence, it is Meenakshi who dictates the gaze and provides the terms on which the encounter with the "other" happens in this case. Right from the beginning, her travel companion, Raja presents as secular and distinctly non-Muslim, going as far as using a Hindu-sounding first name. His Islamic identity is presented as an afterthought which comes to the fore only in a moment of grave risk. His corporeal body becomes the bearer of his identity when Hindu rioters look for Muslims to kill and ascertain the religious identities of their captives by checking for evidence of circumcision.

We need to pause and wonder at how the characters posited as the "other" in both the films are presented without the trappings of a traditional family unit. Meghna is an orphan, with her family making a brief appearance in a flashback scene where we learn of the trauma of her losing her family and village to paramilitary forces. This loss shaped her personhood and course of life. On the other hand, Raja references his family only in passing when he comments about how as a child he really wanted his *ammi* or mother, to wear *bindi* on her forehead like the Hindu ladies he would see. Obviously, men and women in the films mentioned here have very different life experiences and subsequently gender identities owing to which their experiences of travel vary greatly.

UNEQUAL MOBILITIES: WOMEN'S INTERSECTIONAL VULNERABILITIES AND MEN'S PRIVILEGE

The discussion so far indicates that even if both *Dil Se* and *Mr. and Mrs. Iyer* are about women traveling, they specifically show how women travel and how they are perceived while traveling. Further, the two films also demonstrate that traveling women's identities are determined by the many other socio-cultural, political and ethnic markers that one may carry with themselves. The two female travelers discussed here are both women, but they definitely do not have the same universe of experiences, fears, and privileges. We know that "[s]treets are gendered spaces, mediated by caste" (Kannabiran and Kannabiran 1991, 2132). And as well as by race. While analyzing the notorious Nirbhaya case of New Delhi, India (2012), Dey and Orton make a strong case against caste and gender discrimination in India, and the state,

> In India, gender violence is often not only gender related crime but a combined effect of various other factors including caste, class and religion. A hierarchy based on caste, class and geographical location separates women across India and they experience varying degrees of abuse and marginalisation. (Dey and Orton 2016, 2)

They further invoke Crenshaw's theory to underline the situation in India, reiterating her point that, "intersectional subordination need not be intentionally produced; in fact, it is frequently the consequence of the imposition of one burden that interacts with preexisting vulnerabilities to create yet another dimension of disempowerment" (1991, 1250).

Further, Dey and Orton assert how "the nature of violence faced by women differs according to their social class, caste and geography" (Day and Orton 2016: 2). Women from rural areas, lower caste and also from racial minorities are disproportionately more susceptible to violence compared to women from upper caste or class or in urban areas of the country (Anne, Callahan, and Kang, 2013). And this is true for the two female protagonists under discussion in this essay.

Meghna's navigation of the public sphere carries a suggestion of defiance. She appears alone in a train station in the very first scene and confronts us with her subversive presence alone at night. On the other hand, Meenakshi is almost a caricatural representation of a woman who has been confined to the domestic or private sphere, with her parents coming to drop her off at the bus and her father-in-law and husband being in constant communication with her to ascertain her safety on the road. As opposed to Meghna, Meenakshi enacts a form of respectable femininity. Smitha Radhakrishnan asserts that, "In contemporary India, the symbolic capital of the family is further reinforced and legitimated through association with, and reliance upon, respectable femininity. Respectable femininity, then, becomes the embodiment of the family—an embodied symbolic capital that also serves as a primary symbol for Indian culture" (2009, 201). Meghna and Meenakshi in their respective roles corroborate this assertion.

Juxtaposing the above to how minority women have been left out of privileges that come from respectable femininity, we need to shift from talking about a simplistic geography of violence, to an intersectional geography of violence. This is because, as Valentine espouses,

> First to explore in more detail how women's fear and hence use of public space varies throughout the lifecycle, with ethnicity and disability, and in different localities, particularly between rural and urban areas. Secondly, to examine further how individuals and groups appropriate and control public space, with particular reference to gender and ethnicity. (Valentine 1989, 389)

The importance of categories assigned to people, of caste, race, and ethnicity becomes even more urgent when we consider how the framing of "respectability" and minority identities intersect on the road. While Meghna's race is written on her nose and eyes, Raja manages to pass as a Hindu. This is important because, while in the former case, her so-called exoticness becomes a point of fetishization for Amar, in the latter case, it is Raja's ability to pass as Hindu which leads to Meenakshi wanting to form an acquaintance with him in the first place. On the road, as in any public sphere, the first impressions are tantamount and could lead to life-or-death outcomes. Predictably, such physical attributes add to the vulnerability of the woman and the privilege of the man when they are on the road.

OF GENDERED IDENTITIES: WOMEN AND THEIR MALE COMPANIONS ON THE ROAD

If, by the end of the twentieth century, the iconic "angry young man" of 1970s popular Hindi cinema had been replaced by the "creative young man," the first decade of the twenty-first century witnessed the emergence of the metrosexual male protagonist—one largely defined by his physical fitness, grooming and cosmopolitanism. (Gehlawat 2010, 61)

Both the male protagonists in the two films epitomize modernity and cosmopolitanism of India's liberalized nineties. Hence, one notes how both Amar and Raja are well-dressed and stylish, sophisticated and worldly. They are also both engaged in professions which clearly signal a departure from what had hitherto been the standard professions in films. Further, neither of them acts out in quintessential masculine and heroic way that one expects from leading men in Bollywood. There is no violence enacted by these two leading men even amidst the violent context that they are put into.

There is a whole sequence of Amar being beaten mercilessly by Meghna's "guardians" and him taking the punches without retaliation. However, this soft masculinity that seems to characterize Amar must be put in contrast to the masculinity he enacts upon his interactions with Meghna. In spite of her protestations, he continues to stalk and berate her, and then blames her for his obsession with her and his inability to leave her alone. Things come to a head when he accosts her in the middle of a road in Ladakh and forces himself on her, kissing her roughly. Her body, seemingly resisting his advances in the beginning, falls away limply toward the end. This signifies for the audience, in the context of the film, that his forced advances have made her pull down her walls and his desire for her has won her over.

In doing this, however, Amar is just replicating and "perpetuating models of courtship based on the stalking and harassment of women" (Lobo 2018) which has a long history in Hindi film industry. Amar's self-righteous anger toward a woman who has refused his advances is justified by him implying that she led him on, though there is no valid reason for him to base this on. Shahrukh Khan's Amar veers on being the "nice guy," a narrative trope seen commonly in literature and cinema, who tries to rescue the fair maiden even though she never asked for it. Amar's legitimized anger trumps her illegitimated resistance. The "nice guys" represent an alternate soft masculinity which is defined by the pursuit of love, but often, this characterization ends up being a front for covert hegemonic and toxic masculinity. The existence of the "nice guy" trope underlines how in films and popular books, having feelings for a woman while not being a violent or overtly-macho man is presented as enough justification to be granted the love of the female love-interest. Simply put, just presenting oneself as a nice guy is postulated as good enough to be entitled to the regard of any woman one desires. This framing completely neglects the lived reality or the free-will of the love-interest. If the woman refutes the advances of the nice guy, she would then go on to be presented as unkind, unjust, and as in the case of Meghna, cruel and uncaring. Evidently, in *Dil Se* the male travel companion proves once again that his privileges far outshine the vulnerabilities of his female counterpart.

In Laura Mulvey's pivotal work on visual pleasure in cinema (1975), she underlines the male gaze and contends,

> In a world ordered by sexual imbalance, pleasure in looking has been split between active/male and passive/female. The determining male gaze projects its phantasy on to the female figure which is styled accordingly. In their traditional exhibitionist role women are simultaneously looked at and displayed, with their appearance coded for strong visual and erotic impact so that they can be said to connote *to-be-looked-at-ness*. . . . Mainstream film neatly combined spectacle and narrative. (Mulvey 1975, 346)

This statement underlines the framing of Meghna in *Dil Se,* whose real name (if that is at all her name), Moina, too remains unknown to both Amar and the audience until the end. It is the gaze of the male companion which draws out and sketches Meghna's personhood. All the initial conversations she has with Amar are around conjugality and her marital state or the desire to have children: with Amar tempering her obvious agency and strength and emphasizing her femininity and fragility. In the end, we never really get to know Meghna except for what Amar projected onto her. The film almost knowingly posits this all along. Borrowing from Mulvey, even in *Dil Se*, "[a]s the film opens with the woman as object of the combined gaze of spectator and all the male protagonists in the film," Meghna seemingly succumbs to the male protagonist's charm but as the ending of the film shows, neither Amar nor the audience could actually possess her or come to know her: her actions really displaying the limits of "woman as icon" (Mulvey 1975, 348). Moina resists possession, even until the end.

Both Raja from *Mr. and Mrs. Iyer* and Amar from *Dil Se* epitomize the non-secular metro-sexual men, debonair and nonchalant, facing the road and what lies ahead with an eager enthusiasm and relaxed countenance. But unlike Amar, Raja's good Samaritan act does not come with any end in mind. His concerns for Meenakshi are not driven by a desire to possess her or begin a romantic liaison. What is most fascinating is perhaps the infusion of desire and sexuality in the maternal role which Sen does so successfully in her films and the depiction of desiring as just as much a feminine trait as being desired. Bose states, "The key to understanding Sen's films, perhaps, is to accept that they are explorations, rather than pronouncements. The director is clearly interested in the human—gendered—predicament of relationships, and how the individual reveals, and sometimes changes, her identity through them" (Bose 1997, 320). This is why Raja and Meenakshi's tryst begin not with gazing but with conversing. It is conversations that allow the viewers to enter their inner worlds and understand them, humanize them, and de-exoticize them. Even in the scene where Raja takes Meenakshi's photographs, fixating his lens on her and literally gazing at her, it is in fact Meenakshi's gaze that the audience gets to see.

Mr. and Mrs. Iyer does not promise any kind of emancipatory change in the structures that exist in Meenakshi's life. There is not even an indication that she questions it. There is merely a longing for an alternate way to exist: but that too comes with the promise of Raja as her companion. Here again, we construct the road and the idea of wandering away on the road as a masculine project while it remains a feminine longing. Meenakshi's journey is finite and needs to be determined through a purpose, even though Raja can continue on, on the road without having a goal: traveling for travel's sake. If anything, Raja is the westernized, free and spontaneous figure who forms the ideal canvas for Meenakshi to project onto. Thus, in case of Meenakshi, it is the act of gazing that draws out and colors the portrait of her character. It is in her looking and being looked at that we see a complete picture of her personhood. Perhaps that is the kind of conversations we all seek for women traveling on the road and the kind of richness we hope to come back with once the journey is over.

Even the last scene in which Raja symbolically hands over Meenakshi to her husband before proceeding on in his journeys, is pragmatic: one that acknowledges the absolute realities of Meenakshi's life. The triumph of this story comes not with any revolutionary ideas of freedom and liberation for the female protagonist but the ways in which she is able to exercise her agency within the confines of her socio-cultural positions and the ways it can push the viewers to deconstruct ideas of intimacy, motherhood and companionship even within the limits of where we are.

CONCLUSION: FEMININITIES ON THE ROAD

It is impossible to talk about tales of women's journeys in road films, without the prime narrative tool through which these journeys are captured, arbitrated and in many cases, facilitated. Women's distance between public and private space seemingly needs to be mediated and the male companion is the mediator through which these freedoms are most often, dispensed. Very often, the male companion becomes the stand-in for the viewers, leading to us constructing the female traveler through surrogate lens. My essay has attempted to interrogate this very lens and the different perspectives that their changing focus might offer to us.

While both the films I discussed depict women traveling on the road in India, *Dil Se*'s predication of mobility is built around the exploration of masculinity through solving the question of feminine mystic; while *Mr. and Mrs. Iyer* deconstructs the (geographically and culturally) limited purview which predicates the exploration of femininity bound by respectability, tradition and caste. While *Dil Se* posits love as pursuit, with the road itself almost personifying this journey of pursuing a woman, *Mr. and Mrs. Iyer* postulates love as the journey itself, with the two central protagonists coming together to travel. Roads can provide a fertile ground for encounters with the "other" to take place. It is also a rich context through which to explore how the intersectionality of identities, such as race, caste, and gender play out in a public space. The examination of the trope of the male companion is a potent lens through which to deconstruct how women's strengths and vulnerabilities are imagined and played out in road films. On the one hand, they stand as surrogate eyes to project society's perception of women alone on the road within the film, and on the other, they can serve as powerful plot devices that enable the woman traveler to have celluloid existence in different spaces and contexts in a manner that seems convincing enough for the larger societal norms to stomach.

But while these male companions can sometimes empower female protagonists, their presence can also verge on being predatory. Ultimately, any telling of a story where a woman's safe existence on the road is dependent on her perceived respectability or social or romantic positioning with regard to a man (the male companion), still undermines her personhood and agency. And it is this lack of agency that popular cultural media such as Hindi films need to contest and re-visit.

REFERENCES

Berry, Sarah. 2011. "Subversive Habits: Minority Women in Mani Ratnam's *Roja* and *Dil Se*." In *Fashion in Films*, edited by Adrienne Munich, 301–319. Bloomington: Indiana University Press. www.researchgate.net/publication/348884205

Banerjee, Sikata. 2003. "Gender and Nationalism: The Masculinization of Hinduism and Female Political Participation in India." *Women's Studies International Forum* 26 (2): 167–179. doi.org/10.1016/S0277-5395(03)00019-0

Bose, Brinda. 1997. "Sex, Lies and the Genderscape: The Cinema of Aparna Sen." *Women: A Cultural Review* 8 (3): 319–326. dx.doi.org/10.1080/09574049708578321

Brara, Rita. 2010. "The Item Number: Cinesexuality in Bollywood and Social Life." *Economic and Political Weekly* 45 (23): 67–74. www.jstor.org/stable/27807108

Connell, R. W. and James W. Messerschmidt. 2005. "Hegemonic Masculinity: Rethinking the Concept." *Gender & Society* 19 (6): 829–859. doi.org/10.1177/0891243205278639

Dey, Adrija and Bev Orton. 2016. "Gender and Caste Intersectionality in India: An Analysis of the Nirbhaya Case, 16 December 2012." *Gender and Race Matter: Global Perspectives on Being a Woman (Advances in Gender Research)* 21: 87–105. Bingley: Emerald Group Publishing Limited. doi.org/10.1108/S1529-212620160000021006

Ghosh, Shoba Venkatesh. 2009. "Girl Abroad: The Private and the Public in Jab We Met . . ." *Economic and Political Weekly* 44 (17): 58–64. www.jstor.org/stable/40279186

Gehlawat, Ajay. 2012. "'Aadat Se Majboor'/'Helpless by Habit': Metrosexual Masculinity in Contemporary Bollywood." *Studies in South Asian Film & Media* 4 (1): 61–79. doi.org/10.1386/safm.4.1.61_1

Hazarika, Sanjoy. 1994. *Strangers of the Mist: Tales of War and Peace from India's Northeast*. New Delhi: Viking, Penguin Books India.

Mulvey, Laura. 1975. "Visual Pleasure and Narrative Cinema." *Screen* 16 (3): 6–18. doi.org/10.1093/screen/16.3.6

Kannabiran, Vasanth and Kannabiran, Kalpana. 1991. "Caste and Gender: Understanding Dynamics of Power and Violence." *Economic and Political Weekly* 26 (37): 2130–2133. www.jstor.org/stable/41626993

Khan, Shahnaz. 2011. "Recovering the Past in Jodhaa Akbar: Masculinities, Femininities and Cultural Politics in Bombay Cinema." *Feminist Review* 99(1): 131–146. doi.org/10.1057/fr.2010.30

Klinger, Barbara. 1997. "Landscaping the Nation in Easy Rider." In *The Road Movie Book*, edited by Steven Cohan and Ina Rae Hark, 287–306. London: Routledge.

Kohli, Divya. 2016. "Bollywood on Wheels: 10 Movies Starring the Indian Railways." *National Geographic Traveller*, October 6. natgeotraveller.in/railway-reel-10-movies-where-trains-are-the-stars/

Lobo, Alyssa Grace. 2018. "Constructions of Masculinity in Bollywood Promotional Content." *Theses—ALL*. 290, Syracuse University. surface.syr.edu/thesis/290

Phadke, Shilpa. 2007. "Dangerous Liaisons Women and Men: Risk and Reputation in Mumbai." *Economic and Political Weekly* 42 (17): 1510–1518. www.jstor.org/stable/4419517

Radhakrishnan, Smitha. 2009. "Professional Women, Good Families: Respectable Femininity and the Cultural Politics of a 'New' India." *Qualitative Sociology* 32: 195–212. doi.org/10.1007/s11133-009-9125-5

Rai, Rohini. 2021. "From Colonial 'Mongoloid' to Neoliberal 'Northeastern': Theorising 'Race,' Racialization and Racism in Contemporary India." *Asian Ethnicity* 23 (3): 442–462. doi.org/10.1080/14631369.2020.1869518

Schaber, Bennet. 1997. "The Road, the People." In *The Road Movie Book*, edited by Steven Cohan and Ina Rae Hark, 17–44. London: Routledge. www.taylorfrancis.com/chapters/edit/10.4324/9780203137420-7/hitler-keep-em-long-road-people-bennet-schaber

Valentine, Gill. 1989. "The Geography of Women's Fear." *Area* 21 (4): 385–390. www.jstor.org/stable/20000063

Willis, Sharon. 1997. "Crossover Dreams." In *The Road Movie Book*, edited by Steven Cohana and Ina Rae Hark, 287–306. London: Routledge.

NOTES

1. All translations of dialogues from Hindi to English are mine.

2. Trains have featured as the backdrops of some iconic moments in Bollywood with notable examples include hit songs like "Mere sapano ki raani" from *Aradhana* (1969), "Kasto mazaa" from *Parineeta* (2005). As Kohli states, "the train song is almost a genre unto itself, with the locomotive serving as a veritable orchestra with its piercing toots and the chuk-chuk of its wheels" (2016).

3. Brara defines the item song or item number as "a cine-segment comprising an item-girl/boy, a racy song, a vivacious dance and a surround of erotic and immanent exuberance" (2010:67). Very often, the item song is a stand-alone fixture in many Bollywood films and it can exist independently outside the bounds of the plot, subject or location of the film.

PART IV

Troubles of the Outdoorsy Woman
Multiple Genres/Multiple Voices

Chapter 8

Roads, Dreams, and Violence

Tracing the Mental Landscape of India's Domestic Workers

Bonnie Zare and Ditto Prasad

Daily life for women of India traveling along public spaces, whether walking or riding the bus or train, is fraught with challenge. Vulnerability is never far from thought as entitled males on the street may leer, stare, and make comments. Bystanders rarely say anything. The trouble experienced by middle class women is small when compared with working class women, including those in domestic service. Across India, as reported by the Delhi Labour Organization, there are as many as 50 million domestic workers, most of them girls and women. Many of them work for multiple households in a sector or colony, arriving early in the morning and moving from house to house, prolonging their hours on days when extra work is requested. Their low-ranking work makes them more likely to be slighted, insulted, or mistreated.

While these women are literally threatened on the road, this chapter will consider the road of life mentally traveled by female domestic workers. Considering that movement can imply progress and that happiness is often understood as a journey and not a destination, how are these women contending with the repetition of lowly tasks? Whose bodies are deemed worthy enough to be on a life journey of happiness, to even have a journey to call their own? As Jasbir Puar asks in another context, "Where does a body—and its aliveness—begin and where does it end? . . . What is a life? . . . And, who owns it? What defines living?" (Puar 2010, 164).

During the recent period of Covid waves resulting in sudden lockdown conditions, domestic workers lost income and suffered greatly as non-contract workers. Yet, even in ordinary times these workers contend with extreme financial pressure: according to Tripti Lahiri's account of this work, *Maid in India* (2017), a woman, commonly working about six hours a day without counting transportation time, earns an average wage of about Rs. 5000 in a month, which covers only a child's school fees, uniforms, travel and books, leaving the mother with no savings. Adding further injury, many women have little to no say over their working conditions. Never mind anything long term such as maternity leave, domestic workers have no daily rights such as set breaks for lunch or rest. Being granted a sick day is difficult or impossible and receiving leave for an emergency visit to a hometown may not be granted. While sometimes food or clothes are given by a household, a worker cannot count on this, and women as domestic workers state that many times donated food is spoiled or verges on unhealthy. Furthermore, domestic workers in India may face religious discrimination (particularly if they are from minority communities) and certainly confront both caste suspicion and class suppression.

According to workers interviewed by Tripti Lahiri, a frequent practice occurs of accusing domestic workers of theft, sometimes in order to refuse payment that is due. However, worst of all is the emotional, physical and sexual abuse that may occur on the job. Although some states do have a minimum wage for domestic workers in place, a lack of monitoring of the situation allows conditions of exploitation to continue. India badly needs a universal and strictly enforced law which lays out minimum standards of care for domestic caregivers. Some progress along these lines was developing in a few cities: for instance, the National Domestic Workers Union which is headquartered in Mumbai had spread to 16 states, but with the coronavirus health crisis such efforts have stalled.

Finally, the repetitive nature of the work impedes a sense of traveling on the road of life to get somewhere. Drudgery is associated with the work as it is both repetitive and never fully done. Utensils, dishes, floors and clothes are cleaned and yet will need to be scrubbed seemingly the next moment; each day dirt, grease, dust and sweat cover them again. The classic fairy tale Cinderella begins by establishing a young girl as a drudge, one whose sweet attitude cannot erase the lowliness of her tasks, her lack of compensation nor the disdain of people who do not touch the dirt or cinders. Daily and continuous repetition without variety is not perceived as a happy act and this is partly because repeated steps are not perceived as a journey.

Unlike the others in the volume, this essay considers "traveling along a road" as a metaphor for life's daily journey of experience, considering the mental landscape of Indian domestic workers. It investigates the crude ways patriarchal norms threaten movement along a pathway inside their workplace and the ways they must negotiate their potential psychological well-being. The public platforms have few representations of these workers, who themselves often haven't had much chance to become educated or circulate their story widely. In this chapter, we examine a few recent artistic narratives from the small archive which have salience owing to their wide circulation and relatively easy consumption. They are Phantom Praveen's Malayalam film *Udaharanam Sujatha* (2017), Rohena Gera's Hindi film, *Sir* (2018) and Thrity Umrigar's novel *The Space between Us* (2006). Within this small archive, we looked at how domestic workers are shown to perceive their life and whether the idea of happiness as a journey corresponds with their portrayed experience, if such a phrase applies to this situation at all. Can these women workers contest the diminutive space their employers allow them? How do the creative texts grapple with the violence and sexual assault domestic workers often confront?

While boredom, drudgery, and deprivation might be what an audience expects them to struggle with, other challenges abound in the lives of domestic workers. Each text chosen here focuses on a woman's internal conflict over a relationship in her life, and thus her challenges enable the audiences to identify with them. Against the backdrop of intolerably unfair work conditions, we draw on Sara Ahmed's work on the trickery of happiness and Lauren Berlant's notion of cruel optimism to examine to what degree these texts critique the nation's lack of action and the modus operandi of commodifying care and help.

A remake of *Nil Battay Sannata* (slang for "good for nothing"), *Udaharanam Sujatha* is a heart-tugging mother and daughter film showing two family members moving down opposing roads. The widowed mother, Sujatha, gives every ounce of strength and nearly every moment of her day to earn money so that her 15-year-old daughter will continue her education and possibly gain a more certain financial position. Athira, the daughter, is decidedly unlike her patient, diligent and gentle mother, and instead is self-centered, lazy, and movie-star-obsessed. The movie begins at four in the morning as Sujatha awakens. As her daughter continues to sleep, her mother hurriedly starts her walk. The walk takes her along the rail lines, cityscapes, roads, and densely packed elevators to reach a luxurious apartment; the kitchen, however, is a dirty mess from last night's leftovers. Sujatha cleans, washes and cooks before rushing her way back to her house to help Athira reach school. It must be noted the journeys themselves are glossed over. The onerous distance and likely disturbances (including street harassment) from passersby are not captured on screen, almost as if the financially privileged screenplay writer and director are unaware of the vulnerability of women traveling singly on the road and the impediments that may delay or demotivate them.

Instead the film conveys the only true road and destination in Sujatha's mind is her daughter's educational success. However, this road seems uphill all the way, one that is impractical to complete given the mother's lowly status. A key moment that gives shape to Sujatha's dream for her daughter is meeting the highly respected female District Collector, a woman who has risen from humble beginnings and gently tells the mother how one becomes an IAS officer. The Indian Administrative Services (IAS) exam is one of the most difficult exams to clear in India, and requires a candidate to excel in multiple academic disciplines and showcase many officer-like-qualities. In the best circumstances, Athira would have to be not only exceptional but also lucky to attain this rank, and these are not the best circumstances: she lacks motivation to study. In fact, the daughter is fatalistic, believing in the cyclical nature of family traditions and career options. Athira says stubbornly, "Doctor's children become doctors, engineer's children engineers and *vellakari*'s children *vellakari*" [menial worker] (Praveen 2017, 28:59). Wayward and confident, Athira argues with her mother, easily causing Sujatha to wilt into uncertainty. However, eventually Sujatha is mentored and encouraged by one of her elderly male employers, George Paul, a sophisticated wealthy scriptwriter, who reminds her that passing 10th standard is pivotal to her child's avoiding a low-skill job or, worse, no job at all. He has a novel idea: with his help, a place is arranged for Sujatha, who herself had to drop out of school in 9th grade, to join her daughter's school and study by her side in Athira's 10th standard class. Coached to be hopeful by her employer, Sujatha believes if she can be a hard-working student and accept the deep embarrassment of attending school at the wrong age, her daughter may better see the life-long value of getting educated.

Watching the 35-year-old Sujatha be accepted by the youngsters and being in suspense over whether Athira's classroom competition with her mother will truly make Athira into a serious-minded person is central to the film's charm. The scenes in the classroom are brightened by a group of well-cast teen actors, a forbidding teacher, an inspirational song about getting over math block and triumphant announcements about Sujatha's and her daughter's improving exam scores. Notably, it takes the threat of being socially humiliated by having the mother continue to be present in her peer circle to get her daughter to open her books, but when her competitive spirit gets kindled it appears the film will end with the daughter accepting the requirement of studying. True to her earlier lethargy, however, the daughter rejects studying once again, saying she only wanted to do well to get her mother out of the way. Ultimately, Athira must be awakened to her mother's vulnerability dramatically (through a sudden accident and major health scare) to understand she will have to feed herself one day and earn an independent living as well as to see the value of her mother's faith and love. In the last scene, Athira is an adult and has successfully cleared the Indian Administrative Services (IAS) exam.

Sadly, the film's last line does not uphold the dignity of domestic laborers, the words uneasily clashing with the warm treatment of Sujatha and the close ups of her painstaking scrubbing of pots and pans. An interviewer asks the daughter why she chose IAS as a career option and Athira responds, "Because I did not want to be a domestic maid" (Praveen 2017, 2:56:00), a seemingly self-explanatory and unapologetic dismissal of the work done by many millions of Indian women, including her own cherished mother. While the movie's apparent intention is a clarion call for young girls to dream big, it ends up portraying a kind of cruel optimism and sending a regressive message. Lauren Berlant describes cruel optimism as "when you're attached to objects or object worlds or forms of life that fundamentally get in the way of the attachment you brought to them, and of the optimism you brought to them" (2019, 9:24). Sujatha is asked to subsume what she deserves under the banner of motherhood and we are asked to admire her attachment to being a good mother over being a recognized thinker. Sujatha's success depends on her embodying a self-sacrificial and patriotic Mother India. If this is indeed what will save Daughter India, then the culture must continue to reinforce self-abnegation on the part of half of humanity.

"Udhaharanam" in Malayalam means "for example" or "as a testimony," as the title proclaims. Significantly, the example or model for being a good mother is to be an uncomplainingly giving "superwoman." Whether the mother or daughter is traversing public space, the perils of travel are neglected and instead individual heroism is shown as Sujatha obediently goes to at least six different places of work, which also require long walks from one destination to another. Somehow, she also finds time, energy and space to attend an educational institution that is full time. None of this keeps her from thinking constantly about someone else, her daughter, as her repeated worried look, rejection of a suitor, and questions for her employer reinforce at every turn. Here she enacts Berlant's concept of cruel optimism: a phenomenon in which you attach significance to an action as though it results in happiness despite the action being a mere consolation prize or even a deterrent to happiness. At one point, when she loses faith she can acquire sufficient skill in Mathematics to demonstrate competency to her daughter, Sujatha does not even question why and how society deprived her of her initial education. Instead, she demands to know, "What am I, a dustbin that should just receive anything thrown into it?" (Praveen 2017, 57:20). While Sujatha's ceaseless devotion to her child leads to the daughter becoming both productive and lucky in the end, if Sujatha's working herself to the bone had ended in illness or being cheated and being unable to pay off her debts, she would have just appeared as society's dustbin. As Berlant demonstrates in multiple examples, today's market-driven hyper capitalist system refuses futurity "in an overwhelmingly productive present" and many current texts reveal the life of a subaltern person struggling to keep financially secure engaged in "aspirational normativity" (Berlant 2012, 164). How then are we meant to believe Sujatha keeps hoping, keeps cleaning, keeps studying? Berlant says we are asked to digest a kind of deprivation as diurnal in service to our imagination that having "a friend, or making a date, or looking longingly at someone who might, after all, show compassion for our struggles, is *really where living takes place*" (189; emphasis added). Our unfair economic system is shielded from extreme criticism through the promise of intimacy with another, in this case a mother's yearning for her daughter's validation. When Athira finally says, "I am my mother's dream" (Praveen 2017, 1:52:20) the film requires the audience to celebrate a rare stroke of luck and look past the state's neglect of her mother's education.

In contrast to *Udaharanam Sujatha* with several memorable songs, Rohena Gira's film *Sir* is a quiet story despite taking place in the bustling city of Mumbai. Many scenes are wordless or only convey the clink of Ratna's bangles. Ratna is often found folding squares and rectangles—whether tablecloths or clothes—or making food or tea. We see her constantly creating life, using her hands and mind to relieve her employer, Ashwin and his family and friends, from any effort. In an early scene at Ashwin's mother's party, the camera follows her to each cluster of party-goers as she offers starters on her tray, and nearly all of them barely look at her if they notice her presence at all, thus proving how their worlds hardly intersect. There are two invisibles here, one the maid herself and the other, the work she does. As theorists of care work and disability have long been arguing, caregiving should be more highly valued. As Eva Feder Kittay says, caregiving also nourishes the caregiver (Kittay 1999). It is a reciprocal relationship, providing meaning to both parties. But most often, a domestic maid is expected to read the mood of the employer and adjust. The unspecified duties of a housemaid can get normalized to the extent of bearing abuse, sexually, verbally and physically. Ratna is an uncomplaining soul, whose lips sometimes wear a Mona Lisa half smile or half grimace, but who generally glides from room to room "sirring" the "sirs" and "ma'aming" the "ma'ams" without hesitation.

Like Sujatha, Ratna is a widow. She sends Rs. 4000 back for her in-laws and is keen to have her sister stay in school, but is quite restrained throughout the film. At one point she explains that any wrong move by herself would cause her "brother-in-law to drag her back by her hair" (Gera 2018, 50:10), summoning up the picture of yet another Indian woman being abused on the gendered space of the road. Thus she seems to completely accept she must be an avid rule follower. Similar to Sujatha, she also has a dream, but it is for herself. She makes small steps, with the approval of her employer, to learn tailoring as she yearns to pursue a career in fashion designing.

The film's central tension arises from Ashwin's slowly growing romantic feelings for Ratna. We often see Ashwin only from the side or are made to stare at his burdened back as he shoulders the family profession and is micromanaged by his architect father. Indeed, Ashwin seems unhappier than the maid: he has broken the rules of his circle by backing out of a marriage, and he would rather be in America freely pursuing his love for writing. Ashwin leans on Ratna as an intermediary with his Mother who calls and checks on him frequently. One of her duties is to lie about whether he is home, showing that a maid cannot defend her own moral code but must adjust to an employer's whims. Once Ashwin comes home with a friend to eat dinner prepared by Ratna. After witnessing a surreptitious sexual tension between Ashwin and Ratna the friend tells Ashwin, "you can't date your maid, the chick is sweet and she is there for you, but she is your maid, people will never forget she is a maid" (Gera 2018, 1:19:52). To this Ashwin retorts rather rhetorically, "Put that aside for a moment and think" (1:20). Eventually Ashwin admits he is in love with Ratna and asks her to show reciprocal affection by calling him by his name rather than "sir." Ashwin assumes that Ratna would say yes to changing from his maid to his wife: the stellar move in the movie is that she doesn't. His wealth and privilege have not given him the knowledge he needs here. In fact, she, a former maid, cannot become a wife. The perilous space of the public road shadows this imagined moment as she would become a reviled person in the gaze of multiple persons. Labeled a mistake by her employer's family she would also be discarded as a whore by all sections of society including her own.

Sir, unlike *Udaharanam Sujatha*, grapples with the impending violence of stepping out of one's place as a housemaid. The chances of being labelled as a sex worker are very high for a domestic maid in India. While Sujatha is twice associated with sex work, these are passing references rather than threats. In *Sir* Ratna herself continually knows she is one rumor away from losing the respect of the people in the building, whether staff or employers. Thus, if the movie is about love, it is really about Ratna's self-love or degree of self-preservation. Like *Udaharanam Sujatha*, the film does not critique the degree of struggle in Ratna's life nor the state's neglect of people in the service field, instead enabling us to distract ourselves with Ashwin serving as a fairy godmother of sorts, remaining detached from Ratna but granting his Cinderella a spot in a fashion company.

The film's ending is ambiguous. After getting a job in a fashion boutique through Ashwin's arranging it with a friend, Ratna appears a changed woman, a lightness surrounding her. As Ratna emerges onto the terrace of the building she worked at, she receives a phone call from Ashwin. All this while, she had ignored his phone calls because she did not want to pursue a romantic relationship with her own employer. This time, she picks up the call and finally says his name, Ashwin, rather than "Sir." The film ends there, and the future between them is left ambiguous. For those who want a romantic ending, this allows for the possibility of a new connection being forged through her new status. What we can know by hearing "Ashwin" is Ratna's willingness to address her former employer by his name (finally) distances her from being a constant server and establishes her claim to her own identity, asserting herself as newly autonomous.

Bhima, the principal character in Mumbai-born US author Thrity Umrigar's novel *The Space between Us* (2006), is a thinker. She scrubs and cleans and cooks by the hour, but the reader spends long moments inside her reveries, aware of her dreams for her college enrolled granddaughter, Maya, and reflecting on the memories of her husband Gopal's courtship and their time spent raising a daughter and son. Named by her employer as a lower caste domestic worker, Bhima once lived in a serviceable tenement or chawl, but moved to a basti (slum area) after her husband's cruel mistreatment after a factory accident led him first to drink and then to relocating his son and abandoning Bhima. Early in the book we observe this unaccompanied woman's strength, waking beside her pregnant granddaughter Maya, and quickening her way past crowds to the common tap to collect water for the household chores. Throughout her day working for a regal educated Parsi woman named Serabai, the book's other main character, Bhima keeps thinking of her granddaughter with words such as these: "Seventeen would be too young for Maya to deliver a child" and "Of course, she will have to have an abortion" (Umrigar 2006). The juxtaposition of Serabhai and Bhima naturally provides contrast: rich and poor, formal and simple, refined and basic. Furthermore, the employer's daughter Dinaz, is pregnant as well, making both the employer and maid anticipate the arrival of a baby—one in joy and the other in alarm.

The Space between Us is noteworthy for its portrayal of struggle and pain. We are presented with two lives, one full of unadulterated ease and luxury and one full of harshness and deprivation. Though Serabhai is outwardly affluent and privileged, the external show hides a painful marriage. Despite Sera's confidence and poise, she is the target of repeated emotional abuse from her mother-in-law and is treated as a literal punching bag by her husband, Firoz, during his frequent rages. She had, in fact, once ran away from her violent husband only to be brought back by her father, pleading and begging to Firoz to take her in. By contrast, it is the "lowly" Bhima who experiences the happiest marriage in the book. Before factory malfeasance, injury and alcohol ruined Gopal, there were years of the mischievous and flirty Gopal, the man who, cycling furiously, hung onto the bus where his beloved was riding and serenaded her with filmi songs for three weeks, much to the delight of the other passengers. There was the man who loved walking with his wife and two children along the crescent of the sea, buying kulfi and bhelpuri (an ice cream like sweet and a snack made of puffed rice) and looking for the humor in the passing scene. In a parallel to Berlant's conceptualization, Bhima is able to look past the cruelty of her day-to-day situation by dwelling on the satisfaction of being in a dyad, and thinking fondly about how she is luckier in love than so many other women she knows. This is brought to view as she dwells on her most intimate moments, thinking of evenings when Gopal's body found hers: he "never tried to conquer her like she was a mountain" but swam in her "as if she were a river" (Umrigar 2006).

As Bhima's granddaughter steadfastly refuses to name the man who has made her pregnant, the individuals are caught in a Catch-22, wanting to help but not knowing how to proceed. Sera's family eventually arranges for Maya to terminate the pregnancy; nevertheless, the audience, similar to Bhima, plays detective, looking for the person who has transgressed Maya's space. In each chapter, the novel explores the spatial limitations and possibilities between the characters, as announced by the book's title. For Serabai, the separating space between herself and Bhima is valuable and needed. Serabai believes in her own kindly treatment of her maid, congratulating herself on her charitable nature as she has provided well for Bhima's family including Maya's schooling. Across centuries domestic workers have been positioned as objects of control and likewise Sera enjoys the distance she can dictate in her relationship with Bhima. Sipping her tea on a chair, Sera remembers the savage beating her younger self has endured from her husband before his death, and she still shudders at the thought of Bhima, a lower caste woman, rubbing balm on her bruises. Sitting beside her on the ground, Bhima often listens with deep affection to Sera speaking aloud to her. Serabai contemplates enabling the tired Bhima to rest on her couch, yet this image immediately provokes a visceral reaction of distaste. She blames her unsettled feelings on more authoritarian members of the house such as her husband and mother-in-law, but when they are no longer present to set these rules, Sera has to acknowledge her own aversion. Her friends routinely tease Sera for treating Bhima so well, a form of peer pressure that reassures her of her own extra generosity and adds to the illusion she has a remarkable heart. Though able to dislike the moment-to-moment reality of caste which implies such a loyal and helpful daily companion is a lesser human, Sera is unable to dislike the caste system altogether.

Sera's daughter is critical of her mother, scathingly mentioning Sera's inability to let Bhima sit on the couch as similar to a past history of harijans being burnt on stakes. Sera replies, "Dinaz, there is a slight difference" (Umrigar 2006). Sera strongly believes that consistently employing Bhima and providing certain financial assistance to Maya to complete her college education justifies her prejudices. For herself, Bhima is all too aware of the unbridgeable gap between herself and her employer; after all, she is repeatedly reminded aloud of how much she owes to Sera's family. Ever watchful, Bhima comes to know "Serabai better than she knows most of her relatives" (Umrigar 2006). She never assumes or believes the space between them will substantially decrease; yet underneath also believes all members of Serabhai's family feel sufficiently connected to her help, daily presence, and knowledge of her that no one would knowingly injure her family.

Then one day, Bhima learns that the same man, Viraf, Sera's son in law and Dinaz's husband, has impregnated both Dinaz and her granddaughter Maya. When Viraf commits his disgusting crime against the 17-year-old Maya, she was assisting with cleaning in Viraf's house and thus was in a public space, not a home but a workplace to her. Once again we see the sexual vulnerability of subaltern women in India's public spaces. Bhima's horror at discovering her granddaughter has been impregnated by a trusted person is a double betrayal; the hurt of rape and the hurt of a man who for all extents and purposes had acted as a benefactor and near family member to them up to that point. The readers may hope Bhima and Sera might align in detesting this truth, but instead this fact ends their relationship.

Realizing Bhima has learned of his transgression, and looking to remove any reminder of his guilt, Viraf frames Bhima and announces she has stolen a small sum of money from the family. When confronted with Viraf's treachery, Sera figuratively allows a brick wall to move in between herself and Bhima. Bhima loses her job and future prospects, for Sera does not defend her loyal worker and daily companion, instead instantly falling in line behind Viraf, sensing Bhima has been angry since Maya's abortion, and already wishing there was a way for her daughter's pregnancy to be separated from the "shadow of Maya's trials" (Umrigar 2006). Viraf's geographical crossing of the tiny space Maya has, the space of her own body, is too painful for Serabhai to absorb. It is galling to the readers that despite her own experience of being a target of violence, Sera is unable to see Maya was in the same position. Gender solidarity does not pull her away from caste and class allegiance. Bhima, however, is unsurprised. She has always known Sera's liberalism is paired with complacency: we can almost hear her saying to herself that after all, for Sera to absorb Maya's humanity would be to accept her son-in-law's inhumanity, a step too outrageous for her conventional imagination. Although we never witness Dinaz being told of Viraf's act, Bhima senses that even her long-time ally would be wordless, and would not choose to do anything.

Bhima's employer Sera can forgive Bhima for stealing, but she cannot acknowledge Bhima having questioned Viraf's honor. Clearly the space between Bhima and Sera, shortened by Sera's victimization (as Bhima nursed Sera's bruised body) is now greatly lengthened in the same shadow of authoritarian patriarchal crimes. As Sara Ahmed writes, "Happiness has a way of being aligned with others . . . The family is a happy object, one that binds and is binding" (2010, 45). Maya's education made "the fantasy of a good life visible" (Ahmed 2010, 45)—it functioned like a happy object for Bhima. It is this promise of a good life that sustained Bhima's optimism even amid despair and this prospect that Viraf attacked, ultimately violating the lives of four women, yet another pathetic victory for patriarchy. Maya's long hesitancy in revealing the name of the unknown father hung on two cornerstones of their promised happiness—Maya's education and Bhima's job—their "happy objects." The novel's force is driven by a larger critique of India's patriarchal environment that pushed Maya to choose her education and her mother's remuneration over an aggressive voicing of the violence her body had to overcome. This is how Viraf feels he can get away with his violation. The environment creates the trap and makes it easy for the family to jettison Maya and Bhima. In retrospect Bhima reminisces how everybody fails to live up to their promises, whether it be governmental organizations, the factory administration or hospital staff next to her husband Gopal, or the outwardly kind Sera.

Serabai and Bhima fight similar battles but live different lives. After the final retaliation, they are left with fixing the lives of their family members. Each goes in a separate direction: whereas Sera breaks her long unacknowledged commitment toward Bhima and closes ranks, Bhima wanders along the shoreline and makes a choice to show her belief in her dignity is intact. In the closing scene, a sense of reconciliation is achieved as Bhima chooses to honor her memory of a peacemaker, the Pathan balloon maker.

This man from Afghanistan who has been making balloons for children on the beach was known to her and Gopal for the faraway look in his eyes, and the bearing of a man who has seen many lives. Although homesick for his own land and therefore nostalgic, his dedicated practice of slowly making the balloons into shapes for eager children marks him as an artist and someone whose inviolate dignity commands respect. Over time, Bhima had cursed herself for her lack of curiosity at the times she met him, wishing she had been a more ardent seeker of knowledge, a better translator of his contentment. He is not described as happy nor as seeking happiness. Indeed, rather than being on a journey, he seems to represent forbearance; making "a song out of his loneliness" (Umrigar 2016) he demonstrates a tolerance of suffering. The man with the "beautiful brown hands . . . that created poetry out of nothing" (Umrigar 2016) remains a touchstone for Bhima: she recognizes from him that a person can mourn and detach from the mourning, can acknowledge life's brevity and unfairness and yet remain calm and unbowed. Giving all the money she had on her to buy balloons for a moment of happiness, Bhima construes her definition of being happy. While, like a balloon, the joy could pop at any moment, as she runs along the water ignoring others' stares, she feels momentarily as free as a child. Just as the Pathan can never return to his home, at the end of the novel Bhima is exiled from her means of making a home, her employment and employer which was also a home. The novel neither romanticizes anyone's exile nor exaggerates anyone's victimhood, asking us to find a way to create a new paradigm amid uncertainty just as the novelist has done.

In *Ugly Feelings* critic Sianne Ngai reminds readers that canonical works tend to favor high passion over smaller feelings such as pettiness, irritation or extreme boredom. Perhaps this could be why we have so few deep representations of people involved in domestic labor. Stories meant for a wide audience which render the life of a maid tend to highlight compensations having nothing to do with her daily tasks. To withstand the unfair pittance of a wage, a woman is shown instead dreaming of helping a family member escape a similar fate, whether it be a sister at home as in *Sir* or a daughter as in *Udaharanam Sujatha* or a granddaughter in *The Space between Us*. Of the three texts, it is perhaps *Udaharanam Sujatha* that most displays a cruel optimism, for Sujatha lives only for her daughter's improvement: her utter selflessness including the sacrifices in energy she makes to attend school and work for multiple households is taken as a natural action within model motherhood, and her life as a maid can stop because she has created a successful IAS officer-daughter.

The life of a maid is complicated and threatened by employers' long held hierarchical notions about caste, socio-economic status and, in some cases, religious bias. Notably, it is only Bhima whose caste is specifically named. While Bhima is too generous to feel actual joy or schadenfreude at the privileged Sera's pain, her wry observations of Sera's fear of seeming too close to Bhima serve to highlight upper caste and middle-class hypocrisy as well as the humanity and efficacy of the domestic worker. Of these three representations of maids, the person who most helps us see this person as a complex thinker is Bhima, as we follow her multi-layered thoughts and keen awareness of her employer's self-congratulatory kindness.

The nation, by promising a "good life," suggests workers' happiness is always around the corner. The nation keeps maids such as Sujatha, Ratna and Bhima in a static place with very limited options for improving their situation and peddles the message "ache din aayenge" (good days will come). Neither Ratna nor Sujatha expect any appreciation for how they show up for others and yet they are calm and steady, a narrative that reassuringly reinforces the capitalist mantra that if you try harder, you will get farther and become happier. Both do their work well, but it is the *deus ex machina* of a generous benefactor (Sujatha's mentor and Ratna's employer) that helps them obtain some sense of agency. A readiness to be entrepreneurial is insufficient, and if domestic workers were to see the two films, they would likely scoff at the rosy view. The films gloss over the real problems of traveling on public roads in India. The struggle over a relationship in each film occludes the food insecurity and safety concerns workers face and the missing protections the government could provide. With the exception of *The Space between Us*, the road of dreamy optimism appears cruel because it is only when she can rise above the actual matter filling her workdays that a maid really appears to matter.

REFERENCES

Ahmed, Sara. 2010. *The Promise of Happiness*. Durham: Duke University Press.
Berlant, Lauren Gail. 2012. *Cruel Optimism*. Durham: Duke University Press.
Berlant, Lauren and Paul Rand. 2019. "Why Chasing the Good Life Is Holding Us Back." *Big Brains Podcast Episode* 35, 26:22. news.uchicago.edu/podcasts/big-brains/why-chasing-good-life-holding-us-back-lauren-berlant.
Dutt, Yashica. 2021. *Coming Out as Dalit: A Memoir*. New Delhi: Aleph Book Company.
Gera, Rohena. 2018. *Sir*. Platoon One Films. 1 hr., 39 min. www.imdb.com/title/tt7142506/.
Kittay, Eva Feder. 1999. *Love's Labors: Essays on Women, Equality and Dependency*. New York: Routledge.
Lahiri, Tripti. 2017. *Maid in India: Stories of Inequality and Opportunity Inside Our Homes*. New Delhi: Aleph (Rupa Publications).
Ngai, Sianne. 2005. *Ugly Feelings*. Cambridge: Harvard University Press.
Praveen, Phantom. 2017. *Udaharanam Sujatha*. The Scene Studios. 2hr., 7 min. www.imdb.com/title/tt6940692/.
Puar, Jasbir K. 2010. *Prognosis Time: Towards a Geopolitics of Affect, Debility and Capacity*. *Women & Performance: A Journal of Feminist Theory* 19, no. 2 (October): 161–172. 10.1080/07407700903034147
Umrigar, Thrity. 2006. *The Space between Us*. New York: William Morrow and Company. E-book.

Chapter 9

Negotiating Violence and Traversing the City

Female Vulnerability in Delhi Crime *(2019) and* She *(2020)*

Shreya Rastogi and Srirupa Chatterjee

> The right to the city is not simply manifested through changes to the material realm of transport infrastructure to facilitate an effective workforce. It derives from the perceptual realms of belonging and the pursuit of happiness in public space, including the right to treat public space as a place to linger, a destination in its own right, as well as a corridor to traverse on the way to another destination.
>
> —Carolyn Whitzman (2013)

Women's political agency in patriarchal societies is intrinsically linked to their embodiment and is limited by their corporeality. Despite systematic efforts to erase them from the physical and metaphoric *spaces* of public participation, Indian women have taken to the road as defiance, subversion, and an escape from the accepted *placements* dictated to them. Given the history of both patriarchal oppression and gendered violence in India, women's vulnerability in public spaces has necessitated journeys that have to be cautious, planned, and purposive. Predictably, women's forays into public spaces such as roads pose challenges ranging from eve-teasing, death-threats, rape-threats, harassment, and sexual violence to online trolling. In light of such cultural facts, the present essay examines two Netflix dramas that demonstrate how women's bodies are at constant risk within Indian cityscapes by problematizing female embodiment and proving how women are sometimes compelled to conceal their bodies and sexuality to navigate the nation's metropolis. It first examines *Delhi Crime* (2019)—an Emmy award winning web series—which is set in the aftermath of the infamous Nirbhaya case (2012) and follows the investigation, chase, and eventual arrest of the rapists under the charge of its woman officer and protagonist, Vartika Chaturvedi. It then focuses on *She* (2020) which depicts the perils of a young policewoman navigating the city after dark while pretending to be a sex worker. The fictionalized plot of *She* follows Bhumika Pardeshi, a police constable in Mumbai, who is coerced by her bosses into posing as a prostitute in order to nab the drug mafia. The series deftly showcases the fears and perils that befall women who choose to inhabit public spaces at night and must be punished for it by agents of patriarchy.

By analyzing two representative web dramas, this chapter focuses on how Indian media and popular culture have responded to women's perilous journeys on Indian roads. It examines *Delhi Crime* (set in New Delhi) and *She* (set in Mumbai) with regard to three imaginaries of women that the series present. First, it asserts that the multi-cultural metropolis becomes a hotbed of dangers even as it provides opportunities for common women who are always at risk in the city and therefore navigate and map it with the possibility of violence always on their mind. Second, it examines how imaginaries of ideal womanhood exclude economic and social minorities who fall outside the purview of the so-called respectable women and are therefore seen as a threat to the public space itself. If single independent women of lower and middle classes make up one part of this marginalized group, sex workers make up another; and both are viewed as not only inviting violence but also de-sanctifying the public space. Hence, they are deemed unworthy of justice if they happen to fall prey to sexual violence. Third, the essay examines the case of the visually empowered woman or the uniformed policewoman who can navigate the city with comparative ease and is able to exercise relative agency over herself and others while inhabiting the public space. Finally, this chapter also outlines the coping mechanisms and deceits that women are often compelled to employ to escape impending violence and ultimately maintain their presence in the hostile terrain of the Indian metropolis.

EMBODIED SUBJECTS AND THE HOSTILE CITY

Kathleen M. Kirby (1996) rightly notes that women "as active social subjects, are stuck in our skin and anchored by it to particular places" (123). True to Kirby's claims while their embodiment has always dictated women's placements, in India the imaginaries of mother, goddess, and the nation (embodied as woman) are superimposed onto the idea of the makings of a prototypical *good* woman. Hence, writes Meenakshi Thapan (2009) "woman's embodiment is the true repository of purity, sacredness and honour" (11) to the extent that "the female body needs to be appropriated for a sense of national, racial or community identity to persist" (Gedalof 1999, 203). These appropriations range from matters of dress and comportment to restricted mobility and denial of bodily agency as well as romantic and sexual expression. Tellingly, *Lajja*[1] (variously translated as coyness, virtuousness, and shame) is a central tenet of ideal Indian womanhood (Sinha and Chauhan 2013). Analyzing specific episodes from Hindu mythology, Sinha and Chauhan assert that "*lajja* connotes an awareness and expression of socially appropriate behaviour in public, especially for women; transgressions attracting punitive consequences" (137). The ideal image of femininity becomes "that 'way of being' which bestows status, respectability and recognition" (Thapan 12) in general, and is particularly pronounced within the Indian public space.

Contrarily, a woman's alleged slippages in morality under hegemonic patriarchal cultures are viewed as crimes against the collective personage of the public and believed to justifiably incite violent punishments. Mob justice in the form of Khap panchayat judgments, gang rape, public lynching, revenge rape, and violence replace civil law when conservative ideas of Indian femininity clash with more liberal laws of the land even to this day. By the same reasoning, the sexual violation of a purportedly *good* woman's body becomes a public crime. While there are always cultural specificities, these prototypes are hardly typical to India. Kate Manne (2018) defines patriarchy as a "deprivation mindset regarding women being giving, caring, loving, and attentive, as opposed to power-hungry, uncaring, and domineering" (xiv) such that women exhibiting professional ambition or exercising autonomy and sexual agency are branded as "insufficiently caring" and inattentive or "illicitly trying to gain power that she is not entitled to" and finally "morally untrustworthy" (xv). Discussing this problem in the Indian context, Thapan agrees that despite women's growing participation in higher education, professional employment, and financial independence, contemporary urban middle class still inhabits "a safe, patriarchal haven as far as the politics of the family is concerned" (32). Here, claims Thapan, young girls are taught values of "female submissiveness and passivity and particular role-specific identities" which "tend to reproduce gender asymmetry and a classical femininity" (31). Needless to say, these attitudes are reproduced within the nation's public spaces by both men and women.

Indian women therefore must cautiously navigate public spaces and plan their journeys without flouting the dominant imaginaries of ideal womanhood. When alone, their journeys must be purposive and not self-aggrandizing or pleasure-seeking. Shilpa Phadke corroborates that women in Indian public spaces are "carrying something, shopping, heading towards bus-stops or railway stations, but rarely, if ever, loitering around, sitting in a park or *maidan* [public square] or standing at a street corner smoking or simply watching the world go by as one is wont to see men doing" (2010, 5). The sight of a female body out in the dark freely traversing the city leisurely without hurried and purposive comportment—in short loitering—while simultaneously expressing her romantic or sexual self, particularly outside the conjugal bond, becomes an aberration that needs to be uprooted. Hence, while the post-millennial Indian city provides women opportunities for employment, travel, and social mobility, their very presence "unleash(es) male envy, and a crisis of patriarchal expectations" (Atreyee et al. 2019, 6) in the city which harbors a "general animosity" (Bhattacharyya 2014, 1345) toward women.

These feelings of animosity easily translate into attacks against women within hostile cityscapes. In 2019 the National Crime Report Bureau data showed that an average of eighty-seven rapes happened every day in India (*The Wire*) with the conviction rate as low as thirty percent (*Times of India*). It is also noteworthy that these are reported cases, the actual numbers may be significantly higher since marital rape is not yet criminalized in the country and sexual assault by a perpetrator known to the victim is likely to be silenced. In most reported cases the victim is attacked outside the home by a stranger. Public spaces, therefore, represent a "geography of fear" (Valentine 1989, 386) for women who map the city on a threat score based on the perceived possibility of attack. Within the western context, Gill Valentine (1989) asserts that "most women, especially at night, have a heightened consciousness of the micro design features of their environment, and adjust their pace and path accordingly: running past or crossing the road to avoid alleyways, indented doorways, over-grown bushes and other perceived shadowy areas" (386). This is equally true for Indian cities where the threat of assault and the victim blaming that inevitably follows force women to limit their socio-temporal mobility. Suffocated by these conditions Indian women, particularly urban women, have increasingly campaigned online and offline for their right to access public spaces without having to sacrifice their safety.

Demonstrations such as *#IWillGoOut*, *#WhyLoiter*, *Meet to Sleep*, Pinjra Tod [Break the Prison], and *#AintNoCinderella*[2] germinated in Indian cities against the policing of women's behavior in public spaces. Simultaneously, with the rising awareness of women's right to the city international movements like Take Back the Night, *#Me Too*, and *SlutWalk* also appropriated their goals to meet the Indian context. For instance, Kaitlynn Mendes (2015) notes that SlutWalk organizers in Delhi, Bhopal, and Hyderabad used the alternate name of "Besharmi Morcha" (68) to better communicate their opposition to eve-teasing and victim shaming. Most of these consciousness raising events have been made possible only after the mass public outrage following the Delhi Nirbhaya case in 2012 where six men brutally raped and assaulted a nursing student and beat up her male friend in a moving public bus as the duo was returning after watching a film at night. Sociologists agree that it was not only the heinousness of the crime but also the ideal socio-political positioning of the victim as an upper caste, middle-class, urban, nursing student that resonated with the Indian public who went on to occupy the streets in mass protests demanding conviction and death penalty for the rapists. Dutta and Sircar (2013) assert that even the law is complicit in maintaining gender and class hierarchies with its "entrenched conservative sexual morality that makes [only] 'good,' 'chaste,' and 'respectable' women deserving of protection" (300). By these standards Jyoti Pandey (Nirbhaya) was "a classic victim" as she was neither traveling alone, nor "wearing provocative clothes, and you just couldn't point fingers at her" (qtd. in Arya 2015, 58). The case captured the national imagination and media houses adopted campaign journalism to rile their audiences and build pressure on the administration for speedy conviction and trial.

The Nirbhaya case gained popularity and generated significant public debate due to its extensive coverage by the media. It was a watershed moment for the Indian women's movement where for the first time the public was less concerned with the specifics of rape and actively condemned the actions of the rapists. Yet, while the incident led to legislative reform as well as social change, women's fear of the open road remains a significant issue in the country. And understandably only a sustained public conversation can raise awareness and alter mindsets in the long run. In the west, women's travel narratives have increasingly provided the means to carry such discussion forward. Alexandra Ganser (2006) claims that by "reflect[ing] and challeng[ing] cultural realities, being produced and perceived . . . in very specific cultural and historical circumstances" literary narratives open "new discursive fields" and communicate "with their readership" such that "women's literary re-mappings of social space are potentially transformative of gender relations at large" (154). In light of these arguments this essay examines *Delhi Crime* and *She* with regard to three roles that women in the series don in the public space. First, the common everyday woman who maps the spatiotemporal possibility of assault while planning her movement through the city. Her person in the public space becomes a signifier which must demonstrate "signs" of respectability for her to claim safety and protection. Second, it examines the female sex worker, whose profession makes her a threat to the morality of public space. By definition, she is a designated criminal and outside the purview of public protection, and yet is deeply susceptible to sexual assault. Third, the on-duty policewoman whose uniform and identity guarantee her far greater access and safety in the city. This essay examines all such forays depicted in popular media to understand the challenges women face in the Indian metropolis.

WOMEN TRAVELING MISOGYNISTIC LANDSCAPES IN *DELHI CRIME*

Delhi Crime (2019) is an Emmy-winning drama series directed by Richie Mehta and is based on the Nirbhaya rape incident of 2012. Streamed on Netflix, the series spans six days (December 16 to 21, 2012) of investigation and the final arrest of all the accused. The series begins with the victims, Jyoti and her friend Aravind, boarding a bus from the Munirka bus stop at night. While the gruesome rape is not shown, the state of Jyoti's mutilated body is explained in graphic medical terms after the incident. When the dynamic Deputy Commissioner of Police (South Delhi), Vartika Chaturvedi, learns of the crime she is appalled and decides to personally bring the miscreants to justice. The police team with Aravind's help meticulously charts the bus's route and from there begins to gather leads to nab the culprits. As the rapists learn of police action, two of them flee to their homes in rural Rajasthan, and naxal hit Bihar. Meanwhile, intel of the case leaks to the media sparking public outrage and protests in the city. The series ends after the arrest of the final victim with the police team hoping for a fair trial.

Mehta's commitment toward depicting women's experience of public spaces begins in the first episode which features a panoramic view of the city enveloped in the darkness of the night with aggregations of street and car lights illuminating the city in distant clusters. The introduction score presents the point of view of a pedestrian walking the teeming streets, broad highways, and deserted alleyways of the city. The night city is almost entirely populated by men who are commuting, vending or loitering, conspicuously asserting the absence of women. The noir theme constantly juxtaposes the bustle of city life with the economic disparity, anonymity, isolation, and alienation that are characteristic of a modern metropolis. Yet the looming sense of dread, the possibility of being followed, and groped pervades the score as the camera pans through the run-down and packed streets of old Delhi to plush wide lane highways. The voice over informs that "eleven thousand" heinous crimes are reported in Delhi each year adding that "the city looks this way because it has to, because it always has" (ep. 1). Specific devices such as point of view shots (that emphasize the bystander's perspective) filmed using hand-held cameras (Sharma 2019), and the insistence to film in the streets of Delhi rather than movie sets brings the city alive for the audience.

While the series closely follows the meticulous investigation process, the filmography presents a realistic portrayal of Delhi and impresses the experience of navigating its streets as a woman. In addition, Mehta alerts his viewers toward a larger culture of misogyny through subplots scattered across the series. Hence, if inspector Bhupendra Singh (who is investigating the case along with his seniors and is a worried father looking to get his daughter married) is constantly questioned by families of prospective grooms if his daughter is light-skinned enough to make a desirable bride, Neeti (an IPS trainee under Chaturvedi) has a worried mother who wants to sell off their television set in order to ramp up her daughter's dowry. In fact, Chaturvedi herself, on account of her gender, sometimes experiences insubordination from the likes of her juniors such as Vinod Tiwari. The series, therefore, makes a powerful case against the widespread misogyny that not only corrupts all social interactions but also imperils women's presence in public spaces by commodifying them.

Other subplots in the series also highlight the day-to-day experiences of traveling women in Delhi. This is especially pronounced in the case of DCP Vartika Chaturvedi's daughter, Chandini, a high school student who actively plans on relocating to Toronto, Canada for higher education. Chandini represents an upper-middle class, urban, progressive, sheltered teen who despite her privilege is subject to harassment and molestation while traversing the city. She narrates:

> Last month I was getting out of the metro and I saw this guy he had his hand out to intercept my breast, ... to touch me ... I couldn't stop the push of the people and he just grabbed me as I went past him. I looked back and he was smiling at me like some demon ... I just wanted to smash his fucking smiling face. (ep. 2)

The experience of such attacks is all too common in the city to even warrant attention. This anger and fear unite Chandini and her young peers with the hordes of protesters who marched demanding justice for the victim, Jyoti Singh, and sat in night-long vigils. The series brilliantly questions the ethicality of this outrage. While administrative failures and lack of policing are immediately under the public radar, the victim's relationship with her male companion remains a bone of contention, even for the progressive and heroic police officers (who nonetheless share the public morality) investigating the case.

As the accused are nabbed by the police they reiterate that the violence against the couple was incited by their lewd behavior. Jai Singh, the first and main perpetrator narrates:

> We had just planned on looting them. But when we saw her boyfriend having fun with her, we thought we could have fun too ... it all started with her creepy boyfriend. It is because of people like him that our country's traditions are going

to hell. Is this the way to behave with a girl in public. Shameless. And she was having fun too. (ep. 3)

While the police are incredulous of this account at first, repeated assertions by all accused convince them. Aware of the dynamics of public morality at this point, the police try to prevent this information from getting to the public fearing it could jeopardize the case and delay/deny justice. Jai Singh and his mates deem both Jyoti and Arvind guilty of misconduct, but the punishments meted out to them are vastly different. Poignantly, Jyoti's mother asks Arvind "You were both attacked, but she is the only one fighting for her life, why?" (ep. 2). Evidently, it is the imaginaries of ideal womanhood that make the woman's desire to explore the city a greater crime in the eyes of the rapists. Not surprisingly, later Neeti, the young woman officer, while interrogating Jai Singh claims that "it was like his soul was missing" (ep. 7), since the rapists lack all insight whatsoever where a woman and her freedom are concerned. As discussed, the so-called erring female body which symbolizes ideals threatening patriarchal gender norms becomes a greater failure within this scheme of things. And this attests to Kate Manne's statement that "When one's effigy is one's body, one burns right along with it" (68). The victim in *Delhi Crime* is therefore emblematic of the devastating misogyny that feeds patriarchal thinking.

While prominent second-wave American feminists like Susan Brownmiller (1975) and Germaine Greer (1970) assert that rape and sexual violence stem from a desire for power and dominance rather than sex, contemporary theorists like Ann Cahill (2001) argue that the unique gender-specific nature of rape necessitates an embodied understanding of women's lived experience. Cahill asserts that "[s]ubjects do not have bodies; subjects are bodies, and they are sexed bodies" (14). Rape is therefore "laden with political and sexual meanings" which are not merely symbolic and instead "identity and integrity are necessarily connected to embodiment, and embodiment is marked by sexual difference" (14). This explains why the prime accused remains defiant declaring "I don't regret what I did" (ep. 3). Manne asserts that to the misogynist his actions feel "like a moral crusade, not a witch hunt. And it may pursue its targets not in the spirit of hating women but, rather, of loving justice" (63), and in this case of restoring morality.

The series also brings to light how the industrialized metropolis becomes a unique space that shelters the convicts while simultaneously providing a heterogeneous public sphere for progressive debate. The spatial limits of the metropolis juxtapose plush housing colonies against slums with police personnel manning the boundaries at check-points. While the private spaces of the rich and the poor are meticulously segregated, the public space brings together people from all walks of life and the exchange of values breeds discontent and aggression. The character of inspector Sudhir Kumar partly diagnoses the problem explaining:

> The rich have brought more money into the society, but it does not reach the poor. So they try to take it ... Add to it the explosion of uneducated youth here. They have no sex education but get free porn online which affects their adolescent brains. They don't know how to interpret it. They objectify women and wish that the things happening in porn should also happen in their lives. If they don't get it, they take it by force, with no regard for the consequences. After all, they have nothing to lose. (ep. 3)

While this spatial juxtaposition of ideologies may cause discontent, blaming migrants for women's harassment and vulnerability in metro cities, though prevalent, is largely false and deeply colored by classism and regionalism (Dhillon and Bakaya 2014). Migrants to metro cities are often poor daily-wage earners, drivers, and street-vendors. While in the Nirbhaya case the poor perpetuate violence, there is always far greater possibility of the rich and powerful victimizing economically vulnerable women. Tellingly, in the series inspector Bhupendra Singh asserts: "Thank God none of these (convicts) are sons of rich men. Otherwise even an arrest would have been impossible" (ep. 4). The city undoubtedly juxtaposes lifestyles and value systems. However, the direction of crime is not one way and there is no category or class of victim and perpetrator.

Delhi Crime nonetheless emphasizes the vast cultural and lifestyle disparities between metropolitan and rural India. As the chase of the two convicts, Amar and Alok, takes the police teams to hinterland Rajasthan and Aurangabad in Bihar one notes how women in villages cover their heads with their sarees, avoid interaction with men, and even with policemen who visit their houses for investigation; their lives are largely limited to domestic chores. The city juxtaposes these imaginaries of femininity (shared by men of all classes and regions) with the modern and empowered city woman who enjoys leisure and demands a right to the city. The modern metropolis is therefore a breeding ground for cultural conflict between the urban and rural. It is also, however, the same city which allows for the visibility that was afforded to the case. In the public morality of the progressive city hanging out with friends, commuting via public transport, and dating are fairly acceptable and make forces which helped garner sympathy and support for Jyoti's case. Notably, *Delhi Crime* concludes by reminding its viewers how the "incident" or the Nirbhaya case led to an enhancement of "anti-rape laws," "harsher punishment for perpetrators," and the "creation of a fast-track court for victims [of sex crimes]" (ep. 7). Yet, the series also reminds its viewers that misogyny and rape culture is so indelibly inscribed in the nation's cultural landscape that it is too difficult to erase. The series, therefore, collates the myriad impediments that traveling women are forced to consider before accessing the public space which does not guarantee their safety and leaves them open to violence and molestation.

THE PERILS OF STREET WALKING IN *SHE*

She (2020) is a Netflix crime drama written and created by Imtiaz Ali and Divya Johry. The series follows Bhumika Pardesi (Bhumi), a young constable working with the Mumbai Police, who is recruited by the Anti-Narcotics Cell as an under-cover spy. Bhumi is a simple yet resolute woman who provides for her sister and ailing mother. When Bhumi is coerced to pose as a prostitute in order to bust a drug racket, she reluctantly acquiesces and is trained as a spy by the Mumbai Police. While Bhumi projects confidence in the guise of a sex worker she constantly faces the danger of losing touch with her team which would put her at the risk of open violence. After the successful arrest of a criminal named Sasya, Bhumi naturally desires to return to her regular duties. However, she is forced to continue as a spy in order to bust a larger gang headed by a man named Nayak. Bhumi's nightly walks in the city display the enormous threat that sex workers and women at large face within the city. Like in *Delhi Crime* in *She*, too, the night city is devoid of women. Hence, the only women out at night are sex workers, whose very presence in the public space after "respectable" hours removes them from the circle of protection.

The imaginaries of womanhood add to the threats sex workers face in the street. Svati P. Shah (2014) in her ethnographic study on sex workers and migrant female laborers in Mumbai asserts that while there is a vague understanding that sex workers are victims of a biased economic system that pushes them into poverty and sex work as a last resort, it is accompanied by the idea that sex workers could not ply their trade "unless they liked sex" (136). The expression of tabooed female sexuality immediately places sex workers in the category of "bad" women. Such women, therefore, become a threat to the sanctity of public space. Shilpa Phadke (2011) explains that "'[r]espectable' women could be potentially defiled in a public space while 'non-respectable' women are themselves a potential source of contamination to the 'purity' of public spaces and, therefore the city" (n.p.). Shah corroborates that police violence against sex workers is legitimized under the assumption that the presence of sex workers in a residential area is a "collective threat to respectable, middle-class families for whom the area had to be kept 'safe' (i.e., free of sex workers)" (128). However, as Shah notes it is often difficult to even identify sex workers who seamlessly blend into the crowd. Tellingly, Phadke

(2011) explains that the anxiety around the safety of public spaces actually stems "from the potential of confusion in distinguishing respectable women from the unrespectable . . . as it undermines any control on women's presence in public space" (n.p). Given these dynamics of power, any Indian woman accessing the public space after sunset risks being categorized as a "bad" woman, openly inviting violence and assault in the public imagination.

In *She* Bhumi is required to regularly solicit on the streets at night waiting for members of Nayak's gang to spot and hire her. Since she is exclusively waiting for Nayak, she has to refuse all other potential customers. While her trainer assures her that "without your consent no one can touch you" (ep. 2), Bhumi realizes that on the street a prostitute's consent is a non-existent concept. Tellingly, a bewildered client asks, "Why does a prostitute even have a choice?" (ep. 1), while another simply says "You are standing in the market, right? You are paid to have sex. Just go and stop whining" (ep. 1). Another, likewise, comes up and asks if she is willing to "blow" him (ep. 4). Even as Bhumi valiantly faces all risks of sexual assault for sincerely pursuing her duty, she cannot overcome the fears and rape threats that come her way continuously from men who follow her on her nightly duty. Simultaneously, Bhumi knows that for posing as a prostitute she cannot rely on anyone's help if assaulted. Here, ironically, the same imaginaries of womanhood which make public spaces unsafe for women also designate certain women as unrapable (Manne 78). Sex workers, intoxicated women, and minorities therefore cannot be raped as they are either "up for it anyways" or used to sex. Other women who access the city space after dark unaccompanied by men risk slipping into this category and the series demonstrates this dynamic when senior constable Mhatre, Bhumi's colleague and friend whom she calls "Bhau" (older brother), turns on her once he finds her guilty of being comfortable with her sexuality. As Bhumi slowly falls into the pattern of her new job and earns praise from senior officers, the frustrated Mhatre taunts her saying that she "enjoys" her "nightly parades" (ep. 5), implying that she seems to enjoy soliciting clients. The series portrays how Bhumi is reduced to her body by her superiors. The men around her think of her as "just a constable" (ep. 2) while simultaneously exposing her to the international drug mafia—something way beyond her experience and pay grade. Jason Fernandes, Bhumi's boss, reiterates that "all she has to do is stand" in front of the criminals, while the police team will be her "brains and hands" (ep. 3), adding that while Bhumi is almost masculine in her appearance, her "specs [specifications] are right. She is 5'7," bust thirty-four inches, waist twenty-six, hip measurement thirty-six . . . She is an average performer. Follows orders, I think I can control her" (ep. 4). Treating Bhumi as a mindless pawn, the police send her to Nayak without even a weapon or recording device. This makes tracking her location in the city exceptionally difficult.

The only sympathetic voice Bhumi encounters in her night walks is that of a beggar whom she passes every night on the way to work. As per the plan, an undercover cop dressed as a taxi driver drops Bhumi near the train station every night from where she walks on foot across the overbridge, through a deserted and run-down neighborhood that abuts a posh locality where other sex workers solicit at night. A terrified Bhumi is regularly cat-called and stared at by men who see her walking alone at night. A senile beggar who squats near the pavement watches her cross every day and becomes the classic choric voice in the series reminding the viewers of the absurdly tragic world they inhabit. Once when Bhumi is struggling with the moral qualms of posing as a prostitute, the beggar abruptly exclaims, "What is good, what is bad, I earned fifty rupees and had a cigarette. I satiated myself with smoke . . . All of us have to go to the same place one day. I will see all your black deeds one day" (ep. 6), highlighting the fake morality that shames sex workers. It is therefore to this beggar that Bhumi confesses her fear of walking the street at night and also unburdens herself by revealing her undercover operation. In a scene of comic relief, Bhumi harasses the beggar asking him for a permit to sit on the pavement, while he mocks her for claiming to be a cop while being dressed as a prostitute. The beggar unlawfully occupying the pavement and Bhumi dressed as a sex worker share a position of marginality and precarity in the city and are a supposed blight to the public space.

While the series overtly seems to operate under the assumption that a woman may weaponize her sexuality to control space and men around her, its narrative seems to assert the obverse. Though the realization of her sexuality is empowering for Bhumi, it is no defense against the dangers that she encounters on her mission. When potential customers coerce her into boarding their vehicles, Bhumi is open to threats of gang rape and her only assurance of security is the police team tailing her. However, in all the three operations that Bhumi conducts, her team gloriously fails to track her. The metropolis becomes a labyrinth of streets and bylanes that the police is unable to chart. Hence, when Bhumi boards Nayak's car, a wild chase follows in which the goons confiscate Bhumi's belongings and successfully evade the police. At Nayak's residence, Bhumi is strip searched by men, an episode that reeks of the trauma of gang rapes. Later, Nayak learns of her true identity and entraps Bhumi. Left to her own devices with no contact with her team, Bhumi sides with Nayak and becomes a double agent for him. Even as the series ends with the promise of a sequel, it deftly conveys in part one that devices like self-defense, manipulation, and cleverness cannot be strategies to navigate the cityscape; they are at best the last resort for a woman stuck in a life-threatening situation (Hickey 2011). Operating under multiple structures of power, common women like Bhumi may understand or even at times exploit their sexuality but are unable to be the *femme fatale* that popular culture often imagines women spies to be. In fact, for inhabiting a female form such women are often as susceptible to gendered violence as any other person of their tribe. *She*, therefore, reiterates that public spaces pose significant dangers for women.

Rape Culture and the Curious Case of the Uniformed Policewoman

Given the plotlines of *Delhi Crime* and *She*, the perils of traveling women in India appear manifold and layered. There is, however, one class of women that can navigate the city with considerable authority and ease: this happens to be female police officers who present a curious case. Both *Delhi Crime* and *She* follow uniformed policewomen who journey unscathed through perilous zones dictated by rape culture. The uniformed officer's femininity incites little affect when juxtaposed against the powerful state insignia that she carries on her person. This is manifest not only in her uniform but also when undercover in the possession of her identity proof. Simultaneously, the shows are sensitive to the perilous path female officers walk as they are patronized and marginalized by their male counterparts, while nonetheless being assigned with dangerous tasks (Radhakrishnan, Sen and Nihalani 2021; Natarajan 2014). This unique combination of power and precarity undergirds policing for women officers. Nonetheless, the resolute female officers depicted in the two shows under scrutiny present a slim possibility of respite for the state of Indian women in public spaces. By collating the everyday commutes of women against the patriarchal conditioning that ordains their vulnerability, both the web series in this essay unravel the politics of power and presence that govern women's movements in the city.

Delhi Crime features three police personnel Vartika Chaturvedi, DCP south Delhi (played by Shefali Shah), Vimla Bharadwaj, sub-Inspector and Juvenile Welfare Officer (played by Jaya Bhattacharya), Neeti Singh, IPS trainee (played by Rasika Duggal). The characters realistically portray the everyday de-glamorized officers who constantly navigate the city at odd hours in the practice of their vocation and occupy positions of power with relative ease. In the first episode, Chaturvedi instructs Neeti to oversee a check-point and firmly advises: "People should be scared of you. Stare into their eyes if they are doing something illegal, it will show on their face" (ep. 1). These tactics of intimidation work as Neeti confiscates an illegal consignment of ivory on her very first day. For the most part, Chaturvedi herself commands the respect and admiration of her team and traverses the city fearlessly, although she is often terrified for the safety of her daughter, Chandini.

Similarly, Vimala Bharadwaj accompanies her male counterparts in nabbing three of the accused, manipulating them into confessing to their crime. It is also her duty to safely escort the convicts from the jail to the courthouse amid dissenting crowds who are vying for their blood. Neeti is repeatedly sent to contain violent protesting mobs where the female officers are the "first line of defense" (ep. 4) against the mob. This unique role of female officers against the mob simultaneously evades and exploits the imaginaries of womanhood. Women in uniform, therefore, rely on the public morality of the mob which is less likely to attack a woman. Women officers are then empowered, assertive, and physically adept at handling possible altercations. Despite the insubordination or patronizing that they sometimes face from within the force, both *Delhi Crime* and *She* assert that in the city female officers often travel at odd hours, occupy deserted zones, and intimidate criminals.

She, likewise, presents a detailed account of the sexism, violence, and intimidation that a female cop may experience within the force itself. Bumika Pardeshi is selected for the mission due to her impeccable record of service at check-points where she is spotted by Jason Fernandes, her superior in the Narcotics Branch. Remarking on her confidence and body language, Fernandes reveals before Bhumi: "I first saw you at a barricade. You were standing in a corner, very quiet, I could see you were a powerful girl" (ep. 4). The docile and naïve Bhumi experiences empowerment through her profession to the extent that she exploits her agency by illegally raiding a hotel run by her sister Rupa's boyfriend to intimidate him. Later Rupa accosts Bhumi and accuses her of "benefitting from her uniform" (ep. 3). Rupa's jibe at the police uniform is significant, given how important "signs" of respectability are to women's experiences of the public space. The position of a constable affords Bhumi a power that she otherwise lacks in her social interactions. Therefore, the only time Bhumi is intimidated while in uniform is when Sasya makes sexually explicit comments about her during his interrogation (ep. 3). Here Fernandes has to reiterate: "You will have to be strong. As well as confident. How can you let him [Sasya] scare you? You should scare him, control him" (ep. 3). These observations demonstrate that unless deliberately put in situations that emphasize their femininity (as in *She*), the female officer's embodiment does not impede her profession. In fact, armed with the state insignia her forays into the city project more confidence and self-assuredness than the common woman. The common woman, in contrast, is always open to threats of violence, especially gendered violence, if she dares to venture uninhibited into the city. As the narrative takes a different turn in season two, Bhumi continues her nightly trysts and is predictably at the mercy of the vagaries of the road even as she is continually watched both by the police and the narcotics don she initiates a relationship with. *She* in both seasons then reiterates how Indian roads continue to be unsafe spaces for women negotiating them alone.

CONCLUSION

In sum: both *Delhi Crime* and *She* assert that women's insecurity in the public space does not stem from their physical weakness, dress, behavior, or comportment in itself. Rather they are an outcome of the assumptions of ideal womanhood that is superimposed on women by the society at large. While traversing public spaces most women try to mold their behavior into the dominant expectations and map the city in terms of their perceived vulnerability. However, repeated offenses demonstrate that women's dexterity to navigate public spaces is a personal defense mechanism and not a guarantee against violence. Hence, what needs to change is the cultural conversation regarding women's embodiment as well as their rights as free citizens. No doubt, the agitation sparked in the aftermath of the Nirbhaya case made sexual violence an acceptable topic in Indian television debates (Arya 62). This agitation has also made the advocacy of women's right to the public space a family conversation in many Indian homes where it was earlier viewed as a matter of rowdy activism. And yet, a misogynistic rape culture continues unabated in India; the numerous rape cases featured on various news platforms since 2012 attest to this unfortunate reality. Given the current scenario of gendered violence, then, this essay hopes to augment a discussion on the anxieties experienced by journeying women with the help of narratives from Indian media and popular culture.

REFERENCES

Ali, Arif, and Avinash Das, dirs. 2020. *She*. Window Seat Films, Inferno Pictures, Viacom18 Motion Pictures and Tipping Point Productions. www.netflix.com/watch/81187417?trackId=14170286.

Arya, Divya. 2015. "Reporting Sexual Violence in India: What Has Changed since the Delhi Gang Rape?" *Economic and Political Weekly* 50, no. 44: 57–66.

"Average 87 Rape Cases Daily, Over 7% Rise in Crimes Against Women in 2019: NCRB Data." 2019. *The Wire*, September 30. thewire.in/women/average-87-rape-cases-daily-over-7-rise-in-crimes-against-women-in-2019-ncrb-data.

Bhattacharyya, Rituparna. 2014. "Understanding the Spatialities of Sexual Assault Against Indian Women in India." *Gender, Place & Culture* 22, no. 9: 1340–1356. doi:10.1080/0966369x.2014.969684.

Brown C. Mackenzie, Nupur D. Agrawal. 2014. "The Rape That Woke Up India: Hindu Imagination and the Rape of Jyoti Singh Pandey." *Journal of Religion and Violence* 2, no. 2: 234–280.

Brownmiller, Susan. 1975. *Against Our Will: Men, Women and Rape*. New York: Ballantine Books.

Cahill, Ann J. 2001. *Rethinking Rape*. Ithaca: Cornell University Press.

Dhillon, Megha, and Suparna Bakaya. 2014. "Street Harassment: A Qualitative Study of the Experiences of Young Women in Delhi." *SAGE Open* (July). doi.org/10.1177/2158244014543786.

Dutta, Debolina, and Oishik Sircar. 2013. "India's Winter of Discontent: Some Feminist Dilemmas in the Wake of a Rape." *Feminist Studies* 39, no. 1: 293–306. www.jstor.org/stable/23719318.

Ganser, Alexandra. 2006. "On the Asphalt Frontier: American Women's Road Narratives, Spatiality, and Transgression." *Journal of International Women's Studies* 7, no. 4: 153–167. vc.bridgew.edu/jiws/vol7/iss4/10.

Gedalof, Irene. 1999. *Against Purity: Rethinking Identity with Indian and Western Feminisms*. New York: Routledge.

Hickey, Georgina. 2011. "From Civility to Self-Defense: Modern Advice to Women on the Privileges and Dangers of Public Space." *Women's Studies Quarterly* 39, no. 1/2: 77–94. www.jstor.org/stable/41290280.

"India Sees 88 Rape Cases a Day; Conviction Rate Below 30%." 2020. *Times of India*, October 7. timesofindia.indiatimes.com/articleshow/78526440.cms?utm_source=contentofinterest&utm_medium=text&utm_campaign=cppst

Jandial, Shraddha. 2017. "#IWillGoOut: Women across India Take to Streets, Demand Equal Right to Public Places." *India Today*, January 22. www.indiatoday.in/india/story/i-will-go-out-movement-bengaluru-mass-molestation-abu-azmi-956467-2017-01-22.

Khan, Sameera. 2018. "Claiming Parks One Nap at a Time." *The Hindu*, December 25. www.thehindu.com/life-and-style/motoring/meet-to-sleep-by-blank-noise-doesnt-just-trigger-conversations-about-women-space-and-fear-but-also-about-privilege-and-accessibility-of-open-spaces-in-a-city-to-its-citizens/article25828236.ece.

Kirby, Kathleen M. 1996. *Indifferent Boundaries: Spatial Concepts of Human Subjectivity*. New York: Guilford Press.

Manne, Kate. 2018. *Down Girl: The Logic of Misogyny*. New York: Oxford University Press.

Mehta, Richie, dir. 2019. *Delhi Crime*. Golden Karavan, Ivanhoe Productions, Film Karavan and Poor Man's Productions. www.netflix.com/watch/81076758?trackId=14170287.

Mendes, Kaitlynn. 2015. *SlutWalk: Feminism, Activism and Media*. Houndmills: Palgrave Macmillan.

Natarajan, Mangai. 2014. "Police Culture and the Integration of Women Officers in India." *International Journal of Police Science & Management* 16, no. 2 (June): 124–139. doi.org/10.1350/ijps.2014.16.2.33.

Phadke, Shilpa. 2010. *Gendered Usage of Public Spaces: A Case Study of Mumbai.* Background Report for "Addressing Gender-Based Violence in Public Spaces" Project, Centre for Equality and Inclusion, India (CEQUIN).

Phadke, Shilpa, Sameera Khan, and Shilpa Ranade. 2011. *Why Loiter?* New York: Penguin Books.

Pandey, Geeta. 2017. "#AintNoCinderella: Why Indian Women are Posting Midnight Photos." *BBC News*, August 9. www.bbc.com/news/40872788.

Radhakrishnan, Vignesh, Sumant Sen, and Jasmin Nihalani. 2021. "Women Make Up Only 12% of India's Police Force." *The Hindu*, August 29. www.thehindu.com/data/women-make-up-only-12-of-indias-police-force/article36152911.ece.

Satphale, Anup. 2017. "Why Loiter." *The Times of India*, January 18. timesofindia.indiatimes.com/city/pune/why-loiter/articleshow/56640582.cms.

Sen, Atreyee et al. 2019. "(En)Countering Sexual Violence in the Indian City." *Gender, Place & Culture* 27, no. 1: 1–12. doi:10.1080/0966369x.2019.1612856.

Shah, Svati P. 2014. *Street Corner Secrets*. Durham: Duke University Press.

Sharma, Radhika. 2019. "'Delhi Crime' Shot with Non-Judgemental Eye: Director Richie Mehta." *The Week*, March 22. www.theweek.in/news/entertainment/2019/03/22/delhi-crime-shot-non-judgmental-eye-richie-mehta.html.

Sinha, Mala, and Vishal Chauhan. 2013. "Deconstructing LajjA as a Marker of Indian Womanhood." *Psychology and Developing Societies* 25, no. 1 (March): 133–163. doi.org/10.1177/0971333613477314.

Thapan, Meenakshi. 2009. *Living the Body: Embodiment, Womanhood and Identity in Contemporary India*. New Delhi: Sage Publications India.

Valentine, Gill. 1989. "The Geography of Women's Fear." *Area* 21, no. 4: 385–390. www.jstor.org/stable/20000063.

Whitzman, Carolyn. 2013. "Women's Safety and Everyday Mobility." In *Building Inclusive Cities Women's Safety and the Right to the City*, edited by Carolyn Whitzman, Crystal Legacy, Caroline Andrew, Fran Klodawsky, Margaret Shaw and Kalpana Viswanath, 35–52. New York: Routledge.

NOTES

1. *Lajja* may be defined as a sense of civility under which one must "[k]now one's rightful place in society; to conduct oneself in a becoming manner; to be conscious of one's duties and responsibilities; to persevere in performance of social role obligations; to be shy, modest, deferential; and not encroach upon prerogatives of others" (Sinha and Chauhan 2013, 34).

2. *#IWillGoOut* was a nationwide march that was carried out on January 21, 2017 in prominent cities like Bengaluru, Delhi, Pune, Chennai, Mumbai, Kolkata, Hyderabad, Jaipur, Bhopal, Kochi, among others, following an incident of mass molestation of women on New Year's eve in Bengaluru (Jandial 2017). *#WhyLoiter* was a Mumbai based movement which derives its name from a book by Sameera Khan, Shilpa Phadke, and Shilpa Ranade which argued for women's right to public spaces. Under

the movement, women gathered in groups for nightly strolls along prominent streets in Mumbai (Satphale 2017). *Meet to Sleep* began in 2014 with women gathering in public parks for short naps on the grass. The movement aimed at claiming public spaces for women (Khan 2018). *Pinjra Tod* (break the cage) was a student led movement that began in 2015 in Delhi against night curfews imposed by PG accommodation and University campuses on women citing safety reasons. *#AintnoCinderella* was an online movement which began after a stalking incident in Chandigarh where the victim was blamed for driving alone in the city past midnight. As a response women posted their pictures of themselves in public spaces at night with the hashtag *Aintno-Cinderella* (Pandey 2017).

PART V

Struggle for Survival

Working Women and Pitfalls of Indian Roads

Chapter 10

Working Night Shifts, Traversing Neoliberal Roads

Spatial-Temporal Confluence and the Male Gaze

Sucharita Sen

It was exactly midnight. Soumita[1] stepped out of a fourteen-storeyed building in Sector V, Kolkata's Information Technology hub which houses most of the city's BPO (Business Process Outsourcing) industry. India's third metropolitan city was then reeling under a harsh winter, not uncommon for a mid-December night. It was not the usual time for Soumita to leave her office. But a phone call, minutes ago, demanded an early departure. Her ailing father had been hospitalized. The company vehicle would be available, but only five hours later. A deserted street sent a shiver down her spine, more from the ambience of the nightscape than the freezing temperatures. Her phone vibrated a couple of times with signals of low battery before finally running out. The Uber App had notified her that a Swift Dzire was three minutes from the pick-up point. Instead, came a Hyundai. It sped past, stopped and returned to halt in front of her. Inside the car were four men, one of them at the steering. Two men, with their intoxicated voices, offered her a ride. She paced toward her office-building to find no trace of the on-duty security guard. The car closely followed. As it overtook her, three men came out, nearly forcing her into the car. In a moment of discretion, she kicked one of them. Endeavors to free herself were to no avail when the sudden honking of another car disrupted the scuffle. At the insistence of their counterpart at the driving seat, the three men hopped into the car and hurriedly drove away. The honking car was the taxi Soumita had booked. Once in the car, the driver advised her, "Good girls should stay at home during the night."[2]

Narrating her experience, the twenty-nine-year-old call center employee shuddered. Her salary from her call center job sustained her family. Working night shifts necessitated stepping into the streets at odd hours, either in company vehicles or on public transport. It was intimidating. Soumita had commenced the job a month after the 2012 Delhi gang-rape incident had invited worldwide criticism and compassion regarding Indian women's safety in public spaces.[3] Under extreme economic crisis, her parents had reluctantly acquiesced in her decision to accept an offer of employment in the call center. Thereafter, marriage prospects looked bleak. Prospective in-laws were unwilling to accept a daughter-in-law who worked night shifts.

At the heart of patriarchal societies is the ideological commitment to the public-private divide. Housekeeping is ideally considered as the duty of a woman, and the home is believed to be the appropriate space for her existence. This dichotomy was particularly conspicuous in the testimonies of the perpetrators and their defendants in the Delhi gang-rape case. During her documentary-interview, British filmmaker Leslee Udwin (2013) was dismayed at the complete lack of regret among the perpetrators of a crime which had shaken the "collective conscience" of the country, tarnished India's global image and reinforced the national capital's ill-reputation, which, according to recent government reports, tops the list of unsafe places for women (Ministry of Home Affairs 2021). That the rape-survivor was "roaming" around at night, claimed one of the rapists, was an adequate testimony of her being in possession of a questionable moral character. An utterly shocked Udwin took time to swallow the offender's gruesome remark that such girls who transgressed their traditional duties of housekeeping should be taught a lesson. Equally obnoxious were the comments of the defense lawyer who insisted that it was imperative for a girl to return home before dusk and friendship between opposite genders was tabooed (BBC News 2015). The comments triggered nation-wide public outrage. Cutting across any caste-class divide, such patriarchal views are nearly universal in India. What problematizes the spatial dichotomy of the home and the public space are the temporal rules of patriarchy. By patriarchal standards where girls should return home by sunset, the rape-survivor's presence at a Delhi bus stop at night was considered morally wrong.

Violence against women in India has a long history, regardless of whether it is performed in the domestic sphere or the public space. However, despite enduring subjugation, women's preoccupation with traditional works of home-management have undergone a change. This has particularly been facilitated by capitalism, more so with the emergence of globalization and a market-driven economy. India's women increasingly stepped out into the neoliberal public spaces, embracing jobs which violated both spatial and temporal patriarchal restrictions. Feminist literature has focused on the gendered nature of roads, where women's safety is often jeopardized. Gender, Judith Butler (1990) argues, is an act of performance. Men and women perform and enact the socially constructed attributes of gender. Physically embodied are the notions and virtues of masculinity and femineity. Heteropatriarchy determines the roles for each gender, disciplines bodies, and normatively prescribe appropriate behavior in public spaces (Hyams 2003). The body is, then, the locus of production and performance of gender. The delimitation of spaces, public for men and the home for women, reinforces the performance of gendered roles. In a patriarchal society, men are correspondingly less regimented in their mobility than women (Thomas 2005).

As Doreen Massey (1994) and Linda McDowell (1999) have argued, spaces are governed by patriarchal relations of power which excludes women. The city space, argues Susan Reddick (1996, 135), has always been gendered in a way which have tended to exclude women from the public space realm, or include them only in certain patriarchally "scripted" roles. In the context of India, discussions of women's security in public masculine spaces have largely converged into a debate which concludes that it is in the safety of the women that they be kept away from such spaces. Arguably, it is a victory of patriarchal conventions. In an urge to make public spaces more inclusive, Shilpa Phadke (2013, 50) makes a case for a woman's right to step out into the streets, shifting the discourse from women's safety to women's rights. Elsewhere, Phadke has argued that women performed acts of mobility by conforming to socially ascribed codes of dress and behavior. "Veiling," for instance, was a part of patriarchal restrictions, since a woman's body is viewed as a sexual object which can potentially be violated. Nevertheless, veiling did not reduce acts of sexual violence (Phadke 2005). Seen in this light, a woman's body is not just a site for the performance of feminine values, but also a site for the execution of masculine power. Even more than the actual occurrence of crime, it is the fear of being exposed to possible violence which causally restricts women's entry into the masculine public spaces (Stanko 1990; Vishwanath and Mehrotra 2007).

However, it is not only the spatial aspect that curtails women's freedom. Venturing into male spaces in nocturnal hours aggravates women's vulnerability to the male gaze. This essay argues that the obtrusive confluence of space and time in India's neoliberal roads pose a systematic obstruction to women empowerment and reinforces the traditional conventions of patriarchy. Non-traditional jobs like those in India's BPO sector, which will be the focus of this paper, have forced women to venture into the streets at night. However, the nature of such employment and night shifts constantly harbingers stigma and discomfort both at home and in the public spaces. Even more, in an attempt to remedy the vulnerability of women and ensure their safety in the night space, the BPO industry has, time and again, reinforced patriarchal values and conventions.

IN TRANSIT AT THE INTERIM JOB: FLOATING EMPLOYEES IN INDIA'S BPO INDUSTRY

When a customer in New York dials a toll-free number to inquire into the status of a flight, little could they be aware that the call is being routed to a call center, somewhere half a mile across the world. In the wake of globalization, the growth of the information and communication technology (ICT) industry received an exponential surge. This, in turn, led to the growth of the BPO sector, which harnessed the extreme potential of a low-cost English-speaking pool of domestic labor (Ramesh 2004). Call centers are a major subcategory of the BPO sector which specializes in "voice-based services" (Tara and Ilavarasan 2009).

One striking feature of this sector is the army of women employees. Women working in shifts at odd hours of the night is a relatively new phenomenon in the socio-economic scenario in India (Jain 1975; Desai 1977). Although call centers in India also serve domestic firms, they mainly cater to clients from countries like the U. K. and the U. S. A (Singh 2007). Due to the different time-zones, call center jobs are performed primarily at night. Prior to the advent of call centers, sectors like nursing and the hospitality industry also had night shift work. But the bulk of the work was carried out during the day. In contrast, call center jobs begin in the late hours of the evening and continues till early morning (Tara and Ilavarasan 2009).

As stated earlier, call centers brought a phenomenal change in the nature of employment in India's service sector. Emblematic of the neoliberal reforms which India had embraced, call centers breached national boundaries and bore the imprint of a globalized world. There has been a significant number of empirical studies on the growth and impact of call centers in India. Such works have revolved around business research, focusing on information systems, economic factors and human resource management, as well as the globalization and importance of English language in the BPO industry (Gilmore 2001; Bolton 2010). Yet another fascinating area of research around call centers had focused on the question of gender. Such studies spiraled after a twenty-four-year-old call center employee of Hewlett Packard in Bangalore was raped in a car by a man who had disguised himself as her driver. Almost instantaneously, the question of the safety of women commuting to and from work at night came to the forefront. Reena Patel (2010) and Cari C. Kapur (2010) independently contend that the Bangalore incident exposed the challenges of night shifts in patriarchal India. The Bangalore incident terrorized many women and amplified the anxieties of parents about the sending their daughters to work in call centers (Tara and Ilavarasan 2009). In a society where intermingling between genders before marriage has been traditionally frowned upon, the nature of call center jobs demanding that men and women work together throughout the night has largely remained unacceptable (Kapur 2010).

However, in their study, Preeti Singh and Anu Pandey (2005) found that call center jobs were often sought after. These jobs did not require the employee to have a high qualification, yet providing a good environment to work in, decent emoluments and financial incentives, meals and refreshments. Other jobs did not permit the entry of employees with such minimum education, at such attractive perks. Still, argues Tara and Ilavasaran (2009), such jobs are extremely transitory in nature. Neither men nor women desire to remain in this job for a long time. Women working in night shifts are not seen as prospective candidates in a matrimonial alliance. In such cases, a call center job is hardly anything more than an interim job in the period of time between completion of basic studies and finding a suitable groom. Singh and Pandey's 2005 study found that ninety-two percent of the women employees in the call centers were unmarried. McMillian's study, a year later in 2006, showed that eighty-one percent of the women were unmarried. For men, call center jobs are a means of savings to further a higher education, ultimately increasing the prospect of a better job (Tara and Ilavarasan 2009; Sen 2020).

While there is no dearth of empirical studies in the field,[4] there is a conspicuous lack of insights into the intersection of time and space when it comes to call center jobs in India, and how this confluence problematizes women's journey in the streets. This paper aims to contribute to this existing gap by exploring call center employees' travel experiences at night. By examining select media reports of violence against call center women workers across Indian cities, combined with personal interviews of one hundred call center employees in Kolkata, the essay builds up on the discourse of patriarchal violence in neoliberal roads. Data for the survey was collected in Kolkata's Sector V. The initial ten respondents were selected through the methods of purposive sampling. Using the snowball sampling method, I sought assistance from these ten respondents in selecting other potential respondents. Answers were gathered through one-hour interviews where structured, unstructured and semi-structured questions were administered to the interviewees. All the respondents were residents of Kolkata, had an undergraduate degree and came from middle-class backgrounds. While presenting the analysis, all names of the respondents have been changed to maintain strict anonymity. Around ninety percent of the respondents were unmarried, five percent married, and the remaining meagre section had decided to quit their jobs, as their marriage had already been scheduled. This chapter draws upon the experiences of these women's uneasy exposure to the male gaze when they commuted to and from workplace late at night or in the early hours of the day. In the wake of globalization and neoliberal reforms, as India's newly empowered women ventured into the city's night space, they endured a precarious gaze symbolic of patriarchal India's objectification of the female sex.

THE NEW INDIAN WOMAN IN A NEOLIBERAL WORLD: PATRIARCHAL INDIA'S READJUSTMENT TO GLOBALIZATION

In a seminal work, Anne McClintock (1994, 353) has argued that all nations depended on "powerful constructions of gender." McClintock was arguing her case in a colonial context. Post-millennial India has continued to perpetuate similar ideological undertones. The idea of the nation, constructed within a heteronormative framework, imposes the functional essence of women as nurturers and entrusts men with the foremost duty of protecting territory and their women (Oza 2006, 7). By the archetypal gender roles, women are considered as the repositories of culture, a source of both temptations and transgressions. With India's globalization, such constructs and concerns escalated.

The fragile borders and a waning sovereignty altered socio-economic structures in unprecedented ways. Largely reeling under the invasive forces of global capital and neoliberal financial organizations, India desperately attempted to redefine its culture by the moral policing of its women. Globalized India has relocated its control over national identity by reifying sexual and gender identities (Oza 2006). Neoliberal economic and political reforms revolutionized and restructured the market and drew women into spaces of the labor and service sectors, traditionally conceived as masculine. In myriad ways, neoliberalism appeared as an emancipator of women. However, not always did the market operate against the "interests of women" (Elson 1992). Yet, this did not in any way undermine neoliberalism's affinity toward reinforcing conservativism which reproduced the traditional notions of women's work within the family (Molyneux 2008).

The emerging idea of "The New Indian Woman," feminists argue, mirrors this neoliberal ideology. Citing the example of the Hindu Right, India's radical neoliberal avatar, Nivedita Menon (2011) argued that the orthodox patriarchal contentions of the Hindu right have, in no way, been invaded by its gender mobilization. The right wing mobilized women, carefully leaving familial and communitarian ties undisturbed. For example, women came to the forefront within the *Sangh Parivar*, a family unit, which as an institution has largely been patriarchal in India. In a similar vein, Uma Chakravarty

(2008) argues that women's increased entry into public spaces have not unnerved the men, as long as they could be convinced that such changes in existing social structures did not challenge or threaten the unequal power relations within the family. Patriarchy predates capitalism and overshadows neoliberalism, paving the way for what Beatrix Campbell (2014) calls "neoliberal, neo-patriarchy." This, insists Campbell, is a particular form of public gender regime in which inequality in social relationships between men and women are persistently championed and fueled by the political agenda of neoliberalism. The new Indian woman emerges as a gendered subject, only as much subjugated as is necessary for patriarchy to continuously sustain itself, and only as much liberated as is necessary to buttress the apparently emancipatory image of patriarchal neoliberalism.

The new Indian neoliberal woman is liberal, confident, smart, modern and rational. However, she remains culturally rooted. She is to be guarded against unwanted westernization since she is the custodian of Indian culture. An advertisement in SimplyMarry.com, an Indian matrimonial website, for example, epitomizes this idea of the new woman showing a "young woman wearing a South Indian sari and other traditional accessories, such as flowers in her hair, a *bindi* on her forehead, and jewelry. At the same time, she wears a headset, holds a phone in her hand, and is sitting in front of a laptop" (Titzman 2013, 79).

In 2002, *India Today* projected a similar advertisement of a woman on its cover page, wearing a headset with a microphone. "Call Centres, Housekeepers to the World: India's Fastest Growing Industry Employs Millions and Earns Billions," so ran the headlines of the advertisement, yet another glaring paradox of the neoliberal project. Neoliberalism exposed the new modern woman to the male gaze, objectified femineity and made her an item of consumerism. This is, as Comaroff and Comaroff (2001, 8) argued, the "second coming of capitalism in the form of consumerism." In the case of such advertisements, while the notion of modernity is unequivocally emphasized, the underlying tone of traditional values and roles for women, exhibited either through her attire or the use of words like "housekeeping" remain conspicuous. As Noam Chomsky (2011) has commented, neoliberalism not only operates as an economic system, but also as a cultural system.

A state-market-society nexus posed new challenges to the neoliberal woman. The neoliberal market dragged women out of their conventional spaces of home, without addressing the structural inequalities of gender. Call centers were not only fraught with existing inequalities, but they also generated newly-created injustices.[5] Added to this, the neoliberal state was largely reluctant to remedy the existing gender imbalances, for it itself was playing its role of producing women as gendered subjects. The public space already ripe for the objectification and exploitation of women. Amendments to the Factories Act, 1948 enabled the market to employ women beyond the daytime office hours.

The call center employee, who emerged as a representative of a new globalized and modernized woman thus ventured into the labor market at night. As Patel argues, the profane and polluting space of the street at night has the potential to contaminate a woman's body. Since the honor of the family and in a larger discourse, the honor of the nation is located in the sexual purity of a woman, this "nightscape" is seen as being detrimental to women's security. The nocturnal road is, by and large, a masculine space from which the woman ought to be shielded (Patel 2010).

TRAVERSING MASCULINE SPACES, BREACHING PATRIARCHAL FRONTIERS: THE MALE GAZE AND WOMEN'S NOCTURNAL EXPERIENCES ON NEOLIBERAL ROADS

In 2004, the Bangalore rape incident glaringly exposed the issue of women's security in public spaces at night. It was only a debut to the series of such cases which would follow suit. Less than a decade since then, the nightmare of violence against women returned, this time with the gang rape of another call center employee in a pick-up truck in Delhi (BBC News 2014). All call center employees enjoy free pick-up and drop-off services, arranged by the company. However, as Tara and Ilavarasan (2009) have shown, often the company vehicles do not drop employees at their doorstep, but at a location more convenient for the larger group of passengers. In the Delhi case, the young woman was abducted and raped by five men in the early hours of the day after an office cab dropped her off near her home (BBC News 2014).

As India's metropolitan cities continued to grow and employ women in night shifts, companies themselves were entrusted with the duties of securing the safety of women. Women's entry into the public space was unwanted yet could not be restricted. But this has not been India's only claim to some of the seminal paradoxes it features. In tune with the neoliberal rhetoric, in society's best interest public resources were used to facilitate and protect private investors. Off-shore outsourcing expanded the labor market and increased employability, with the booming private sector juxtaposed against sluggish public sector opportunities. Again, neoliberalism with its increased prospects of migration, argues Himani Banerji (2016, 15) forced the growth of slums, poverty, crime, violence and dehumanizing conditions of livelihood. At the same time, neoliberal policies also envisaged a new way to envision urban areas. In the early 1980s, for example, the "broken-window theory" inaugurated debates both in social science and the public sphere in the United

States. Certain visible signs of crime like anti-social behavior and civil disorder created an urban environment that stimulated disorder by aggravating and escalating into more serious crimes. Thus, was recommended moral and community policing (Kelling and Wilson 1982).

But the theory and its implementations in U.S. cities had wider implications. Such policies, Marine Dasse (2019) argued, in their bid to secure the streets was often tantamount to social and spatial exclusion which jeopardized civil liberties. In New York, for example, policies which drew upon the broken-window theory entailed getting rid of the undesirables (the homeless and other people perceived as problems) who tarnished the image of the public spaces, particularly the urban streets. In the Indian context, Phadke's (2013) research points to a similar kind of social exclusion of women to secure them and also check the ruinous image of India's public space as being dangerous to women. To prevent crimes, criminals were not policed, but women who could potentially become the victims were increasingly policed. In a country where the morality of rape survivors and women working night shifts is questioned, hegemonizing and controlling the women by monopolizing public roads as masculine realms is hardly arduous. The safety of women in public spaces was guaranteed by segregating their spaces from those of the men. This included securing separate seating arrangements for the women in public transport, running special trains for them and most importantly, separate washrooms and changing rooms.

However, delineating spaces (given that complete exclusion of women was not feasible) were not enough to guarantee the safety of women who worked night shifts. Crimes were being reported on the streets, more on vehicles, while commuting to and from the workplace. Thus came a new legislation making it compulsory for a male colleague to accompany women in company vehicles. In addition, no woman employee was to be dropped off last or picked up first. In many ways, this was a gross denial of the women's right to a safe environment. Instead, it was a neoliberal reinforcement of patriarchal dichotomies where in a public space, the presence of a male cohort was deemed crucial to guarantee the protection of women. This was also the reiteration of the men's responsibility to protect the women. In the Delhi gang-rape case, for instance, the trials saw the defense lawyers unscrupulously blaming the survivor's fiancé for failing to protect her.

Meanwhile, as newspaper headlines were screaming to wake the country's women from the slumber of being tolerant to patriarchal intolerance, a twenty-four-year-old employee of Convergys BPO was abducted at gun-point by two men on the Delhi-Gurgaon Expressway. Gang-raped in the moving car, and later dumped in Gurgaon, the incident came as a horrific reminder of the vulnerability of women in the public spaces at night (Kumar 2013). In yet another incident, a twenty-two-year-old BPO employee in Bangalore,

India's IT hub and response to the Silicon Valley, was raped in a minibus (*The Hindustan Times* 2015). Two years later, a twenty-one-year-old call center employee was gang-raped by an auto driver and his accomplice in Chandigarh. Around 8 pm, she had hired an auto to go home from work (India.com 2016).[6]

My own survey points to call center women's unwelcoming prospects and unenviable experiences. While working night shifts, male employees took short recesses from work and visited nearby tea stalls. Female employees refused to even accompany them, much less attempting to venture out alone. Incidents of women employees being recipients of catcalling from stray bikers at the tea stall were enough to act as deterrents. Even at the workplace, the cubicle within the four walls of the office appeared comparatively safer to women than the public space of the roadside stall. In their neighborhoods, warding off disrespectful advances from errant men was a recurrent challenge. As domestic problems increased on account of her night shifts, one married employee had decided to resign from her job. Suhasini's husband and her in-laws were outraged by her working hours, which kept her away from home at night.

Even more conspicuous was the negative attitude of taxi drivers. Antara had to wait for nearly five hours before she could avail the company vehicle. When she chose to return home on public transport, experiences were bitter. Drivers frequently passed remarks on "what she was doing outside her house so late in the night." As she relaxed in the taxi after a twelve-hour shift, she heard the driver mumbling about how "women who transgressed the boundaries of home at night and loitered in the streets were immoral."[7] Taunted for her presence in the public space of the street at night, Antara soon gave up the idea of availing public transport. Instead, she preferred to wait for her company vehicle, even if it was less convenient. Many women employees were being compelled by their families to resign from their job as it was diminishing their prospects of finding a suitable groom (Sen 2020). Less qualified girls were then left to decide between economic empowerment or a good matrimonial alliance. Still others speculated on searching for a lower paid teaching job, since that was seen as a more desirable occupation for girls.

Few employees were terrified of walking to their homes after their company vehicle dropped them off at a walkable distance from their doors. Many waited in office till late morning, before availing public transport when the streets were crowded enough. After she had commenced employment at a BPO, Nandita's brother escorted her from her door to the company car, which picked her up from the entrance to the narrow lane on which her house was located. This tendency of avoiding certain routes at night or asking a male relative or friend to accompany a woman reflects a concerted effort to comply to patriarchal impositions. Women viewed themselves as imposters in the night space and preferred to adapt themselves to social limitations.

Feminist geographers have constantly urged that the male gaze in the public space largely generated a sense of fear. This fear which women experience is a product of systematic structural violence (Pain 2001). Such threatening situations also serve as grotesque reminders of women's vulnerability in public spaces, and assist in restricting women to the household, particularly at night (Koskela1997; Rodó de Zárate, 2014).[8] Gendered violence in the streets or the threat of harassment is then, as stated earlier, an exertion of patriarchal power and masculine ownership of a monopolized public space. Here, it is worth reiterating the policies of the neoliberal state to contain violence against women in nocturnal streets. As mentioned earlier, regulations like no first pick-up or last drop-off of the women employees is suggestive of the state's endorsement of the vulnerability of women in such spaces. Women will be safer in the public space, only when accompanied by men. Since women's safety is jeopardized in such spaces, her mobility needs to be restricted and monitored. In myriad ways, the male gaze on nocturnal streets thus impaired women's journey. From bus stops to taxis, women have constantly been the recipients of verbal and physical abuse, eve-teasing and sexual harassment.

CONCLUSION

In the late hours of a February night, Geetanjali sat in her company vehicle awaiting the arrival of her male cohort. As Abhrajit walked in, the car sped off. It was Geetanjali's last "working night" at her office. Geetanjali and Abhrajit were getting married. Geetanjali's parents were relieved. Abhrajit's parents were determined. Abhrajit would continue with his night shift. Geetanjali should resign. So was settled a month before their marriage. Not that Geetanjali was unhappy. Her marriage was an escape from the daily scrutiny of her neighbors. After the deadly incident of eve-teasing on her doorstep by a group of ruffians in the "not-so-safe" neighborhood, Geetanjali had enough. Her night-shifts raised eyebrows. Her character did not have to face the litmus test; that it was dubious was a forgone conclusion. So were the fates of many call center employees who were compelled to venture into the night space by virtue of their jobs. Neighbors speculated on the nature of their work; night work for women is equated with possessing an immoral character.

This essay has thus explored the convergence of space and time which systematically restricts the mobility of women by exposing her to the male gaze. As an impediment to women's empowerment, the spatial-temporal intersectionality actively generates a sense of fear. In patriarchal neoliberal roads, women's journeys are challenging since empowerment and subjugation merge to complicate the issue of women's safety. Empowerment pulls them out of home into the streets at night, necessitated by emerging forms of work in a neoliberal market. At the same time, patriarchal limitations crystallize in neoliberal roads and contests women's empowerment. Women workforce in call centers is one of the prime victims of a paradoxical empowerment, where gendered roads, patriarchal violence and societal surveillance curtails women's freedom, jeopardizes her safety and forbids the exercise of her rights.

ACKNOWLEDGMENT

Part of this essay originates from the survey I had conducted as part of my M.A. dissertation at Presidency University, Kolkata. I wish to thank all my professors at Presidency University, Kolkata, particularly Madhura Shamkant Damle, Abdus Samad Gayen, Zaad Mahmood, Pradip Basu and Nandalal Chakraborty for their kind assistance. I also remain indebted to Sekhar Bandyopadhyay, my PhD supervisor at Victoria University of Wellington, for constantly guiding me in my research and writing.

REFERENCES

Banerji, Himani. 2016. "Patriarchy in an Era of Neoliberalism: The Case of India." *Social Scientist* 44 (3): 3–27.

Basu, Kaushik, ed. 2007. *The Oxford Companion to Economics in India*. New Delhi: Oxford University Press.

BBC. 2013. "Delhi Gang Rape: Four Sentenced to Death." *BBC News*, September 13. www.bbc.com/news/world-asia-india-24078339.

BBC. 2014. "Delhi Call Centre Worker Gang Rape: Five Convicted." *BBC News*, October 14. www.bbc.com/news/world-asia-india-29611483.

BBC. 2015. "Delhi Rapist Says Victim Shouldn't Have Fought Back." *BBC News*, March 3. www.bbc.com/news/magazine-31698154.

Bolton, Kingsley. 2010. "'Thank You for Calling': Asian Englishes and 'Native-Like' Performance in Asian Call Centres." In *The Routledge Handbook of World Englishes*, edited by Andy Kirkpatrick, 550–564. London: Routledge.

Bradley, Tasmin. 2017. *Gender, Oppression and the Politics of Neoliberalism*. London: I.B. Tauris.

Butler, Judith. 1990. *Gender Trouble: Feminism and the Subversion of Identity*. New York: Routledge.

Campbell, Beatrix. 2014. "Why We Need a New Woman's Revolution." *The Guardian*, May 25, 2014. www.theguardian.com/commentisfree/2014/may/25/we-need-new-womens-revolution.

Chakravarty, Uma. 2008. "Beyond the Mantra of Empowerment: Time to Return to Poverty, Violence and Struggle." *IDS Bulletin* 39 (6): 10–17.

Chauhan, Chanchal. 2016. "Call Centre Employee Gang-Raped: 4 Years after Nirbhaya Incident, How Safe Are Women in India?" *India.com*, December 16, 2016. www.india.com/news/call-centre-employee-gang-raped-4-years-after-nirbhaya-incident-how-safe-are-women-in-india-1708642/.

Chomsky, Noam. 2011. *How the World Works*. London: Penguin.

Comaroff, Jean and John L. Comaroff. 2001. "Millennial Capitalism: First Thoughts on a Second Coming." In *Millennial Capitalism and the Culture of Neoliberalism*, edited by Jean Comaroff and John L. Comaroff, 1–58. Durham: Duke University Press.

Dassé, Marine. 2019. "The Neoliberalization of Public Spaces and the Infringement of Civil Liberties: The Case of the Safer Cities Initiative in Los Angeles." *ANGLES: New Perspectives on the Anglophone World*, 8.

Desai, Neera. 1977. *Women in Modern India*. Bombay: Vora and Co.

Elson, Diane. 1992. "Male Bias in Structural Adjustment." In *Women and Adjustment Policies in the Third World*, edited by H. Afshar and C. Dennis, 46–68. London: Macmillan.

Gilmore, Audrey. 2001. "Call Centre Management: Is Service Quality a Priority?" *Managing Service Quality* 11 (3): 53–119.

Hyams, Melissa. 2003. "Adolescent Latina Body Spaces: Making Homegirls, Homebodies and Homeplaces." *Antipode: A Radical Journal of Geography* 35 (3): 536–558.

Jain, D. 1975. *Indian Women*. New Delhi: Ministry of Information and Broadcasting, Publication Division.

Kapur, Cari C. 2010. "Rethinking Courtship, Marriage and Divorce in an Indian Call Centre." In *Everyday Life in South Asia*, edited by Diane P. Mines and Sarah Lamb, 50–61. Bloomington: Indiana University Press.

Kelling, George L. and James Q. Wilson. 1982. "Broken Windows: The Police and Neighbourhood Safety." *The Atlantic*, March. www.theatlantic.com/magazine/archive/1982/03/broken-windows/304465/.

Koskela, Hille. 1997. "'Bold Walk and Breakings': Women's Spatial Confidence versus Fear of Violence." *Gender, Place and Culture: A Journal of Feminist Geography* 4 (3): 301–320.

Kumar, Ajay. 2013. "Another Rape in Delhi-NCR: Call Centre Employee Abducted, Gangraped in Gurgaon." *India Today*, March 7. www.indiatoday.in/india/north/story/gangrape-in-moving-car-call-centre-employee-abducted-in-gurgaon-155543-2013-03-07.

Massey, Doreen. 1994. *Space, Race and Gender*. Minneapolis: University of Minnesota Press.

McClintock, Ann. 1994. *Imperial Leather: Race, Gender, and Sexuality in the Colonial Contest*. New York: Routledge.

McDowell, Linda. 1999. *Gender, Identity, and Place: Understanding Feminist Geographies*. Minneapolis: University of Minnesota Press.

McMillin, Divya C. 2006. "Outsourcing Identities: Call Centres and Cultural Transformation in India." *Economic and Political Weekly* 41 (3): 235–241.

Menon, Nivedita, ed. 2011. *Gender and Politics in India*. New Delhi: Oxford University Press.

Molyneux, Maxine. 2008. "'The 'Neoliberal Turn' and the New Social Policy in Latin America: How Neoliberal, How New?" *Development and Change* 39 (5): 775–797.

Oza, Rupal. 2006. *The Making of Neoliberal India: Nationalism, Gender and the Paradoxes of Globalization*. New York: Routledge.

Pain, Rachel. 2001. "Gender, Race and Fear in the City." *Urban Studies* 38 (5–6): 899–913.

Patel, Reena. 2010. *Working the Night Shift: Women in India's Call Centre Industry*. Stanford: Stanford University Press.

Phadke, Shilpa. 2005. "'You Can Be Lonely in a Crowd': The Production of Safety in Mumbai." *Indian Journal of Gender Studies* 12 (1): 41–62.

Phadke, Shilpa. 2013. "Unfriendly Bodies, Hostile Cities: Reflections on Loitering and Gendered Public Space." *Economic and Political Weekly* 48 (39): 50–59.

Ramesh, Babu P. 2004. "Cyber Coolies in BPO: Insecurities and Vulnerabilities of Non-Standard Work." *Economic and Political Weekly* 39 (5): 492–497.

Ruddick, Susan. 1996. "Constructing Difference in Public Spaces: Race, Class and Gender as Interlocking Systems." *Urban* Geography 17 (2): 131–152.

Sen, Sucharita. 2020. "Tradition-Technology Wedlock: The Paradoxical Modernisation of Matrimony." *South Asian Survey* 27 (2): 172–190.

Singh, Preeti and Anu Pandey. 2005. "Women in Call Centres." *Economic and Political Weekly* 40 (7): 684–688.

Stanko, Elizabeth A. 1990. *Everyday Violence: Women's and Men's Experience of Personal Danger*. London: Pandora.

Tara, Shelley and Vigneswara Ilavarasan. 2009. "'I Would Not Have Been Working Here!': Parental Support to Unmarried Daughters as Call Centre Agents in India." *Gender, Technology and Development* 13 (3): 385–406.

The Hindustan Times. 2015. "Bengaluru Police Arrest 2 Men in BPO Employee Minibus Rape Case." *The Hindustan Times*, October 6, 2015. www.hindustantimes.com/india/call-centre-employee-gang-raped-in-bangalore/story-hhS7Y8fJub34Sy6WyhwXfO.html.

Thomas, Mary E. 2005. "Girls, Consumption Space and the Contradictions of Hanging Out in the City." *Social and Cultural Geography* 6(4): 587–605.

Titzman, Fritz Marie. 2013. "Changing Patterns of Matchmaking: The Indian Online Matrimonial Market." *Asian Journal of Women Studies* 19 (4): 64–94.

Viswanath, Kalpana and Surabhi Tandon Mehrotra. 2007. "'Shall We Go Out?' Women's Safety in Public Spaces in Delhi." *Economic and Political Weekly* 42 (17): 1542–1548.

Zárate, Maria Rodó de. 2014. "Managing Fear in Public Space: Young Feminists' Intersectional Experiences Through Participatory Action Research." *Les cahiers du CEDREF [Online]* 21.

NOTES

1. All names have been changed while discussing the findings. The field data was collected in Kolkata, India during November–January 2016.
2. Cited and translated (mine) from interview dated December 17, 2016.
3. On December 16, 2012, a young paramedical student (later titled *Nirbhaya* by the Indian media) was raped, beaten and tortured in an off-duty charter bus in Delhi. After the crime, the woman and her fiancé were thrown out of the bus. Nirbhaya succumbed to fatal injuries.
4. The empirical studies, as discussed, have mainly focussed on surveys among the call-centres in North Indian cities like Delhi and Gurgaon, Western Indian cities like Mumbai and South Indian cities like Bangalore. There have however been negligible studies on the ballooning call centre industry in Kolkata. This paper partly draws upon the survey conducted among female employees in Kolkata's BPO sector.
5. Research on the neoliberal market and labour relations have focussed on women as a provider of cheap labour, low pay and workplace harassments, coupled with increased vulnerability of women at home as traditional family relations have been challenged by the women's new working status and their financial independence. See Tasmin Bradley, *Gender, Oppression and the Politics of Neoliberalism* (London: I.B. Tauris, 2017).
6. "Call Centre Employee Gang-Raped: 4 Years after Nirbhaya Incident, How Safe Are Women in India?" *India.com*, December 16. Accessed on July 27, 2021. www.india.com/news/call-centre-employee-gang-raped-4-years-after-nirbhaya-incident-how-safe-are-women-in-india-1708642/.
7. Cited and translated (mine) from interview dated December 21, 2016.
8. See Hille Koskela, "'Bold Walk and Breakings': Women's Spatial Confidence versus Fear of Violence," *Gender, Place and Culture: A Journal of Feminist Geography* 4, no. 3 (1997): 301–320. See also Maria Rodó de Zárate, "Managing Fear in Public Space: Young Feminists' Intersectional Experiences Through Participatory Action Research," *Les cahiers du CEDREF [Online]*, 21 (2014).

Chapter 11

Women Journalists Negotiating Space in India's "Small" Cities

Ranu Tomar

How do we understand the city? The dwellers of a particular city are the best resource to know more about a city. As Shilpa Phadke (2005) writes, "Life in a city has often been described as filled with ambiguity, replete with a sense of possible threat and the inevitable negotiation of risk" (43). Thus, the presence of women journalists in a city and their interaction with city spaces and surroundings are significant aspects of their experiences. It is these experiences, obtained through personal interviews with respondents, which have been critically discussed in this chapter[1]. Accordingly, this chapter explores the experiences of women journalists[2] in four different "small" cities of Madhya Pradesh (India), namely, Bhopal, Indore, Jabalpur and Gwalior, in an attempt to engage with the feminist understanding of urban spaces and outline critical debates on gender and women's mobility.

The spatial context is not just about space but more about socio-cultural process of making and remaking the cities and their dwellers. In this regard, Henry Lefebvre (1991) writes, "Social space is a social product" (26). Lefebvre also posits that "the space thus produced also serves as a tool of thought and of action; that in addition to being a means of production it is also a means of control, and hence of domination, of power" (1991, 26). Discussing space from a sociological and feminist perspective, Doreen Massey (1994) critically comments that "construction of place is articulated consideration of patriarchal relations" (181). In the light of such spatial discourses, this chapter attempts to understand women's experiences of being in city spaces, and examine how they negotiate their right to the city as an individual and as a journalist. The first-hand accounts of women journalists facing blatant sexism and misogyny both in professional spheres and male dominated public spaces that informs the central argument presented in this chapter.

WOMEN JOURNALISTS IN SMALL CITIES: REPORTING BIG ISSUES?

The notion of the "small" city often brings a sociological image to mind filled with conventional and traditional ideas. Also, the understanding of small cities gives a generalized sense of less urbanized spaces and a more conventional lifestyle. As a researcher, I myself have experienced these socio-cultural realities of a small city. According to the Government of India Census (2011) "Out of 468 Urban Agglomerations (UAs)/Towns belonging to Class I category, 53 UAs/Towns have a population of one million or above each. Known as Million Plus UAs/Cities, these are the major urban centres in the country. Around 160.7 million persons (or 42.6% of the urban population) live in these Million Plus UAs/Cities."[3] In the context of this study, all four cities—Indore, Bhopal, Gwalior, and Jabalpur—come under the category Million Plus Urban Agglomeration city. This is a useful context to understand existing realities that women journalists have shared through their narratives.

That said, it seems hard to define a small city. Through this study, I attempt to develop an understanding of India's small cities based on the lived experiences of women. Here I turn to L.P. Repina (2009, 27) who is cited in Tyapkina (2011, 3–4):

> [T]he new urban history and sociology moved away from traditional approaches (biographic, typological, autonomous and local) toward a contextual approach that presented a new understanding of the place and role of cities and urbanization in human history. The city appeared before the scholar as a complex object which united multiple functions in itself but was also a part of a larger whole. The city became a spatial incarnation of its social connections and cultural specificities.

True to issues of "spatial incarnation" of cultural values, women journalists face dual challenges as they work in a small city, first as women and second as journalists. It becomes significant to highlight the experiences of women journalists as "small city journalists," a title which they find undermines their capacities as professionals in this field. Certainly, one cannot ignore the social, economic, and cultural realities of small cities which have uneven development and are not in the race to become metropolitan cities anytime soon. Smaller Indian cities are often looked down upon, and the journalists I spoke to were very aware of being small-city dwellers. In fact, many of them had an internalized belief that their issues were not important enough. In addition to this, in small cities the safety of women is a serious concern as mobility of women in public spaces remains less. A Delhi-based NGO "Breakthrough" conducted a study in Hyderabad, Delhi, Mumbai, Kolkata Hazaribagh district (Jharkhand), Gaya district (Bihar) and Jhajjar district (Haryana). It confirms that around 78.4 percent experience violence in public spaces whereas this does not include the violence women face while using public transport ("Seventy Eight Percent" 2021). Breakthrough clears that particularly women, identified violence as a broad term, consisting of physical, mental, verbal and sexual abuse. This study affirms that patriarchal and misogynistic practices are culturally embedded in society making women vulnerable in public spaces.

The nature of journalism in metropolitan cities is different because there it is all about the issues, political processes, and negotiations going on in those respective geographies and political spaces. Here it is important to examine the choice of work women journalists make in their cities vis-a-vis existing journalistic hierarchies regarding the traditional binary of soft versus hard beats. I present here the narrative of one such journalist, Upasana:

Upasana: For a Hindi newspaper a woman working on the Defense beat was not easy to digest and my work got both criticism and appreciation. I continued working but still, I face many challenges to survive with this beat in this field. It has been a hard choice made by me and because I have chosen it so I am entitled to all risks and arrangements required to cover any assignment in such sensitive locations. Borders are very sensitive zones and I do this work out of my passion. Such a choice in itself has brought additional challenges as I work in Hindi Print media. For them (male employers) I am a valuable reporter in a small city because I am a woman and I am fearless and open to go to cover Defense issues. At the same time, I know how less I am paid and overloaded with work because I chose this.

Interestingly, during my work, while covering Defense issues I have found that borders provide a more secure and respectful/dignified environment for a woman journalist as compared to a Hindi-newspapers' office and work culture. Most of the time, I make my own travel arrangements including tickets, hotel booking, and other related stuff for assignments. During the most dangerous period, I covered Jammu and Kashmir in my own life-risk situation. I am sure if I would have been working in some big city I would have been given more facilities and benefits.

Upasana's narrative demonstrates that when a woman finds her professional working environment unfit, it is a challenge to sustain her work under highly gendered circumstances. Generally, Hindi media houses still shun taking on the economic-reimbursement expenses responsibilities of the women journalists who have to travel for their work assignments while risking their lives. Unfortunately, given the financial crunches this issue is hardly acknowledged by human resource management within such presses/media houses. Even though women feel more secure while being on their assignments if they find themselves more confident at their work, neither of these issues ever get addressed within office settings.

When it comes to understanding the beat-specific facilities to be given to journalists within an organization, no women journalist I interviewed could clarify the actual policies existing for them in their office. It can be said that it is a deliberately maintained information gap in order to affect and restrict women journalists' bargaining power with respect to their rights or safety within the workplace. Another journalist, Bhavna, corroborates the complex gender dynamics involved in this.

> Bhavna: Covering an election is always considered something beyond the capacity of a woman and thus we rarely get the opportunity to cover news related to elections. The seniors make such elections sound like such a dangerous thing to report so that women stay away from them. Because here it is assumed that women can't handle analytical reporting like covering elections. After spending years in journalism while covering certain local political issues I understood that media organizations tend to favor political parties. Also, male lobbying is very tight so as not to allow women journalists into election reporting. Any woman who manages to get into it is seen as a threat in this biased journalistic world. It is important to understand why women are prevented from covering elections; perhaps being a woman the inequalities and hierarchies of caste and class are better understood and thus I can report well on the ongoing equations. But somehow being in a small city, one's chances and opportunities are shrunk because a male is more powerful to be decisive and to declare who should cover what and why. The situation is changing now but very slowly.

Bhavna's narrative describes a Catch-22 situation wherein in the name of safety women are often keep away from centers of power. Further, her experience of working with Hindi print media in a small city shows how mostly male journalists segregate news beats between the so-called soft and hard issues. For instance, covering gender, even with respect to elections translates as a "soft" news story but other issues related to elections are considered "hard" news. This practice results in less coverage of women's issues in media. Kalpana Sharma (2010) writes that a gendered lens enables us to have a deeper understanding of all issues ranging from policies, politics, and business that have an impact on both men and women. Denying or restricting women's access to election news reveals the many-layered gender issues in politics that are not touched upon which directly eliminates coverage of debates around gender. Basically, in a hierarchical newsroom where the male view dominates, women's work and their opinions are dismissed as being illogical and unimportant. Arguing against this Kalpana Sharma (2010) mentions that women are missing from news coverage because journalists do not understand how patriarchy functions determining gendered work for men and women. As expected, patriarchy reduces the value of women's work which is reflected in news coverage. And such problems do not arise only out of misogynistic professional spaces but also of sexist public spaces where women journalists find it hard to negotiate their way. This is why it is necessary to understand the vulnerability of women journalists facing physical threats in public spaces too. The National Crime Records Bureau (NCRB) data for crimes against women for the year 2019, reveals a rise by 7.3 percent in crime against women, particularly sexual crimes and rape (xii). Commuting for work makes women vulnerable than men which asserts prevalence of gender-based violence in streets and on roads. Ruchita is yet another woman journalist whose take on this issue attests to women's difficult experiences of public spaces.

> Ruchita: No wonder this Hindi print media can make a "Hindu family environment" at the workplace too like a "parivaar" or "Kutumb" (extended family). Such a nature of the workplace promotes more conventional values towards family and expects women to be submissive and less argumentative; no liberating space for women is allowed in the workplace despite them being journalists.

Obviously, here the submissive woman in the workplace is not accorded the safety she deserves in the public space. Ruchita's narrative has been the most powerful expression to show dissent of a woman journalist directly explaining the conventional character of the Hindi Print media. While understanding from Ruchita's experience, one can argue that Hindi print journalism reinforces the dominant gender roles in the media workplace. The construction of a "family-like" workplace reiterates the gendered and age-based hierarchy found within the institution of the family rather than inculcating ethical professional values. It is significant to understand that patronizing a woman does not let her emerge an entitled being like a male to claim her rights. Ironically, patronizing women at workplace reinforces the patriarchal power structure which places women as inferior gender. This is a dominant practice which basically keeps women debarred from being an individual professional having autonomous system to negotiate for herself even in the public spaces. Writing for hard beats in journalism is thought of as being beyond a woman's intellectual abilities. The segregation of beats and subjects is projected in a very abstract manner. The set-up of the Hindi print media shows a conventional approach that holds women solely responsible for household and care work and therefore journalistic work is cast as an extension of women's domestic engagement. This, by extension, also means that she is better confined at home and the public sphere is not to be accessed by her.

Francesca Orsini (2002) writes that many Hindi writers and intellectuals are people "who thanks to their strategic position as Hindi experts, [can] pursue their cultural agenda and force it upon the public" (174). This constructed nationalized identity has been used by elites although only in a subordinate way as the higher echelons of society engage with the discourse in English language print media. Labeling women journalists as limited to Hindi print media can be seen as a deliberate effort to keep them under-represented and under-reported. Orsini writes that "Hindi's claim to be the national language of India was an ideological construct" (2002, 26). Thus, promoting conventional values in the name of culture and tradition is often done in an effort to make Hindi and Hindi print media focus on a right-wing ideology to reinforce a specific socio-cultural agenda. The character of Hindi nationalism is patriarchal and coercive which is why women are at margin not accommodating their existence in public spaces. Women are constructed a vehicle of cultural values and their obedience thus ideological reinforcement disempowers women's freedom and liberty an individual. We should not ignore that Hindi print media's workplace are sight of ideological operation which propagates regressive patriarchal values.

The demarcation between a small city and big city women journalists by Hindi Print media enunciates the politics of a variety of issues in the traditional binary of soft versus hard beats. In the Indian context, this is also indicative of the fact that cities have multiple realities dependent on socio-cultural and geographical circumstances which follow gendered power relations placing women vulnerable. The public spaces exclude women risking their safety and security thus accessing public spaces by women remains a matter of courage more against women's right to public space. It needs to be critically understood that most of the time women end up making choice for work, education and mobility considering question of safety and security. It also results in making compromise which limits women's exposure and experience too. Monk and Hanson (1982) explain that landscapes reflect ideologies supporting distinct gender roles and inequalities of power suggesting that women and men attach different meanings to landscapes. They both experience the landscape in different ways. It directly controls the participation of women journalists in reporting and coverage of issues concerning women and their views in news. It perpetuates a male-centric view in news coverage with the strict binary of news beats as hard and soft beats. Women journalists' choice of work is not considered significant while assuming that women coming from small cities lack exposure. Experiences of women journalists echo the conventional pattern of choice of work which is reinforced by not allowing women to experiment with new areas of reporting. Though women have been negotiating in their own interests despite the hazards and impediments, they are limited by being constantly pushed back as small city journalists.

EXPERIENCING CITIES: QUESTIONS OF SAFETY

It has been a journey from home to work and from work to public space; the negotiation establishes that women are gendered bodies vulnerable to male violence. Michael Waltzer (1986) defines public space as "the space which we share with strangers, people who are not our relatives, friends or work associates" (cited in Valentine 1989, 386). Women across cultures find that their personal space is threatened by catcalls, comments, and physical advances from strange men in public. Incidents of sexual violence against women are strictly used to limit their mobility leading to further construction of the city as unsafe spaces for women. Streets are also viewed as unsafe spaces for women as they face sexual harassment, stalking, and male-gaze perpetuating a constantly threatening environment for women out in these spaces. Being out in public, a woman is perceived merely as a body controlled by patriarchal values that limit her, making her responsible for her own security. The narrative of another journalist named Sangeeta proves a case in point.

> Sangeeta: Security and safety issues are always considered a woman's responsibility, even if you are working with a big-brand newspaper. Once you are out in public, your professional identity is not visible on your body thus chances of being molested, eve teased, or raped are always as high as for any other woman who is out. Here being a small city one cannot expect too much organizational support for women journalists. There is no pick-and-drop facility. It is always a personal arrangement supported by either family or friends if we are on late-night assignments.

> Though there are cooperative male colleagues who are caring and ask us to leave for home in time by 9:30 or 10 pm. All long-distance assignments are done alone; sometimes photographer accompanies us to the place of the event. Generally, women are asked to leave early for home. Usually, women journalists are not sent on any outgoing assignments as it requires a lot to arrange for them for their security thus they are confined to city reporting only. Even in city reporting, sometimes, some places are not women-friendly and one might not feel safe going for coverage. Many a time either a photographer is accompanied by a woman journalist or it's all up to the individual to take the risks if signing up for the assignment. Somewhere the professional task does not allow you to think of risks.

Sangeeta's narrative adds to the discourse on "risk" that a woman faces which then feeds into restricting her professional freedom while being in public spaces. Ensuring safety is always a personal effort for women while returning from the office as the organization does not offer any pick and drop facility. In small Indian cities, women are told to leave home early from the office as a safety measure whereas it is reinforcing restricted mobility on them. Sangeeta's experience also elucidates the limited work choices given to women, limiting their professional growth and opportunities.

Lewis and Maxfield (1980), Brower et al. (1983; cited in Valentine 1989, 388) write that when a woman is out beyond her own local environment, she judges her safety in the area based on certain preconceived images about the area and its residents. She receives certain social behavior from her physical surroundings; for example, a sense of incivility as vandalism is inappropriate or threatening behavior is considered a possible fear while being out. Thus, a woman usually cannot afford to assume safety in public space which is occupied by others too. The structural violence in public spaces and its internalization by both women and men makes space exclusionary to women and controls their mobility. Shilpa Phadke et al. (2011, 54) write that "women are inevitably cast in the role of potential victims to be protected and the discourse becomes not about women's right to the city, but about risk, fear and danger." The narrative of a journalist, Anisha, adds to this argument as she shares:

> Anisha: Jabalpur is a very inactive-slow city. Here males are dominating and think they can do whatever they like. Even in the media, there are colleagues with the same mentality.

> When the country was raising voices against the perpetrators of rape in the "Nirbhaya Case,"[4] people and media in Jabalpur were in deep slumber, after almost two weeks they thought that they should do something for women's safety in their city too thus they organized some workshop and talk only in women's college. This is an irony of the city that always women are taught to be responsible for their behavior and dressing sense to be safe. The violence against women is completely understood as women's fault because it is understood that on moving out, they invite incidents like rape. It's a common attitude here that women are preached here more to stay traditionally value-oriented. We are not given out-station assignments because we are women from Jabalpur and we need to stay within city limits. It's easier for the people here to blame women who are frequently out in public in big cities because they are seen as the major reason to incite violence against them. In any way, the moral guidelines and controlling attitude are taught to all of us while saying that "mahaul ganda kar diya hai ladkiyon ne, jitani ladkiyaan bahar hongi utna yada crime hoga" which translates as "women have spoiled the whole milieu/environment, the more women are out, the more there is crime-violence against them."

This response from Anisha deciphers the particular character of the city Jabalpur, where men cannot accept the presence of women in public spaces; their opinion is that women should not be out beyond a certain time. Interestingly, the code for "city-limits" is taken as a socio-moral limitation describing the code of conduct of a particular city in this context. Such teaching and preaching of women are a systematic approach that patriarchy deploys to delimit women through educational institutions, media, and the state. Noting such problems, Shilpa Phadke et al. (2011, 27) write:

> "Respectable" women could be potentially defiled in a public space while "non-respectable" women are themselves a potential source of contamination to the purity of public spaces and therefore, the city. For the so-called "respectable" women this classification is always fraught with some amount of tension, for should she transgress the carefully policed "inside-outside" boundaries permitted to her, she could so easily slip into becoming the "public" woman the threat to sacrality of "public space."

Anisha's narrative previously discussed informs that women who are seen in public are considered a threat to patriarchal family values. Thus, the demarcation of "inside-outside" is made to morally police women in the family. Clearly, gender relations are organized and reinforced through controlling women whereas men remain the powerful gender at every level. Kalpana Viswanath et al. (2007) write that "inequality between the sexes and the systemic discrimination that women and girls face in a patriarchal system limits their movements and ability to negotiate public spaces. This limitation affects women's lives in numerous ways-right and access to education paid work and the freedom to move around. These must be seen as violations of basic rights of women to live and work in cities" (1543). It is this patriarchal mindset that justifies rape culture while targeting women and their freedom in public spaces. Moreover, it allows the custodians of patriarchy to comment on women's clothes and the time of the day they choose to access public spaces while showing complete rejection of women's autonomy. Even metro cities like Delhi fail to accept women's presence in public. For women, the city and its localities do not allow a friendly space to walk or be out in the evening. Access to public space is further delimited in terms of class, age, and caste. To save their own freedom and mobility, women tend not to share their troubles and challenges posed in the form of stalking, threats, and harassment.

The basic character of the four Indian cities discussed in this chapter reflects conventional values which forbid women's mobility. Women journalists from Bhopal and Indore have expressed their relative freedom to access city spaces with a sense of safety because the visibility of women is higher. Whereas the experiences of women in the other two cities were markedly different. As women journalists from Jabalpur and Gwalior informed, safety concerns in these cities were higher as the visibility of women in public is less due to a patriarchal and traditional environment.

WOMEN JOURNALISTS: NEGOTIATING UNSAFE CITY SPACES

Assessing what kind of spaces offer freedom to women or discriminate against them is a significant aspect of feminist geography. City and its social and cultural boundaries play a key role in shaping gender relations in certain spatial contexts. Roswitha Mueller (2002) writes citing Elisabeth Wilson (1992) that the independence of women has been always a source of anxiety in a patriarchal society and this becomes particularly acute in the context of the city (42). Citing Wilson's book, The Sphinx in the City (1992), Mueller (2002) describes how women have been held responsible for chaotic elements of the city since Roman times when Juvenal focused his attack on the immorality of Roman life primarily on the conduct of women (32). Their lack of virtue was figured as the root cause of Rome's decadence. Wilson also mentions that the presence of women in cities and in city streets has been historically questioned. Moreover, controlling and surveillance within city life have been directed particularly at women.

Undoubtedly, then, the hierarchy of gender-based power structure regulates mobility of women in society. India witnesses a "culture of misogyny" (Bhattacharyya 2015, 1345) that is why women feel out of place in public spaces. In my study, women indicated that small cities have a conventional approach, and thus here women have to face difficulties being working women. A city's socio-cultural environment regulates women's mobility and behavior. The predicament of a lone working woman in a small Indian city is thus articulated by Apeksha:

> Apeksha: Being single and living alone is not a good thing in small cities. Women are coming from other cities here but they have to face problems because many residents of the city do not like giving accommodation to a single woman and this journalistic job doesn't have timing thus they are not seen as good women. Even for landlords, a woman has to maintain a "suitable" image to continue her stay in a particular place. Sometimes being a well-informed woman helps but it costs otherwise too as you are called a "clever woman." My father was not comfortable with my shifting to Gwalior. I have lived alone and I had to be extra careful because being single and living alone is taken as if you are here to spoil the environment in the locality or colony. Sometimes I get late to reach my place and my landlady does say that "ladaki waali baat hai . . . itane der tak aati ho . . . mohalle wale kya sochate honge" (it's the matter of being a girl, if

you come late in evening, colony residents might be thinking it otherwise). I try my best to keep her at convenience with my nature of the job. I have to do so that my landlord perhaps allows me despite my profession.

According to Apeksha, small cities are hesitant to accommodate single working women as they don't have social security and they are often tagged as "free-bad" women. Journalistic jobs like Apeksha's bring freedom, but society does not accept such freedoms and a woman has to follow a code of conduct so that she can continue with her work and stay in a given small city. Apeksha also claimed how "being single" is perceived as a threat. Critiquing such cultural dispositions, Shipla Phadke argues that:

> [S]taking a safety claim is critically dependent on being able to demonstrate that one is worthy of being protected. This demonstration takes varied forms from the wearing of symbols of matrimony to the presence of protective men and the carrying of bags and other parcels to illustrate the purpose. As is apparent such demonstrations are symbolic rather than materially effective for instance the presence of men in their roles as fathers, husbands or brothers merely marks women off as unavailable rather than provides them with the guarantee of physical safety. (2007, 1512)

Such demonstration of being worthy as per social norms shows the structural vulnerability of a woman where concerns for her safety are negligible and if anything she is warned of the risk of sexual violence within cities and public spaces.

The city as a collective has a moralistic/judgmental attitude toward women which directly limits the mobility and visibility of women in accessing public space in general. In this context, Phadke et al. also write that "public-private division of space decrees that the rightful place of respectable women at night is within their homes and not in public space" (2011, 26). As per the working hours of the profession, a woman who comes late and has an outgoing lifestyle is taken as a threat by local people too. Her narrative brings out the language used to warn her or reinforce her fear of being out till late evening. This for Shilpa Phadke et al. leads to concerns about the safety of women or specifically their "sexual safety" and not safety from theft or accident, or even murder because women's sexual safety is rather connected to ideas of "izzat" and honor of the family and the community (2011, 53).

The local culture of a particular city impacts journalism and perceptions about women journalists. Their professional identity as a journalist helps women get respect from local people but when it comes to accommodation and arrangements of living, they are socially judged. Shilpa Phadke argues that "middle class women are central to any discussion on safety both as desirable urban subjects and also as the symbols of national honour to be protected from the potential contamination posed by others in public space" (2007, 1511). It is important to understand that the construction of fear and safety is gendered indicating sexual safety issues that demarcate outsiders as others and insiders as respectable. Nayna's take on this provides some compelling insights.

> Nayna: It has become easier for us to explore our city through such a job of being in journalism. Especially the upcoming mall culture, cafes, and restaurants have made our outings more frequent. For women, it is important what kind of place we are in and which locality. I feel that malls have given us a kind of free space. These days it is quite easier for us to fix up meetings at places which are usually located in decent areas of the city. Indore as a more advanced city has many malls, coffee shops, and such places where women are more comfortable going.

Interacting with the newly emerging public spaces in cities has made women more confident in their approach to being in these spaces as they now assure themselves of being in public. Further, processes of urbanization in India have introduced new spaces which are to some extent safer for women to be in public like malls, coffee shops, and restaurants. Here it conveys a critical point when the subjectivities of respondents find malls and coffee shops as public spaces. Nonetheless, scholars like Shilpa Phadke bring out the embedded patriarchy of the public space by arguing that:

> It is important to point to reiterate that new spaces of consumption like coffee shops and malls are not public spaces but privatized spaces that masquerade as public spaces. Limited access to such private-public spaces creates a veneer of access for women, pre-empting any substantive critique of the lack of actual access to real public space. While these space might give individual women an opportunity to hang out it does not in any significant way change the limited nature of women's access to public spaces nor does it adequately challenge the dominant idea that women's proper place is in the private. (2011, 46–47)

In general, differentiating the embodiment of public-private spaces is not clearly understood because of the conventional understanding of the places which does not liberate particularly women. Dominantly, open spaces or geographic areas are taken as public spaces whereas malls and coffee shops are entangled with the understanding of these new public spaces which are private spaces with limited access to women. Undeniably, women on the move find that new spaces especially malls, coffee shops, and restaurants are becoming their most preferred locations which offer freedom in their given social-cultural context of small cities.

Negotiating with the available city spaces, women journalists find the new urban space enabling their freedom and safety. As Erving Goffman (1976) cited in Shirly Ardener (1981) suggests that space reflects "social organizations" exerting their own influence, similarly cities in the context of my research also speak of the gendered reality of the space (2). Narratives establish that women journalists find Bhopal and Indore relatively liberal when it comes to the visibility of women in new urban spaces whereas Jabalpur and Gwalior, smaller and less developed cities, still have limited spaces accommodating women within the public sphere. This is true for women seeking accommodation to accessing city spaces for journalistic work. Their experiences demonstrate patriarchal socio-cultural geographies for women.

SENSE OF BELONGING: STRUGGLE FOR SELFHOOD?

The sense of belonging is a need and a process both for one's growth in daily urban practices with work life too. Despite having families, women who are working in their cities cannot claim a sense of belonging. Their engagements tend to be dealing with being a "woman" as a constructed social category rather than a professional in a city. Probyn (1996; cited in Fenster 2005, 243) has emphasized the significant aspects of belonging as not just of being, but of longing or yearning. The Oxford Dictionary describes "belonging" through three meanings which are first, to be a member (of a club, household, grade, society, state, and so on); second, to be resident or connected with; and third, to be rightly placed or classified to or fit in a specific environment. These aspects assert membership elements of belonging and multiple dimensions.

Going by this definition, women in the city are a social category where family is there but when it comes to the state woman becomes a political category that requires citizenship. The belonging brings a contested space in terms of citizenship. Phadke et al. (2011, 9) argue that cities and definitions of citizenship have always been based principle of exclusion—on grounds of class, religion, race, age, sexual preference, and property ownership, among others.

For women journalists in the context of this chapter, a sense of belonging speaks about the place where they these women were born, have grown up, and are now working. Their narratives revolve around more day-to-day life in their city with reference to their work and domestic space. With regard to public spaces, it is known that "[w]hat Certeau constructs as a model of how we make a sense of space through walking practices, and repeat those practices as a way of overcoming alienation" (Leach 2002, 284; cited in Fenster 2005, 243). Appropriately, de Certeau identifies the process through which a sense of belongingness is created including a process of transformation of a place. The everyday practices built up attachment and emotions for a given place. The fundamentals of accumulated knowledge, memory, and intimate corporal experience of one's life develops a sense of belonging and attachment. With time sense of belonging also changes with growing experiences. Roshani's narrative elucidates this better.

> Roshani: For me, a sense of belonging comes with my work. Journalistic job makes us engaged in the city for work purposes but when it comes to seeing ourselves as a part of the city, it remains missing. Thus professional belonging is very much there but personal belonging is missing. Here I specifically mean social upbringing which trains us to be married as a woman and belongs to a man but once a woman is working it becomes more about work rather than associating with the city as an individual because ultimately a woman must or should belong to a man. Being a professional brings more isolation and a lack of social life and the city also gives less space excluding women as an individual.

For women journalists, the sense of belonging is important as it helps to seek a social support system in hours of need. Also, the feeling of belonging makes one feel included in the city. Being an insider in the city does not offer a woman acceptance in the city where her work gives her a professional association but a sense of belonging is more socially constructed associating marriage as belonging to a man rather than belonging to oneself in the city. In her narrative another respondent, Apeksha, mentions the social upbringing of a woman which teaches her to belong to a man which has been the structural placement of a woman where she is sacrificing her aspirations and desires.

> Apeksha: Gwalior is a less developed city and it is a crime-prone city too. Many a time my professional position as a journalist brings me more protection. I do not belong to this city which helps me to know the city from a new perspective. Though my professional engagement is more with the city as my news sources and networking for professional assignments are very strong here but I do miss my friends and more personal support system to feel more accepted. Though it is very strange to expect immediate acceptance, for women it is always a negotiation even in the case of belonging to a particular city. I chose to be working over household work. That is how I wanted to be in this field to explore more but still, I am not over the lack of clarity between domestic and work life. It seems a continuous fight within me where it makes me uneasy. This city Gwalior seems more traditional and conventional. Perhaps being anonymous helps more rather than being a woman feeling like belonging nowhere.

Knowing a particular city through one's professional identity helps to critically understand the city. Here, women journalists are trying to point out the absence of a social support system or even acceptance that might have transformed their relationship with the city.

Yuval-Davis et al. (2006) write that belonging is an emotional attachment, a feeling of being "at home" (2). On similar lines, Michael Ignatieff (2001; cited in Yuval-Davis et al. 2006, 2) writes that belonging is about feeling "safe." Politics of belonging function with specific political projects aiming at constructing belonging to particular collectivities. Yuval-Davis et al. (2006) argue that citizenship and identities including culture and tradition with all signifiers of borders and boundaries have central roles in the discourse of politics of belonging (3). Respondents described Gwalior as being infamous for being a dacoit infested region, an area which has been a male-controlled and crime prone where a woman journalist feels like an "unbelonger" but shows courage to work in the such city without having a sense of citizenship or belonging. Shilpa Phadke critiques this by claiming that:

> [I]n various spaces the risks that are created by belonging and not belonging are different. In conflict situations like riots, in pragmatic terms, it is safest for a woman, if she has to be in a public space, be in a neighbourhood belonging to her own community where she is dressed or coded in ways that immediately identify her as belonging. However, in peaceful times it is often the insiders, those who belong, who are expected to conform and are censured if they do not do so. (2005, 53)

Being an insider of the city as a local resident does not offer much freedom as there are many known people, close-knit relatives, and social circles. Thus mobility and freedom remain so limited with professional mobility. Women journalists find "anonymity" to be a mask to hide their perceived fears and feeling of not belonging to the city.

The notion of "anonymity" that has been brought by the journalists in their narration is relevant. Being anonymous might give a woman journalist more freedom in the city. The participation of a woman in a male-occupied space might require anonymity as it gives one more liberty. Viswanath et al. (2007) write that the anonymity of a city's public space offers the space and freedom helping in escaping family or traditional community boundaries (1542). But for women, this freedom is hindered by the increasing rate of violence against women thus women prefer to be anonymous to have more freedom in accessing the city. Further, in this context, Anna Secor (2004) writes that anonymity may be a tactic covertly helping women to transgress the everyday spatial hegemonies. Citing Judith Garber's (2000) critical suggestion on anonymity in urban living, Secor (2004, 360) mentions that anonymity may be a defensive tactic for those who are looking for freedom from persecution but in the long run identity replaces anonymity as the goal of urban living.

In order to understand the location of a woman in the realm of her own journalistic professional city of work, her negotiation to be recognized as a citizen of the city directly collides with the notion of anonymity. The dichotomy of "identity" where on the one hand the political identity of citizenship is a contested space and on the other hand the notion of "anonymity" needs to be observed when it comes to being in a male-occupied public sphere. In the context of my research, there has been an emerging debate over belonging to a place, profession, or self which raises critical questions on shifting the meaning of identity, freedom, and family with their respective journalistic profession. For these women who I have interviewed, their longing for a stable identity with stable emotional attachment (Yuval-Davis et al. 2006) has been a socio-political engagement with their spatial mobility. It opens debate on the notion of belonging which displays patterns of spatial mobility emerging through experiences of women journalists failing to specify their sense of belonging to any particular city. Unfortunately, among these four cities Bhopal, Indore, Jabalpur, and Gwalior none can fulfill the longing of these women journalists to enable their feeling of belonging and safe in these cities.

CONCLUSION

Negotiating with the dominant values of the small Indian city and its patriarchy poses a challenge to women journalists where urbanization processes have brought mixed realities of socio-cultural processes with them. For women journalists conceptualizing the city from various points of view portrays a lacuna between the city and their freedom to access public space fearlessly. Small city journalism poses a challenge to women journalists as male journalists' hierarchy controls and limits their choice of work. Issues and news beats indicate controlling mechanisms to make women confined to conventional values and gender stereotyped roles. The fabric of Hindi print media echoes its nationalist values through the use of media and its ideologically charged environment. Where women are treated more as value-keepers at the workplace too rather than working on concerns of their choice. Moral policing and preaching of values are quite visible through the experiences of women journalists. It also shows that the construction of the divide between big city and small city journalism is institutionalized to limit issue-based journalism. It reinforces the sense of inferiority among women journalists doubly; first, as a women journalist undermining her choice of work; and second, regulating a woman's work according to small city journalism which presumes that women are weak at logical and analytical reporting, unlike big city journalists.

It is critical as women are unable to claim the city completely as per their needs and leisure. Especially, according to the respondents, Jabalpur and Gwalior are the cities that have little space for women having more restricted patriarchal city limits. There has been an emerging question on relative safety and freedom existing in big cities and small cities for women journalists which reveals that there is persistent risk and danger of being out in public spaces in cities. Somewhere urbanization has been giving women access to public spaces. Cities like Bhopal and Indore seem to provide new public spaces which women associate with a sense of freedom and relative safety. These capitalist-economic processes are bringing materialism and infrastructure to the cities which are basically providing shallow freedom and limited access to public spaces and mobility. Nonetheless, women and journalists appreciate these spaces.

In addition to existing cultural dynamics, the lockdown period during the Covid years revealed systematic vulnerabilities of women which further reduced their negotiation for mobility. During lockdown all means of public transportation were shut down and women who were largely dependent on public transportation were deeply troubled since they did not own private vehicles. According to the Institution for Transport and Development Policy (ITDP 2017) 58 percent of women in India depend on public transport to get to work. The absence of safe and reliable means of public transport heightens their social exclusion (Bell 2016; Hamilton and Jenkins 2000). Regrettably, women's right to public spaces and their mobility has been restricted by the threat of violence resulting in making compromises in their choices regarding education, work, home and leisure. And all this was only heightened in the recent past owing to the huge limitations brought on by the pandemic.

The much-debated issue of belonging brings out the socially constructed meaning of belonging that always privileges a man. This debate further elucidates the exclusion of the woman from her city and her citizenship in terms of having equal access to public spaces like the man. Women therefore deserve and need both freedom and safety in public spaces to establish their political identities as citizens in claiming cities as their own to explore, live, and celebrate.

REFERENCES

Ardener, Shirly. 1981. *Women and Space: Ground Rules and Social Maps*. London: Oxford University Women's Studies Committee.

Bell, Karen. 2016. "Bread and Roses: A Gender Perspective on Environmental Justice and Public Health." *International Journal of Environmental Research and Public Health* 13 (10): 1005. doi.org/10.3390/ijerph13101005.

Bhattacharyya, R. 2015. "Understanding the Spatialities of Sexual Assault against Indian Women in India." *Gender, Place and Culture* 22 (9): 1340–1356.

Fenster, Tovi. 2002. "Gender and City: The Different Formations of Belonging." In *A Companion to Feminist Geography*, edited by Lise Nelson and Joni Seager, 242–256. Hoboken, NJ: Wiley-Blackwell.

Hamilton, Kerry and Linda Jenkins. 2000. "A Gender Audit for Public Transport: A New Policy Tool in the Tackling of Social Exclusion." *Urban Studies* 37 (10): 1793–1800. 10.1080/00420980020080411.

Lefebvre, Henry. 1991. *The Production of Space*. Translated by Donald Nicholson-Smith. Carlton: Blackwell Publishing.

Massey, Doreen. 1994. *Space, Place and Gender*. Cambridge: Polity Press.

Monk, Janice and Susan Hanson. 1982. "On Not Excluding Half of the Human in Human Geography." *The Professional Geographer* 34 (1): 11–23. doi:10.1111/j.0033-0124.1982.00011.x.

Mueller, Roswitha. 2002. "The City and Its Other." *Nature Art and Urban Spaces* 24 (2): 30–49. doi:10.1353/dis.2003.0028.

National Crime Records Bureau. 2019. "Crime in India 2019." Ministry of Home Affairs, Government of India. https://ncrb.gov.in/sites/default/files/CII%202019%20Volume%201.pdf.

Orsini, Francesca. 2002. *The Hindi Public Sphere, 1920–1940: Language and Literature in the Age of Nationalism*. London: Oxford University Press.

Phadke, Shilpa. 2005. "You Can Be Lonely in a Crowd: The Production of Safety in Mumbai." *Indian Journal of Gender Studies* 12 (1): 41–62. doi.org/10.1177/097152150401200102.

———. 2007. "Dangerous Liaisons: Women and Men: Risk and Reputation in Mumbai." *Economic and Political Weekly* 42 (17): 1510–1518.

Phadke, Shilpa et al. 2011. *Why Loiter? Women and Risk on Mumbai Streets*. New Delhi: Penguin Books.

Secor, Anna. 2004. "There Is an Istanbul That Belongs to Me: Citizenship, Space, and Identity in the City." *Annals of the Association of American Geographers* 94 (2): 352–368.

"Seventy Eight Percent Women Experienced Violence in Public Places, Reports Survey." 2021. *Deccan Chronicle*, March 6. https://www.deccanchronicle.com/nation/current-affairs/060321/78-of-women-experienced-violence-in-public-places-study.html.

Singh, Nadia and Areet Kaur. 2022. "The COVID-19 Pandemic: Narratives of Informal Women Workers in Indian Punjab." *Gender, Work, and Organization* 29 (2): 388–407. doi.org/10.1111/gwao.12766.

Sharma, Kalpana. 2010. *Missing: Half the Story: Journalism as if Gender Matters*. New Delhi: Zubaan.

Tyapkina, Olga. 2011. "Small Towns as a Phenomenon of Historical Urbanization from a Western European Methodological Perspective." In *Disappearing Realities on the Cultural Consequences of Social Change*, edited by A. Dwyer and M. Bucholc, 1–9. Vienna: IWM Junior Visiting Fellows' Conferences.

Valentine, Gill. 1989. "The Geography of Women's Fear." *Area* 21 (4): 385–390. www.jstor.org/stable/20000063.

Viswanath, Kalpana and Surabhi Tandon Mehrotra. 2007. "Shall We Go Out? Women's Safety in Public Spaces in Delhi." *Economic and Political Weekly* 42 (7): 1542–1548. www.jstor.org/stable/4419521.

Wilson, Elizabeth. 1991. *The Sphinx in the City: Urban Life, the Control of Disorder and Women.* Berkeley: University of California Press.

Yuval-Davis, Nira. 2006. "Introduction Situating Contemporary Politics of Belonging." In *The Situated Politics of Belonging*, edited by Nira Yuval-Davis et al., 1–14. London: Sage Publication.

NOTES

1. Much of this study has been carried out as part of my doctoral project titled "Understanding Women Journalists Experiences of Working in Hindi Print Journalism in Cities of Madhya Pradesh" at the Tata Institute of Social Sciences, Mumbai, Maharashtra, India. The dissertation was awarded a PhD in 2017.

2. For purposes of confidentiality all identities of interviewees have been withheld and pseudonyms have been used in this chapter. The interviews were conducted between 2014–2015.

3. Census of India 2011.

4. The 2012 Delhi gang rape case involved a rape and fatal assault on a 23-year-old woman that occurred on December 16, 2012 in Munirka, a neighborhood in South Delhi, India.

PART VI

Traveling Solo, Traveling Strong
Women Braving Neoliberal Roads

Chapter 12

Travel with Care

Reinforcing Patriarchy through Tips for Solo Female Travelers in India

Kiranpreet Kaur Baath

Wearing a wedding ring and saying you're married, and due to meet your husband shortly, is another way to ward off unwanted interest.

—"Women Travellers in India—Lonely Planet" (2021)

In most places, it is best not to venture out alone after dark. While booking flights, trains, and buses, choose options that get you to your destination in daylight. If its unavoidable have someone from your hotel/homestay come meet you.–

—Neha Dara (Dara 2017)

Travel and the genre of travel writing—directly linked to cultural exchange, knowledge of self and the other and power and authority—has provided an opportunity for women to escape the domestic spaces and explore self and the world. By enabling women to adopt the role of traveler and travel writer, which was largely associated with masculinity, travel employs agency to women by rescuing them from a static mapping of women's bodies and spaces by the male "gaze." For a long time, they, either Victorian women or other colonial migrants, have been traveling in groups or with their husbands. Recently, almost a decade ago, the trend of solo traveling has proliferated among female travelers. Solo traveling provides women an opportunity to push the boundaries of patriarchal structures of power and allows women to negotiate a space for self. Indian women, ever been a part of travelers and explorers, are now taking up the challenge of traveling solo around the world as well as across India.

Nonetheless, to understand the place and possibilities for solo women travelers in a global patriarchal or at least male-dominated space, let me take the readers through three Facebook pages: *Solo female travelers*, *Finding Carla* and *SAWTA*. Though these pages are not primarily related to Indian roads and Indian solo female travelers, still they demand attention as they symbolize and voice three different understandings about women traveling alone. The first one, *Solo female travelers*, earlier known as the "First FB group for women who travel solo," is a Facebook group started in 2015 with a vision to "empower" women to travel and "explore the world solo . . . on their own terms" (Club 2015). Though the group was started for English solo travelers only, it has attracted acceptance from all over the globe, so much so that it has now 144,600 members. Such worldwide acceptance of a group encouraging, arranging, and documenting solo female travelers demonstrates the rising interest of women in solo traveling. According to the O.A.T (Overseas Adventure Travel) report more than "60,000 women traveled solo between 2018 and 2019" (*Over 85% of Solo Travelers are Women—Adventure Travel Reports* 2020). Google trends have also recorded that searches for "solo female travel" have gone up by 52 percent (Kow 2018) from 2016 to 2017, and most recently it has further gone up by 230 percent in 2019 (Roberti 2019, 4; *Solo Travel Statistics and Data: 2021–2022* 2022). Karen Lawrence, in her seminal work, *Penelope Voyages: Women and Travel in the British Literary Tradition,* has discussed that travel tropes and the genre of travel writing has played a vital role in allowing women to negotiate their place in society by allotting "more (and new) territory to women's province and replace[ing] the static mapping of women as space with a more dynamic model of woman as agent, as self-mover" (Lawrence 1994, 18). This observation, though made for British women, is indeed true for all women across the globe who had been suppressed, gazed upon, or made to agree to gender stratification. It is established, through a study of 194 solo women travelers, that the reason for traveling solo by women was "to explore new experiences, gain new-knowledge and understand different ways of thinking and being in the world"; out of five major reasons "experience, escape, and self-esteem" were most prominent ones (Chiang and Jogaratnam 2006, 59–60). These women, through their solo journeys, "transgress gender norms" which, consequently, empower other women to employ "a form of gender power" (Ghose 1998, 133). Therefore, the growing trend of solo female travelers in a way motivates other women to claim agency and directly indulge in cross-cultural exchanges and knowledge that eventually lead to power and authority through visibility and gaze. Indian women have also started undertaking solo travel and using digital platforms, such as blogs and social media accounts, to document their new experiences and claim agency in dictating their space. This group, *Solo female travelers*, therefore resonates with the demand and need for solo female travelers. By arranging trips, holidays, and solo travel for women, along with giving them a space to connect with like-minded people and document their experiences, the Facebook group validates the presence of solo women travelers and also motivates other women to join the cadre and reclaim their space through mobility.

Alternatively, women traveling alone have never been accepted by patriarchal power structures, due to which female bodies, trying to push the boundaries of patriarchal understanding of travel tropes and genre, have faced violence, abuse, and witch-hunt. Women on the move are either seen as vulnerable, or morally corrupt and thus inviting men for sexual advancements, or just easily available objectified bodies deserving to be violated or even eliminated. The second Facebook page in discussion *Finding Carla* validates the travel for "solo women" as a "particularly risky undertaking." Charlotte Macdonald has documented this behavior of patriarchy against Victorian women travelers: though these women started "traveling to the colonies" for "a young woman to set out 'alone' was regarded as a *particularly risky undertaking*" (Macdonald 2015, 10; emphasis added). This belief has managed to survive well into the twenty-first century as well. Lauren Haigh, in her article "Female Travellers: A Unique Risk Profile," has noted that "the number of females travelling alone is on the rise, but so is women's unease" (Haigh 2020). Megan Specia and Tariro Mzezewa, in an article published in *Independent*, states "more women are travelling solo, but that doesn't take away the danger" (Mzezewa 2019b). This "unease" and "danger" spans a wide spectrum of threats posed in public spaces to solo women travelers: from being uncomfortable with male stares and uninvited efforts to talk to being groped, teased, and sexually harassed in public transport and places that many times has led to rape and even death. *Finding Carla* is a page that was started in December 2018 after Carla Stefaniak, a 36-year-old Florida woman, went missing from her Airbnb hotel in Costa Rica. After finding that Costa Rican authorities were not making enough efforts to find Stefaniak, her family started this page a week later as a search mission to find the whereabouts of Stefaniak. Her body was discovered soon, and now the security guard has also been sentenced to a sixteen-year term for raping and murdering her. However, the page exists to date; now it has become a place for putting missing information of other travelers in the public domain. The presence of this page in itself interrogates the "empowerment" and "encouragement" the first page (discussed earlier) tends to provide to women for traveling solo. The picture portrayed by Hostelworld, one of the largest holiday booking companies, by stating that "Solo travel was once seen as brave and risky for female travelers, but . . . it is now an adventurous, exciting experience that allows them to feel free with no one else to worry about or please" is ruptured by *Forbes* report stating "[b]ut the sobering reality is that this can be a risky endeavour" (Bloom 2017). Stefanaik is not a solitary case, rather such incidents are reported frequently and some even go unreported globally. However, the situation is even worse in patriarchal societies, such as India, where women's mobility is linked to promiscuity. According to the NCRB (National Crime Record Bureau) report of 2020, 77 rape cases on average per day were recorded, and 62,300 cases of kidnapping and abduction were recorded in that year (Bureau 2020, x–xii). So, the question arises: should the women take "encouragement" from the social media pages, such as *Solo Female Travelers*, and continue claiming agency in structuring their own space; or they should refrain from visiting dangerous roads as it happened after the high-profile Delhi Gangrape[1] in 2012. It was reported that after the incident, the number of women traveling to India dropped by 35 percent (Advani 2013, 2); however, the way the behavior of Indian women traveling in India was altered has not been reported—I doubt if it was even thought as a subject of study! If they refrain from traveling "dangerous roads" then another question is: where are the "safe roads'? Most of the time violence against women is carried out at home: according to WHO (World Health Organization) report, 38 percent of murders of women are committed by an intimate partner, globally only "6% of women report having been sexually assaulted by someone other than their partner" (World Health Organization 2021). Nonetheless, by warning women against "dangerous roads" or "dangerous countries" or "dangerous areas and time" the discourse of gender vulnerability and femininity is circulated. These discourses, as rightly suggested by Sara Mills, has constructed travel "as physically dangerous and a site for sexual threat" (Mills 1991, 103). Similar image of "dangerous" Indian roads, specifically after the Scarlett Keeling[2] rape and murder case in Goa and the Delhi gangrape case, has helped patriarchal society to dominate and instruct women to either be away from public space or depend on the male counterpart to use the space or take the responsibility of knowing and "doing" everything "right" to be safe.

The third Facebook page, *SAWTA* (Safety for all women traveling alone), speaks to and about this responsibility of women to be "safe" by providing safety tips for women traveling alone on foreign roads; thus signifying efforts of sustaining solo women traveling (2018). In the twenty-first century when there is "increased financial independence amongst women" and they have "created unconventional careers" (Chaudhary 2020, 297) as travelers and travel bloggers, the need to develop ways to navigate through the "physically dangerous site" of solo traveling has become essential. The page started in October 2018, allows space for the contributors to share their fears, experiences as well as safety tips depending on their socio-cultural understanding of gender relations in a particular travel destination. Even though the page is highly appreciable due to its constructive role in enabling women to travel safely, still, it, and other such pages, convincingly indicate that for a woman to travel alone is not simple leisure, but rather a complicated project that needs planning, risk management, and psychological skills. A woman is expected to research the destination, not only for the places to visit, but for how solo traveling women are seen and treated in that place; she is then expected to read the mind of male counterparts or *travelees* wherever she goes: it is a recurring tip to believe your intuition, and be conscious of male stares as well as behavior; and finally, she is expected to have a risk management plan in place. Certainly, these are wise steps to be taken while traveling in a foreign place but the problem is they don't transcend gender. Rarely, or even never, a male solo traveler is instructed to be conscious of female stares, or female advancements in terms of efforts to talk or touch or to dress according to societal or cultural norms. It is not to say that men are not under threat of any kind of violence, but, I propose, that their security is most of the time seen as a law-and-order situation; whereas that of a woman is seen as a socio-cultural problem, which means that situation is seen as avoidable if a woman can travel with care. Due to this, women traveling alone are burdened with all the responsibilities of staying safe—this automatically signals that women should find and learn ways to navigate the patriarchally constructed public spaces where a female body *will be* subjected to masculine violence. This perhaps is the reason for the president of WorldAware, a global risk management provider, to state that "it is 100% easier to be a man traveling than a woman" (Bloom 2017). It appears as if the first Facebook page discussed in this study is about the reason for traveling solo and the second one is a warning against doing the same, however, the third one is a rescue and provides a way for women to travel solo while reinforcing gender stratification. This gender stratification, further, hampers the mobility of women or allows them conditional mobility only, thereby interrupting the cause forwarded by the first page. Solo women travelers thus are sort of trapped in a circular model of the necessity of claiming agency and challenging patriarchy, perceived threats of disagreeing to social expectancies, agree to patriarchal conditions to navigate "safely" through their spaces to claim agency.

In this chapter I argue that the digital and print guides for travelers, designed to provide them with appropriate information and cautions about the destination, reinstate the process of instructing women about male authority and significance. Though the Indian women's travel accounts, either printed or digital, are indeed a testimony of solo women being capable of taming "dangerous" roads, still, the tips provided by online magazines, such as *Lonely Planet* and *National Geographic*, advise women to follow a strict list of recommended tricks and safety guards, as demonstrated in the opening quotes, is not only emblematizing the space of Indian roads as dangerous for women but also disrupt the authority of women as capable of traveling alone, rather it reinforces the need of male persona to accompany a woman on her journey. The agency allotted to women by travel and the genre of travel writing is ruptured when women are made or at least advised to follow "terms and conditions," often pretending to save them from violence and sexual threats, of traveling solo. This not only controls their mobility and thus their experience of travel, but also forwards gender stratification. In this paper, I argue that though the travel tips available on digital platforms are to facilitate travelers, in operation, they reinforce and reinvent the male authority and supremacy by constructing Indian roads as highly gendered spaces. Also, instead of looking at law and order situations, educating men on gender equality, or developing a guide for men to behave in public places, it seems that travel tips blogs and advisories work toward pronouncing gender vulnerability, which is in itself a paradigm and the by-product of inequality. I will read some of the blogs by leading Indian women travelers, where they share their experiences on Indian roads, and the online travel tips to study how and to what extent these tips influence the travel experiences of women on and off the road and the way they reinforce gender stratification.

In the next section, I study Indian roads as constructed gendered spaces, and later I read safety tips provided by leading travel magazines and blogs by solo females traveling on Indian roads to analyze the relationship between travel tips and gender stratification.

INDIAN ROADS: GENDERED SPACES

According to the UN report "Violence against women . . . are not isolated 'incidents,' private family matters or sacrosanct 'local customs' but "are based on the patriarchal system that establishes relationships of power and domination between men and women" (Impe 2019, 8). Traditionally, India is a conservative and patriarchal society, with a skewed sex ratio (Phipps 2017). This "skewed sex ratio" itself speaks about the perceived supremacy of male child in Indian households who is seen as the carrier of patrilineality and thus more relevant to this patriarchal social structure. However, to understand the relationship between power and domination, the very core of the circulation of this discourse of supremacy needs to be understood. Michel Foucault suggests that every society has its regime of truth—which in itself is a "system of ordered procedures for the production, regulation, distribution, circulation, and operation of statements"—as well as its "general politics of truth" in terms of accepting some discourses as truth and others as not (Foucault 1980b, 131, 133). Once the "truth" has been normalized by society, that is it is taken as a *divine rule*, the individuals become subject to that truth, which means, according to Foucault, it now sets up laws. The discourse of truth decides, conveys, and propels the effects of power (Foucault 2003, 25), which means that the knowledge formulated and circulated in the form of the "truth" is relational to power: "the exercise of power perpetually creates knowledge, and conversely, knowledge constantly induces effects of power" (Foucault 1980a, 51–52). Indian patriarchy also has, through the "ordered procedures" of culture, religion, and traditions, forwarded a "truth" that validates and accepts men as superior and higher in the hierarchy, leading to violence against women starting from female foeticide and infanticide that results in "skewed sex ratio."

The "truth" in a patriarchal society establishes that gender is natural and even more natural are gender norms. For instance, Gender norms, generally in all patriarchal societies, dictate that "women prioritize family and men prioritize career," which validates the "male bread-winner norm" casting "men as primary-or-higher-earner in the house" (Gonalons-Pons and Gangl 2021). In India, primarily due to this gender norm, men are referred to as "head of the family" and "*pati-parmeshwar*" (husband is god), and father and brothers are seen as protectors of daughters and sisters; in contrast, women are seen as responsible for domestic space, serving men of the family. These gender norms feed into the discourses of masculinity and femininity: masculine becomes a symbol of protector, superior, provider male; feminine becomes a symbol of vulnerable, inferior, receiver female. These roles are performed through "stylized repetition of acts," which further produce the effect of gender, that according to Judith Butler, is "the mundane way in which bodily gestures, movements, and styles of various kinds constitute the illusion of an abiding gendered self" (Butler 1990, 191). Consequently, the performativity of these roles produces the discourses of masculinity and femininity, which are then circulated through social interactions between genders, furthering the process of masculine superiority. Since these discourses, by evading the constructed nature of gender identity, reinforce a "truth" of gender being natural, thus they declare the performance of gender as a natural "law" (Ridgeway 2008; West and Zimmerman 1987) for the working of the society. A study around marriages and separation has demonstrated that couples do perform gender roles according to societal expectations: they "follow scripts that signify and accentuate men's masculinity and women's femininity." The failure to carry out gender roles leads to "confusion, sanctions and stigmatization," therefore individuals feel "pressure to account for gender non-normativity" which they do through "exaggerating gender normativity in other domain" (Gonalons-Pons and Gangl 2021). This "law" then is seen as *demanding* and *deserving* to be maintained for the effectual operation of the society. If a female member of the family is seen as evading gender norms, that may be as minimum as making decisions of her career, men start feeling the need to practice masculinity in another way- often through laying rules of mobility, timing and choice of clothes. The urgency to impose and operate these rules of domination and subjugation, as well as performing masculine authority in controlling female bodies, may lead to the use of "violence against women as a way of maintaining power and dominance over women" (cited in Diamond-Smith and Rudolph 2018). Also, the customs, such as dowry, and women as prestige carrier of the family that informs the gender-based normative rules and roles such as the preference of the male child, looking at the girl child as a financial burden, act as a catalyst in commodifying the female bodies and reduce gendered relationships to mere transactions. The female body is either "sexually objectified or seen as belonging to the men in their lives, this prompts a dehumanisation of women which allows others to perpetrate violence against" female bodies conveniently (Behrana 2021). Phumzile Mlambo-Ngcuka, executive director of UN Women, has affirmed that there exists evidence demonstrating that "women face risks that men don't face in public spaces, at home, or wherever they may be" and this, according to her, is largely due to "the underlying gender stereotypes, social norms, entitlement and patriarchy" (Mzezewa 2019a). It is because the "accepted truth" of male supremacy, now seen as a law, allots the power to male members of the society, to make or approve every decision of the society, including that related to female bodies in terms of education, clothing, marriage, or holidaying. As Foucault, in his theory of Panopticism, suggests that human behavior is controlled through normalization of power norms which are assured through "dissymmetry, disequilibrium, distance": the dominant and dominated are trained to believe the supremacy of power invested in the dominant (Foucault Autumn 2008). Women also, after being in a panoptic discipline mechanism created by patriarchy, start taking responsibility for playing gender roles and adhering to gender norms. Gender stratification thus evolves as a core value of the society, empowering men to take charge of female bodies, and instructing women to obey the subjugation.

Gender stratification reinforces patriarchal hierarchy in the society (Hesse 2020, 9), and as Pierre Bourdieu argued, there "is no space, in a hierarchical society, that is not hierarchized and which does not express social hierarchies and distances in a more or less distorted or euphemized fashion" (Bourdieu 2018, 107). Indian roads, also, become the site of expressing hierarchies. India has noticeable cultural, social, and political variations across different geographical regions. This makes the country a favorite destination for solo female travelers and one of the "most complex" too (Bloom 2017). The complexity arises due to cultural, social, and traditional variety, nonetheless, there remains homogeneity in dividing Indian space as public and private. In India, public space, which is the space of "transcendence, production, politics, and power," is seen as the space of men; whereas private space, which operates as the domestic front and "the sphere of reproduction," is considered as women's space (Siwach 2020). Male occupying a space of politics and power, thus, is entitled to produce, govern and implement the rules to control public space. Therefore, they exercise the power manifested through public space by keeping the "outsider," who are women in this case, away from these places. It then results in "social practices which see certain activities and certain spaces as male preserves" (Storey 2001, 160), thus acting to transmit inequality. Indian roads are compulsively seen as male preserves: though women are visible on roads specifically in a metropolis, still the image of "footpaths spilling over with old and young women watching the world go by as they sip tea, and discuss love, cricket and latest blockbuster" is imagining a utopia whereas "men hanging out . . . stop[ing] for a cigarette at a paanwala or lounge on a park bench . . . to stare at the sea or drink cutting chai at a tea stall . . . wander [ing] the streets late into the night" is a familiar sight (Shilpa Phadke 2011, vii). Thus Indian roads, like other gendered spaces, are also instrumental in adhering to and reaffirming "patriarchal systems of power," which reinforces "male dominance" (Spain 1992, 4). The "prevailing status distinctions that are taken for granted" (Spain 1993) are reinforced, reproduced, and recirculated on Indian roads. Men are empowered to dictate rules for women using Indian roads, and women are made responsible to legitimize their presence in that space. If a woman is unable to do this, then her act is termed as "loitering"—a term that comes with massive negative connotations. Through these terms, their presence on roads "is conjectured to entail dishonor and shame as well as questions of sexual virtues" (Walby 1989). Thereby forwarding the case of "respectability"; Doreen Massey sees the absence of flaneuse in contrast to flaneur as a result of linking this "respectability" to "mobility" specifically seen as "wander[ing] around the streets and parks alone" (Massey 1994, 234). The case for controlling the mobility of women then is shaped as a way to uphold her "respectability" as well as saving her from "the threat of male violence" (Massey 1994, 233). Thus, when an incident of violence against women takes place on roads, specifically those in patriarchal societies such as India, the victim is seen as culprit. For this reason, though violence on roads is also carried out against men, but the violence against women stems largely out of the hierarchical structure that sees women as subjects of male dominance as well as instinctively sees public places, such as roads, as male spaces. This furthers the validation of exclusion of female bodies from the Indian roads making the Indian roads highly gendered spaces.

TRAVEL TIPS AND TRAVEL BLOGS: CONDITIONS OF "SAFETY" AND TRAVELING

Based on a survey of 550 respondents, in 2018, Reuters declared India as the "world's most dangerous country for women due to high risk of sexual violence," the war-torn countries Afghanistan and Syria are second and third (Goldsmith 2018). Nonetheless, to sustain the encouragement and interest in women for solo travel, demonstration of which can be seen on social media platforms—as *Solo Female Traveller* discussed earlier—the online, easy to access, travel guides and blogs enlist number of tips on traveling in India as a solo woman. These travel tips, as will be discussed in this section, are designed around the idea of instructing/suggesting to women the ways to be "safe" while traveling solo in India. This, in a way, suggests that any irresponsibility in using tips will make women "unsafe," which means prone to direct or indirect violence; not only does this tend to make the mobility of women conditional but also tend to reinforce patriarchal authority on public spaces by underpinning gender stratification.

Even though these travel tips, and any research done before exploring a foreign land, is a commendable and responsible way of traveling. Nonetheless, these gender-oriented tips for safety appear as a way of informing women about the expectations of society from a particular gender and dictating them to match these expectations as a condition to travel safely. When women are categorically instructed to "do some research" and understand "culture, customs, and traditions" (Hewitt 2021) to avoid offending someone—it means primarily not to offend male members of the society because they are the ones who own the public spaces, and the safety of a woman depends on the attitude of these men. The majority of travel tips published on travel websites such as *Wanderlust, Intrepid Travel, National Geographic,* and *World Nomads*, concentrate on instructing women to "dress[ing] conservatively," "behave[ing] appropriately in public," "accompany[ing] women as much as possible" and "not travelling at night" (Phipps 2017; Childs 2017; Pearce 2021; Dara 2017). Even the welcome kit issued to foreign travelers in India included safety tips for women. Mahesh Sharma, then tourism minister, said "In that kit, they [women] are given dos and don'ts . . . these are very small things like, they should not venture out alone at night in small places, or wear skirts" only "for their safety" (Safi 2016). Ranjana Kumari, the director of the Centre for Social Research, Delhi, reacting to Sharma's "irresponsible statement" called it the reflection of "the syndrome of blaming women" (quoted in Safi 2016). As Jessica Nabongo suggests that the approach of telling "women what not to do to avoid being attacked instead of telling men not to attack women" is a way to find a "convenient scapegoat" (quoted in Mzezewa 2019a). The statement made by Sharma is reflective of the common patriarchal attitude of investing power in men to protect public spaces from any perceived immoral behavior of women, "the outsider." In India, a country where women mobility is still linked to promiscuity, such statements give men an authority to judge women on the basis of their clothes and mobility and make women responsible for adhering to the norms of accessing the public space. Thereby shifting the responsibility of gender vulnerability on the victims rather than the culprits.

As Sharma said "for their own safety" women accessing Indian roads are expected to know and value, as in other gendered spaces, "a behavioural code of conduct" that includes a "definite physical look, proper decorum, non-verbal communication, proper attire, etc." (Siwach 2020). Neha Dara reports that certain actions, such as "drinking alcohol, dancing with men, staying out late, wearing small clothes, rank high among them" and are "considered as 'unbecoming' for women in Indian culture" and thus women who are traveling alone are considered as "immoral" and "available" (Dara 2017). The article, rather almost all the articles and blogs about travel tips for solo women travelers, clearly mentions "dress conservatively" as a primary tip. Almost all have maintained that covering yourself will help in warding off unwanted attention—revealing clothes are seen by local men as "an invitation." However, a blog, *Hippie in Heels,* implicitly suggests that covering up may not work all the time. Rachel Jones in this blog on her Indian travels recounts that in "the overnight local buses and sleeper class trains . . . no amount of clothing/hiding made me feel covered enough" (Jones 2014). Priyanka Dubey, an award-winning journalist, while traveling to work on a story for her reportage on rapes in India, was "groped in the night by a group of men on a train" (Mohta 2019). This gives the impression that probably "covering" your body works in daylight, and women should seek another alternative tip to travel "safely" at night. This demand for another tip related to a "safe" time to travel for women is answered in all blogs homogenously as by Dara's blog that says: "not to venture out alone after dark" (Dara 2017). Nonetheless, this tip also sounds insufficient after reading Baruna Goswami's blog on travel tips, where she suggests "never travel alone in an empty bus, even during day hours" (Goswami 2020). This indicates that a solo woman traveler should be conscious about not only the clothing, and time of travel but also the place of mobility. Aparna Parikh however wrote that overcrowding of public transports makes women more vulnerable (Parikh 2018). Also according to a 2011 survey by Jagori and UN women on sexual harassment in Delhi, it was established that 51.4 percent of women reported being harassed on public buses (Choudhury 2021). This suggests that if empty buses are not safe, so are crowded buses. To address this problem, the next tip appears almost homogeneously in all travel blogs: *Intrepid travel* suggests taking taxi services with women drivers only, and if taking public transport "ride in the women's carriage only" (Intrepid); *Wanderlust* in addition to this, also suggest women to take an upper berth in sleeper trains for additional safety. Kartik Pandey goes a step further to suggest: "Be around other women. Opt for an all-women hostel or dorm, sit next to a female on a bus or any other public transport and join a female-only group on a social media site, especially wherein the members know the place you are going to" (Pandey 2020). These travel tips appear suggesting women to only move and interact in women space and avoid male spaces.

This conditional access to safety and public spaces validates what Robert Aldrich, has suggested that gender has always "influenced what travellers can and cannot do, and where they can and cannot go" (Aldrich 2019, 520). Travel tips are not only instrumental in proposing "the perceived travel risks and travel constraints [that] have negative effects on cognitive and affective destination images" (Kaba 2021, 478) but also persuade women that "public places are where men are most likely to commit violent acts against them"; this evolves "personal fears" that further "hamper their mobility" (Condon, Lieber, and Maillochon 2007). It is not to suggest that "the perceived travel risks" never turn into reality, rather the stories of violence or an attempt of violence against women have recurrently been documented by solo female travelers. For instance, Sreshti Verma, in her blog, writes about her experience in Macleodganj. She writes that in the market:

> I had already spotted a shady man who looked completely out of place. I felt his eyes on me, but I am from Delhi, even aunties stare the shit out of us. The man had started following me. He pretended to talk on the phone so I wouldn't notice. By now, I just wanted to rush home. Screw hotel, I wanted home. The distance between us almost vanished when I suddenly felt his hand grabbing my behind. (Verma 2016)

Nonetheless, the dramatic circulation of these stories through media reiterates "the narrative that women are not safe in public spaces" (Shilpa Phadke 2011, 10) which further leads to hampering the mobility of women. Not only do their families feel unsafe for them to travel alone but women get intimidated too. As Shivya Nath, a travel blogger writes that "hearing fearful stories of faraway places can make anyone reconsider traveling solo"; she narrates that, even if she is an experienced solo traveler still "listening to my mother's endless apprehensions can dampen my spirit" (Nath 2015). Similarly, the range of tips, as discussed above, by travel websites, portrays if all places, all times, and all spaces are dangerous for solo female travelers. Women's mobility in patriarchal public spaces, such as Indian roads, then becomes a matter of affordability, that is to say, what and how much risk one can afford to take to travel solo. These public spaces then become "spaces of contest" as women "literally have to fight their case" for accessing these spaces (Siwach 2020)—writing travel tips is a form of negotiating the conditions to access the public spaces.

Even in an urban metropolis, such as Bombay, where women using public spaces is visible site, women "do not share equal access to public space with men" (Shilpa Phadke 2011, viii). Not only does this fear for women's safety "allows even more brutal exclusions from public space in the guise of righteous desire to protect women" (Shilpa Phadke 2011, 11–12), but also demands women to have a strategic plan to navigate through these "dangerous" avenues. Other than instructing women to dress conservatively, not travel at night, and while traveling look for women companions, these travel tips also recommended women to "ask a male travel companion . . . to accompany you if you need to leave your compartment overnight" (Intrepid). Furthermore, to tackle all the perceived threats related to time, place, and space of mobility, women travelers are even suggested to "consider pretending to have a husband" or "keep an imaginative lover waiting" (Fergusson 2019). This tip though is given to keeping the unwanted attention of "local men" off, nonetheless, it reinforces an attitude that reproduces and validates gender stratification and declares public places as male spaces where women can only enter either in a company of a male companion or by abiding by the behavioral and other instructions outlined by patriarchy for women. These tips to travel safely, therefore, become a way to further a case of "neo-traditionalism" that "locates women back in the private space of the home" (Shilpa Phadke 2011, 10).

CONSCIOUSLY FEMININE: CHALLENGING THE VEIL WHILE EMBRACING IT

In the late nineteenth century Pandita Ramabai Saraswati (1888–1889), a social activist, started traveling across India and abroad and producing her experiences in the form of travel narratives. Since then, Indian women, such as Rosy Thomas (1958), Savitri Devi Mukherjee (1980), Anees Jung (1987), Monisha Rajesh (2012), and Jahanvi Acharekar (2015), have taken in stride to travel and write their experiences. Earlier, traveling and travel writing conformed to masculine ideals of valor and sexuality (Bird 2016), this was seen as a masculine endeavor, nonetheless, women by traveling solo and documenting their success stories were, and are, producing an alternative narrative. The blogs by solo Indian women travelers, such as Shivya Nath, Sreshti Verma, and Mansi Singh, demonstrate the eligibility and ability of

Indian women to travel solo. Also, since "travel functions as a defining arena of agency" (Smith 2001, ix), these solo women travelers claimed agency and challenged gender stratification, and the patriarchal authority over public spaces by claiming equal ownership of the Indian roads. Nonetheless, the travel tips, by making their mobility conditional and dependent on patriarchal norms, tend to interrupt this agency. Women solo travelers, then to safeguard this agency and the authority, claimed through travel and travel writing, chose to navigate between challenging and adhering to the gender norms.

Women travelers and travel writers, who opted to "stay away from home and perform tasks considered as masculine," globally, right from the Victorian era, were "likely to be labelled as immoral" (Kassis 2015, 38). Their condition, according to Victorian patriarchy was similar to that of "the fallen woman," who as suggested by Lynda Nead, was once a "respectable woman" but "fallen" due to her choices and decisions (Nead 1988, 95). This "respectability," as discussed earlier, has helped, and is still helping, patriarchy to dictate the "respectable" choices for women, including the use of public spaces. Earlier, as well, women using public spaces, specifically roads, without "legitimate reason" were witch-hunted through recurring images of "fallen women" that tended to legitimize violence against women and also blame women for violence against women. In the twentieth century, feminist reformers sought and fought to revert this idea of a "fallen woman" as a culprit of society to a victim of "male lust and exploitation" (Odem 1995, 3). Though this demand resonated with the idea of "New Woman" that validated the "woman leaving home" as opposed to the "angel at home" image of "respectable women." Still, the status of women, in this twenty-first century, in public spaces, specifically in societies with a higher degree of gender stratification, remains that of an "outsider" or lesser "being" than men, and therefore women are still expected to adhere to the patriarchal rules for accessing the public sphere "safely." Consequently, either, to uphold their "respectability," or to avoid this threat of violence, women in these societies, have been persuaded to avoid male spheres and roles, or adhere to the rules laid by the masculine hegemony and patriarchal authority of accessing that sphere, such as roads. Even though Indian women have long been traveling and writing, still the uncontested equal ownership of Indian roads have yet not reached even the metropolis, such as Bombay. There is a compulsive demand as well as a need for women to demonstrate that "they have a legitimate reason to be where they are" (Shilpa Phadke 2011, 8). In case there is no "legitimate reason," the female body is seen as "asking for" violent punishment, an example of that was seen in the case of the Delhi gangrape, and the attitude of society toward the victim despite public outrage. Jyoti Singh's, famously known as Nirbhaya, rape on a moving bus in Delhi, which eventually led to her death, is "a catalyst for new awareness of patriarchal structures in society that limit women's movement" (Hesse 2020, 1).

Even if women are not explicitly instructed to remain in private space, still through conditional mobility and reinstating men, even an imaginative man, as the savior of women, the gender-based distribution of space is naturalized. The travel tips, advocating women to depend on men or segregate them from men through "dedicated" spaces, imply gender segregation as well as stratification by pronouncing men as either protectionists or predators and women as "victims." Nath suggests, "relentless victimization"—that portrays women "neither as strong nor as safe as men"—is a "root cause of so many challenges faced by women" (Nath 2013). Through the effect of naturalization,[3] women "subconsciously accept their subordinate position by abiding by rules of gendered spaces and indirectly enable men to reaffirm their advantage in society" (Spain 1992, 15). It also inculcates a behavioral pattern among women, who unconsciously as well as consciously start protecting their bodies from the "male gaze" and gender-based violence. This answers to the behavior of women in metropolis, such as Bombay, where even if women are "visible as commuters on public buses and trains," still they wear "visible *mangalsutras* that mark them as married," "have their files clasped carefully to their chests in the classic posture of defensiveness," keep their "cell phone close" to them, "almost without being aware of it, every woman reflects deeply about how to access public space" (Shilpa Phadke 2011, 6, 7, x). According to Foucault, this controlled behavior leads to the power that is "visible and unverifiable" which means women continuously feel under surveillance, under a "gaze" of patriarchal society, and consciously believe that any effort to break the norms will then result in inviting danger and violence. It can be understood through Foucault's theory of Panopticism, which says:

> The Panopticon is a machine for dissociating the see/being see dyad: in the peripheric ring, one is totally seen, without ever seeing; in the central tower, one sees everything without ever being seen. . . . A real subjection is born mechanically from a fictitious relation. . . . The efficiency of power, its constraining force have, in a sense, passed over to the other side—to the side of its surface of application. He who is subjected to a field of visibility, and who knows it, assumes responsibility for the constraints of power. (Foucault Autumn 2008, 6,7)

This when applied to travel tips, which is a form of suggestion for traveling with care, it becomes evident that women are led to assume this responsibility for the constraints of power. Undoubtedly the travel tips are provided for "safety" but do they solve the purpose? The answer to this can be found in Shilpa Phadke's experience while traveling with a friend through Agra, Gwalior, Jhansi, Orccha, and Datia in North India:

We were well aware of the need to plan the minutest details. Our hotels and guesthouses were booked in advance. The train tickets were reserved mindful of delays. We could not leave before it was light or arrive after dark. Our clothes were chosen to be as little out-of-place as possible. As urban *bal-kati auratein* (short-haired women) we could not hope to blend in completely but nor did we want to draw undue attention. . . .

Nonetheless this did not mean we were not harassed. In our guesthouse in Agra, we put a chair under our door handle as we heard repeated knocks on the door well after midnight. At the Gwalior fort we finally succumbed and hired a guide . . . , his presence "protecting" us from many offers of guidance and other things. At the palace-fort in Orchha we held our breath when a group of men loudly talking to each other and verbally harassing us went by without doing more. As they passed us, both of us saw vivid images of gang rape in our minds. That holiday passed off without anything worse than verbal harassment and strange and leering looks. Despite the pleasure we found in our travels, there was a sense that as women we did not have access to the full range of travelling pleasures. (ix–x)

Solo female travelers remain in the interstices of effect of Panopticism and will break the Panopticon. These tips of traveling "safely," reinforcing the "fearful" stories of attack and violence, make women feel "fearful of travel," which is "a modern form of *purdah* (seclusion or secrecy), with sexist and misogynistic undertones" (Ward 2020). Nath acknowledges that online forums, such as *Lonely Planet*, "flooded with safety concerns" (Nath 2011) for women traveling solo in India, circulate the discourse of threat and violence against solo women travelers. On the one hand, she challenges the discourse as well as the *purdah* it imposed on women by "choose[ing] not to read media reports propagating fear about traveling in countries labeled unsafe" (Nath 2015). On the other hand, she also affirms that "dress conservatively"—a form of "covering up, a *purdah*" (Nath 2016)—is a useful safety tip. Not only do the women, in an effort to adhere to safety tips, reinforce a form of *purdah*, but also the efforts made by the society for women's security revolve around this in the form of "women only" spaces. Alka Kaushik, a Delhi-based travel blogger, expressed her discontent over the "women only" hotel started by Oyo by writing "I feel that the society which failed to assure women security, is now trying to build walls around women to make them feel secure."[4] These walls are nothing but a form of *purdah* imposed on women which in a way restricts their mobility to a specific zone. Even though Kaushik acknowledges the threats and inconvenience of being a woman traveling in male spaces, she still feels suffocated by the "siege" around her. She advocates traveling with men and women for that is where, according to her, society exists (Kaushik 2015), thus challenging the gendered segregation. Nonetheless, she also reinforces that as a solo woman traveler she remains alert about "not to take any risk" and thus, adheres to the norms of dress, behavior, and time of travel. Therefore, redirecting solo women travelers to the zone of conditional mobility.

CONCLUSION

These travel tips, that in a way agree on the conditional mobility of women, empower the social and civic structures of the society to evade real gender-based violence by shifting the focus to the way women dress, carry out the mobility as well as cultural exchange. As much as travel has given agency to women to claim voice, power, and authority; their gender and gender-related violence, therefore, become a tool for the patriarchal society to interrupt that agency of women as solo and independent travelers and explorers. Since "[b]odies are used to act out roles in various settings, which confirm and resist wider sets of expectancies" (Cresswell 1999, 176). Therefore, through solo female travelers oscillating between adhering to and challenging these norms—expectancies of patriarchy are confirmed. It is now evident that both the travel tips as well as "fearful stories," which tend to educate and caution women about their "dangerous" journeys, actually end up hindering women's mobility; nonetheless, women, to reclaim agency, negotiate between adhering to and, simultaneously, challenging the gender norms.

REFERENCES

Advani, Rahul. 2013. "India: A Destination Nightmare for Tourists? Implications of Sexual Violence." *ISAS Insights* 214: —8. www.files.ethz.ch/isn/166940 /ISAS_Insights_No__214_-_India_A_Destination_Nightmare_for_Tourists _10072013140704.pdf.

Aldrich, Robert. 2019. "Gender and Travel Writing." In *The Cambridge History of Travel Writing*, edited by Tim Youngs Nandini Das, 520–534. Cambridge: Cambridge University Press.

Behrana, Maheen. 2021. "India: Can We Turn the Tide on the Epidemic of Violence against Women and Girls?" *Candid Orange*. Accessed September 9, 2021.

Bird, Dunlaith. 2016. "Travel Writing and Gender." In *The Routledge Companion to Travel Writing*, edited by Carl Thompson. Oxon: Routledge.

Bloom, Laura Begley. 2017. "10 Most Dangerous Places for Women Travelers (And How to Stay Safe)." Forbes. www.forbes.com/sites/laurabegleybloom/2017 /07/28/10-most-dangerous-places-for-women-travelers-and-how-to-stay-safe/?sh =23cb6eda2448.

Bourdieu, Pierre. 2018. "Social Space and the Genesis of Appropriated Physical Space." *International Journal of Urban and Regional Research* 42 (1): 106–114. doi.org/doi.org/10.1111/1468-2427.12534.

Butler, Judith. 1990. *Gender Trouble: Feminism and the Subversion of Identity.* New York: Routledge.

Chaudhary, Sanchari Basu. 2020. "Flânerie in Female Solo Travel: An Analysis of Blogposts from Shivya Nath's the Shooting Star." *Rupkatha Journal on Interdisciplinary Studies in Humanities* 12, no. Themed Issue on "India and Travel Narratives" (3): 296–302. doi.org/10.21659/rupkatha.v12n3.35.

Chiang, Chu-Yin, and Giri Jogaratnam. 2006. "Why Do Women Travel Solo for Purposes of Leisure?" *Journal of Vacation Marketing* 12 (1): 59–70. doi.org/10.1177/1356766706059041.doi.org/10.1177/1356766706059041.

Childs, Lorinda. 2017. "6 Easy Tips for Solo Female Travel in India." Intrepid. www.intrepidtravel.com/adventures/tips-for-solo-female-travellers-india/.

Choudhury, Disha Roy. 2021. "Why Women Stay Silent about Sexual Harassment in Public Spaces." *The Indian Express*, February 15, Life-Style. indianexpress.com/article/lifestyle/life-style/women-sexual-harassment-public-places-transport-7183030/.

Condon, Stéphanie, Marylène Lieber, and Florence Maillochon. 2007. "Feeling Unsafe in Public Places: Understanding Women's Fears." *Revue française de sociologie* 48 (5): 101–128. doi.org/10.3917/rfs.485.0101. www.cairn.info/revue-francaise-de-sociologie-1-2007-5-page-101.htm. www.cairn.info/load_pdf.php?ID_ARTICLE=RFS_485_0101.

Cresswell, Tim. 1999. "Embodiment, Power and the Politics of Mobility: The Case of Female Tramps and Hobos." *Transactions of the Institute of British Geographers* 24 (2): 175–192. www.jstor.org/stable/623295.

Dara, Neha. 2017. "Should Women Travel Alone in India?." Travel. Accessed February 10. www.nationalgeographic.com/travel/destinations/asia/india/should-women-travel-solo-india-tips.

Diamond-Smith, Nadia, and Kara Rudolph. 2018. "The Association between Uneven Sex Ratios and Violence: Evidence from 6 Asian Countries." *PloS one* 13 (6): e0197516-e0197516.doi.org/10.1371/journal.pone.0197516.pubmed.ncbi.nlm.nih.gov/29856763. www.ncbi.nlm.nih.gov/pmc/articles/PMC5983495/.

Fergusson, Asher and Lyric. 2019. "A Study of the World's Most Dangerous Countries for Women Traveling Alone Reveals the Good, the Bad and the Ugly." *Solo Female Travel* (blog), *Asher and Lyric*. www.asherfergusson.com/solo-female-travel-safety/.

Foucault, Michel. 1980a. "Prison Talks." In *Power/Knowledge: Selected Interviews and Other Writings 1972–1977*, edited by Colin Gordon. New York: Pantheon.

———. 1980b. "Truth and Power." In *Power/Knowledge: Selected Interviews and Other Writings 1972–1977*, edited by Colin Gordon. New York: Pantheon.

———. 2003. *Society Must Be Defended: Lectures at the Collège de France 1975–1976.* Translated by David Macey. Edited by Mauro Bertani and Alessandro Fontana. New York: Picador.

———.2008. "'Panopticism' from Discipline & Punish: The Birth of the Prison." *Race/Ethnicity: Multidisciplinary Global Contexts* 2 (1): 1–12. muse.jhu.edu/article/252435.

Ghose, Indira. 1998. *Women Travellers in Colonial India: The Power of the Female Gaze*. Delhi: Oxford University Press

Goldsmith, Belinda. 2018. "India Most Dangerous Country for Women with Sexual Violence Rife—Global Poll." *Reuters*, June 26.

Gonalons-Pons, P., and M. Gangl. 2021. "Marriage and Masculinity: Male-Breadwinner Culture, Unemployment, and Separation Risk in 29 Countries." *American Sociological Review* 86 (3): 465–502. doi.org/10.1177/00031224211012442.

Goswami, Baruna. 2020. "21 Tips For Solo Female Travelers in India." *IndianVisit* (blog), *Indian Holiday Pvt Ltd*. www.indianvisit.com/blog/solo-female-travel-in-india/.

Haigh, Lauren. 2020. "Female Travellers: A Unique Risk Profile." *International Travel and Health Insurance Journal* 203. https://www.itij.com/latest/long-read/female-travellers-unique-risk-profile

Hesse, Sandra. 2020. "Gendered Spaces in India: Processes of Claiming Space through Feminist Street Art in Delhi." Master"s of Education, Institute for English/American Studies, University of Potsdam. www.uni-potsdam.de/fileadmin/projects/wci/Gendered_Spaces_in_India_Hesse.pdf.

Hewitt, Rachel. 2021. "For Women to Feel Safe in Public Spaces, Men's Behaviour Has to Change." *The Guardian* (Opinion). Accessed September 25.

Hill, Amelia. 2017. "Two Men in Scarlett Keeling Murder Case in India Face Court Again." *The Guardian*, February 9, News. www.theguardian.com/world/2017/feb/09/two-men-in-scarlett-keeling-case-in-india-face-court-again.

Impe, Anne-Marie. 2019. *Reporting on Violence against Women and Girls: A Handbook for Journalists*. Paris: UNESCO.

Intrepid. "Safety Advice for Women Travellers in India." Intrepid Travel. Accessed November 15, 2021. www.intrepidtravel.com/en/women-safety-india.

Jones, Rachel. 2014. "14 Tips for Solo Female Travel in India." *Hippie in Heels* (blog), *Wordpress*. hippie-inheels.com/tips-for-solo-female-travel-in-india/.

Kaba, Bahar. 2021. "Foreign Solo Female Travellers' Perceptions of Risk and Safety in Turkey." In *Hidden Geographies*, edited by Marko Krevs, 475–494. Key Challenges in Geography. Switzerland: Springer.

Kassis, Dimitrios. 2015. *Representations of the North in Victorian Travel Literature*. Newcastle upon Tyne: Cambridge Scholars Publishing.

Kaushik, Alka. 2015. "Why 'Women's Exclusive' Tag Does Not Appeal to the Nomad in Me!" *LyfInTransit* (blog). alkakaushik.com/2015/10/24/why-womens-exclusive-tag-does-not-appeal-to-the-nomad-in-me/.

Kow, Nicole. 2018. *The Solo Female Travel Trend: The Experiences and Priorities they are Chasing*. TrekkSoft (Online), May 11. www.trekksoft.com/en/blog/solo-female-travel-trend-experiences-and-priorities.

Lawrence, Karen. 1994. *Penelope Voyages: Women and Travel in the British Literary Tradition*. Ithaca, NY: Cornell University Press.

Macdonald, Charlotte. 2015. *A Woman of Good Character: Single Women as Immigrant Settlers in Nineteenth-Century New Zealand*. Wellington: Bridget Williams Books.

Massey, Doreen. 1994. *Space, Place and Gender*. Cambridge: Polity Press.

Mills, Sara. 1991. *Discourse of Difference: An Analysis of Women's Travel Writing and Colonialism*. London: Routledge.

Mohta, Payal. 2019. Meet the Journalist Documenting India's Unreported Rape Cases. *Open Democracy*. Accessed September 20, 2021. https://opendemocracy.net/en/5050/meet-the-journalist-documenting-indias-unreported-rape-cases/.

Mzezewa, Megan Specia and Tariro. 2019a. "Adventurous. Alone. Attacked." *The New York Times*, March 31.

———. 2019b. "More Women Travelling Solo but That Doesn't Take Away the Danger." *Independent*. Accessed March 3, 2021. https://www.nytimes.com/2019/03/25/travel/solo-female-travel.html.

Nath, Shivya. 2011. "On Solo Travel & Indian Women." *The Shooting Star* (blog). the-shooting-star.com/travel-india-alone/.

———. 2013. "Why I'm Not Celebrating International Women's Day." *The Shooting Star* (blog). the-shooting-star.com/why-im-not-celebrating-international-womens-day/.

———. 2015. "How I Conquer My Solo Travel Fears." *The Shooting Star* (blog). https://the-shooting-star.com/travel-india-alone/.

———. 2016. "Practical Ways I've Learnt to Stay Safe while Travelling Alone." *The Shooting Star* (blog). the-shooting-star.com/practical-ways-ive-learnt-to-stay-safe-while-travelling-alone/.

National Crime Record Bureau. 2020, September 13. *Crime in India 2020 Statistics*. Ministry of Home Affairs. New Delhi: Government of India. ncrb.gov.in/sites/default/files/CII%202020%20Volume%201.pdf.

Nead, Lynda. 1988. *Myths of Sexuality: Representations of Women in Victorian Britain*. Oxford: Basil Blackwell.

Odem, Mary E. 1995. *Delinquent Daughters: Protecting and Policing Adolescent Female Sexuality in the United States 1885–1920*. Chapel Hill: The University of North Carolina Press.

Over 85% of Solo Travelers are Women—Adventure Travel Reports. 2020. IGN24 (Online), January 14. industryglobalnews24.com/over-85-of-solo-travelers-are-women-adventure-travel-reports.

Pandey, Kartik. 2020. "25 Safety Tips for Solo Women Travellers in India." *Travel Tips and Hacks* (blog), *fab hotels*. www.fabhotels.com/blog/safety-tips-for-solo-women-travellers-in-india/.

Parikh, Aparna. 2018. "Politics of Presence: Women's Safety and Respectability at Night in Mumbai, India." *Gender, Place & Culture* 25 (5): 695–710. doi.org/10.1080/0966369X.2017.1400951.

Pearce, Sophie. 2021. "10 Honest Tips for Solo Female Travel in Varanasi." Third Eye Traveller. Accessed October 20, 2021. thirdeyetraveller.com/solo-female-travel-guide-varanasi/.

Phipps, Anna. 2017. "5 Practical Tips for Solo Female Travellers in India, Including What to Wear." Wanderlust. www.wanderlust.co.uk/content/solo-female-travel-india-practical-tips-what-to-wear/.

Ridgeway, Cecilia L. 2008. "Framed Before We Know It: How Gender Shapes Social Relations." *Gender & Society* 23 (2): 145–160. doi.org/10.1177/0891243208330313.doi.org/10.1177/0891243208330313.

Roberti, Janice and Nick Waugh. 2019. *Solo Travel Trends Report.* Solo Traveler (Online). solotravelerworld.com/wp-content/uploads/2018/12/Solo-Travel-Trends-Report_Full_v3.pdf.

Safi, Michael. 2016. "Female Tourists Should Not Wear Skirts in India, Says Tourism Minister." *Guardian* (India), August 29. www.theguardian.com/world/2016/aug/29/india-female-tourists-skirts-safety-advice.

SAWTA (Safety for All Women Travelling Alone). 2018. www.facebook.com/SAWTA-Safety-for-All-Women-Traveling-Alone-489038611584339/?ref=page_internal.

Shilpa Phadke, Sameera Khan, and Shilpa Ranade. 2011. *Why Loiter?: Women and Risk on Mumbai Streets.* New York: Penguin Books.

Siwach, Prerna. 2020. "Mapping Gendered Spaces and Women's Mobility: A Case Study of Mitathal Village, Haryana." *The Oriental Anthropologist* 20 (1): 33–48. doi.org/10.1177/0972558X20913680. doi.org/10.1177/0972558X20913680.

Smith, Sidonie. 2001. *Moving Lives: Twentieth-Century Women's Travel Writing.* Minneapolis: University of Minnesota Press.

Solo Female Travelers Club. 2015. Facebook. www.facebook.com/groups/solofemaletravelers/.

Solo Travel Statistics and Data: 2021–2022. 2022. Solo Traveler (online). solotravelerworld.com/about/solo-travel-statistics-data/#More_Sources_of_Solo_Travel_Statistics_and_Trends.

Spain, Daphne. 1992. *Gendered Spaces.* Chapel Hill: The University of North Carolina Press.

———. 1993. "Gendered Spaces and Women's Status." *Sociological Theory* 11 (2): 137–151. doi.org/10.2307/202139. www.jstor.org/stable/202139.

Storey, David J. 2001. "Territory and Locality." In *Territory: Nations, State and the Claiming of Space*, edited by David J Storey. Oxon: Routledge.

Verma, Sreshti. 2016. "How I Was Attacked and How I Fought Back as a Solo Female Traveller." www.tripoto.com/mcleod-ganj/trips/how-i-was-attacked-and-how-i-fought-back-as-a-solo-female-traveller-578de9b7d5b59.

Walby, Sylvia. 1989. "Theorising Patriarchy." *Sociology* 23 (2): 213–234. www.jstor.org/stable/42853921.

Ward, Mariellen. 2020. "Is India Safe for Women Traveling Alone?" *World Nomads* (blog). www.worldnomads.com/travel-safety/southern-asia/india/womens-travel-safety-in-india.

West, Candace, and Don H. Zimmerman. 1987. "Doing Gender." *Gender & Society* 1 (2): 125–151. doi.org/10.1177/0891243287001002002. doi.org/10.1177/0891243287001002002.

"Women Travellers in India—Lonely Planet." 2021. www.lonelyplanet.com/india/narratives/practical-information/directory/women-travellers.

World Health Organization. 2021. *Violence against Women.* www.who.int/news-room/fact-sheets/detail/violence-against-women.

NOTES

1. On December 16, 2012, a 22-year-old physiotherapy student was brutally beaten, tortured and gang-raped on a moving bus in Delhi, the capital city of India. Jyoti Singh, the victim also named as Nirbhaya, died thirteen days after the incident.

2. Scarlett Keeling was a 15-year-old Briton who was found dead on Anjuna beach, Goa in 2008. She was on a "trip of lifetime" with her family members. Her death was initially declared as an accident by the police, but later, after a campaign by her family, the second post-mortem report in March 2008 confirmed that Keeling was drugged and sexually assaulted before drowning in sea water (Hill 2017).

3. The effect of naturalization is associated with "the durable inscription of social realities onto and in the physical world: differences produced by social logic can then be seen to arise out of the nature of things." *See*.

4. The blog is written in Hindi, in this quote I provide my translation of the blog article on solo travel.

Conclusion

WOMEN AND THE ROAD: POSSIBILITIES AND PROMISES

Indian feminist scholars, Shilpa Phadke, Sameera Khan, and Shilpa Ranade begin their book *Why Loiter* by asking the reader to:

> Imagine an Indian city with street corners full of women: chatting, laughing, breast-feeding, exchanging corporate notes or planning protest meetings. [Then to] [i]magine footpaths spilling over with old and young women watching the world go by as they sip tea, and discuss love, cricket and the latest blockbuster. [And finally to] [i]magine women in saris, jeans, salwars and skirts sitting at the *nukkad* reflecting on world politics and dissecting the rising sensex. [Eventually, they claim][:] *If you can imagine this, you're imagining a radically different city.* (2011, vii; emphasis in the original)

Despite the utopic underpinnings of such a vision, the authors urge Indian women to assert their claim to Indian public spaces by embracing the risk to loiter "without purpose and meaning ... without being asked what time of the day it is, why [they] are here, what [they] are wearing, and whom [they] are with" (219). Clearly, the authors propose loitering as the "fundamental act of claiming public space and ultimately, a [matter of] more inclusive citizenship" (178). Among the many aggressive online and offline campaigns following the notorious Nirbhaya incident, the "Why Loiter" movement started in 2014 and was spearheaded by theatre artist and author, Neha Singh. Tellingly, it grew out of the ideas propounded by Shilpa Phadke, Sameera Khan, and Shilpa Ranade's book published in 2011. Without banners, charts or identifying markers, the activists of "Why Loiter" campaign wander the streets of Mumbai, take midnight bicycle rides and night-time walks, nap on park benches, and laze around in chai shops thereby normalizing their presence in public spaces, and "turning the male gaze back upon itself to notice what it perceives as normative and nonnormative within public space" (Lieder 2018,

150). Along with such offline protests, the #whyloiter hashtag campaign urged Indian women to go out and loiter aimlessly in public spaces and post photographs on online platforms such as Instagram, Twitter, Facebook, and Snapchat (Jha 65). The campaign garnered immense media support and thousands of attendees signed into the "Why Loiter" Facebook page (www.facebook.com/people/Why-Loiter/100064256066567/) with similar events organized in cities such as New Delhi, Bangalore, Mumbai, Srinagar, Jaipur, Chicago, Hong Kong, Bharuch (Gujarat), and Uttarakhand (Jha 70).

In addition to "Why Loiter," other Indian campaigns such as "#Boardthebus," "Meet to Sleep," "Blank Noise," *Pinjra Tod*," "Take Back the Night," "Besharmi Morcha" (Indian equivalent of SlutWalk), "Freeze the Tease," and "Hollaback," among others, powerfully protest against restrictions on women's mobility, misogyny, the rape culture, and rampant violence against women while also celebrating women's claim to safe public spaces. #Boardthebus started as an offshoot of protests following the violent gang rape and death of Jyoti Singh on a bus in New Delhi, India. Initiated by a global human rights organization called Breakthrough with the aim of "regaining public space" (Fickes 2014), the activists asked the participants to board a public bus, take a selfie and share it on social media (Fickes 2014). The movement was intended to raise awareness regarding the "acute sense of insecurity" (Tara 2011, 72) women experience on public transport in the national capital territory. On similar lines, the performative "Meet to Sleep" campaigners challenged "the vulnerability of the female body" (Lieder 2018, 152) in public locations by organizing sleep outs in public parks. Initiated in 2015 by "Blank Noise," a Bangalore based community that seeks to end street harassment, the "Walk Alone Akeli Awaara Azaad" (alone, wandering, free) campaign invites women to walk alone in a place they never have been before. Their website (www.blanknoise.org/walk-alone-akeli-awaara-azaad) exhorts: "The action calls to confront fear and build a relationship of ownership and belonging instead of fear" with streets and public spaces (Action Heroes Walk Alone). Another powerful campaign, *Pinjra Tod* (Break the Cage) (www.facebook.com/pinjratod/) is a collective movement by women students from colleges across New Delhi, India against misogynistic hostel regulations and curfews that limit women's mobility and freedom. "Hollaback," the anti-street harassment movement, which started in New York in 2005, also finds its indigenous variations in major cities of India. Notably, anti-street harassment documentary *Jor Se Bol* (Speak Out Loud) (2011) produced by Akshara Centre, an NGO based in Mumbai for women's empowerment, urges men to stop the harassment (locally termed as "eve-teasing") of Indian women on buses, train stations, schools, and colleges. Along with such local campaigns, global hashtag activism including #MeToo, #EverydaySexism, #BeenRapedNeverReported, among others, have found a powerful response within India with survivors of gendered violence actively engaging in digital feminist activism by sharing personal stories of sexual violence and harassment on social media. Concerning this, gender and media studies expert Kaitlynn Mendes along with her colleagues Jessica Ringrose and Jessalynn Keller point out that hashtag activism on social media is "doing meaningful and worthwhile work in building networks of solidarity . . . [that] often transforms into a feminist consciousness amongst hashtag participants, which allows them to understand sexual violence as a structural rather than personal problem" (2018, 238). Without a doubt, it can be argued that the offline and online activism by women's rights activists across the world is engaged in creating radically altered public spaces devoid of sexual violence, harassment, and misogyny for all women.

Within India, in addition to collective feminist activism, government-initiated plans such as "Pink Taxis," taxi cabs chauffeured by women, operates from major cities such as Bangalore, Delhi, and Kolkata in India to offer safer commute for women. Other initiatives by the Government of India to ensure women's safety include the Nirbhaya Fund. The Department of Economic Affairs, Ministry of Finance, administers the non-lapsable Nirbhaya Fund for programs that ensure safety and security of women in India. Further, the Ministry of Women and Child Development functions as the nodal authority to appraise/recommend proposals under this scheme. Under the Nirbhaya Fund Scheme, Safe City Project (safecity.mha.gov.in/) by the Ministry of Home Affairs aims to create safe, secure, and inclusive city spaces for women to pursue opportunities without the fear of gender-based violence. The 181 helpline is a twenty-four-hour emergency response system to provide assistance to women facing violence or threats of violence in private and public spheres. "Investigation Tracking System for Sexual Offences" is an analytical tool launched by the Ministry of Home Affairs to monitor and ensure the timely completion of investigations in sexual assault cases and to track sex offenders across the country. The Ministry of Women and Child Development has in the past introduced One Stop Centers to provide integrated assistance and psycho-social support to women affected by violence. Along with the Government of India, the National Women's Commission works tirelessly to ensure the safety and security of Indian women in domestic as well as public spaces. As powerful as these interventions are in ensuring women's safety within Indian public spaces, what also needs to change is a larger culture of misogyny that afflicts women's rights and freedoms of mobility. This book is an attempt in that direction; it hopes to add to discussions surrounding women's right to the road and their freedom to explore public spaces.

It is important to note that when sexual crimes and violence are reported in public spaces, the immediate public response is to demarcate these spaces as dangerous and to delimit women's access to them. Rather than restricting women's mobility, recent feminist campaigns and digital activism demand overarching strategies to continuously monitor public spaces to make them a more inclusive and less hostile. More important, they assert the need for awareness and sensitization against sexual violence and misogyny to develop from the grass roots and reach the highest levels of the nation's socio-cultural structures such that the vision of street corners occupied by women loitering and engaging in various activities throughout the day and night becomes a reality. Adding to such efforts, this compendium of critical essays addresses the necessity to engage with women's journeys and creates a powerful call of social awareness so that women's experience of public spaces is not impaired by the fear of assault and violence. In sum, this volume aspires to create theoretically informed discursive paradigms that ultimately bolster the possibilities and promises for women as they take to Indian roads.

REFERENCES

"Action Heroes Walk Alone towards Freedom from Fear." *Blank Noise*. www.blanknoise.org/walk-alone-akeli-awaara-azaad

Fickes, Ted. 2014. "Breakthrough's Board the Bus Campaign Reaches Millions across India." *Mob Lab*, June 23. mobilisationlab.org/stories/breakthroughs-board-the-bus-campaign-reaches-millions-across-india/

hooks, bell. 1989. *Talking Back: Thinking Feminist, Thinking Black*. Toronto: Between the Lines.

Jha, Sonora. "Hashtag Activism and the Claim for Public Space by Women in India through the #whyloiter Campaign." In *New Feminisms in South Asian Social Media, Film, and Literature*, edited by Sonora Jha and Alka Kurian, 63–84. New York: Routledge.

Lieder, K. Frances. 2018. "Performing Loitering: Feminist Protest in the Indian City." *TDR/The Drama Review* 62, no. 3 (Fall): 145–161. muse.jhu.edu/article/702228/pdf

Mendes, Kaitlynn, Jessica Ringrose, and Jessalynn Keller. 2018. "#MeToo and the Promise and Pitfalls of Challenging Rape Culture through Digital Feminist Activism." *European Journal of Women's Studies* 25, no. 2 (May): 236–246. doi.org/10.1177/1350506818765318

Phadke, Shilpa, Sameera Khan, and Shilpa Ranade. 2011. *Why Loiter? Women and Risk on Mumbai Streets*. New Delhi: Penguin Books.

Tara, Shelley. 2011. "Private Space in Public Transport: Locating Gender in the Delhi Metro." *Economic and Political Weekly* 46, no. 51 (December): 71–74. www.jstor.org/stable/23065551

Index

acid attack, 1, 9, 51–52.
    See also Chhapaak;
    Priya's Mirror
adventure, 1, 13, 75, 79–80, 98–100, 105, 116, 118, 121–22, 127, 224
alienation, 83, 170, 214
anonymity, 189;
    of a city, 215–16, 170
Article 15, 123–26
autoconstruction, 44–46
awareness, 55–56, 111, 162, 167–69, 236, 246, 248

Bangalore, 84, 188–89, 192–93, 199n4, 246–47
belonging, xi, 34, 36, 38, 42, 165, 230, 246;
    in the city, 213–17
binaries, 16n1, 33–34, 37, 80
Blank Noise, 246
Bollywood, 9, 10, 26, 52, 71, 73, 77–82, 88, 92n27, 103, 113, 117, 122, 134–35, 138, 143, 148n2
BPO. *See* Business Process Outsourcing
Business Process Outsourcing, 12, 185, 187–88, 193–94, 199n4
bus stations, 23

call center, 186, 188–89, 191–92, 194–96;
    employees, 189, 192, 195
campaign, 52–53, 55, 62–64, 169, 244n2, 245–46
capitalism, 38, 91n11, 186, 191
care work, 156
caste, 10–11, 28–29, 81, 85–86, 105, 107, 115–117, 119, 122–28, 132, 137–38, 140–42, 146, 152, 158, 159, 160, 162, 169, 186, 204, 209
celluloid, 10, 97, 135, 146
Chamar, 41
Chhapaak, 5, 10, 52, 60, 95, 98, 107–111, 116, 123–27
cityscapes, 12, 34, 37, 48, 78, 81, 153, 165, 168, 176
clothes, 19, 24, 42, 101, 119–120, 124, 152, 156, 169, 209, 230, 233, 238
consumerism, 79–80, 191
Covid, 151, 217
crimes, 4, 10, 51, 57–58, 108–11, 160, 167, 170, 173, 193, 247;
    against women, 4, 8, 205

Dalit, 41, 115, 123–27
Delhi Crime, 5, 11, 165–66, 169–70, 172–74, 177–79
Delhi gang rape, 19, 54, 63, 81, 219n4.

See also Nirbhaya
development, 40, 57, 77, 82, 84–85, 87, 202, 217, 247;
neoliberal, 82
Desai, Kishwar, 5, 8, 19–29
Devineni, Ram, 9, 52–56, 59–60, 62, 64–67
Dil Se, 10, 132, 135, 137–41, 144, 146
disappearance, 24, 26, 28, 42
documentary, xi, xvi, 60, 63, 186, 246
domestic labor, 155, 162, 188
domestic violence, 1
domestic worker, 11, 151–53, 158–59, 162

empowerment, 10, 25, 62, 81, 99, 105–06, 115, 133, 178, 187, 194–96, 225, 246
eve-teasing, 4, 23, 95, 117, 124, 165, 168, 195, 246

female body, 6, 25, 95, 103, 167, 172, 227, 230, 236, 246
female kinship, 8, 19–20, 26, 29
feminist activism, x, 246–47
feminist geographer, xvi, 2–3, 10, 12–13, 16n1, 21, 38, 43, 57, 102, 108–9, 133, 195
flaneuse, xii, 9, 73–75, 77, 88, 231
foreign tourist, 40;

girl, 25
gender-based violence, 7, 20, 51, 54, 64, 66, 205, 237, 239, 247
gendered public space, x, 2, 4, 6, 9, 12, 24, 116;
roads, 137, 196
gender roles, 12, 99, 101–103, 107, 116, 124, 190, 205–206, 229, 230
gender stratification, 224, 227–28, 230, 232, 235–36
Goa, 8, 19–20, 22, 24–26, 226, 244n2
Government of India, 16n2, 202, 247
guidebooks, 13, 105, 106
Gujarat, 42, 48, 136, 246

Gurgaon, 78, 82–86, 123, 193, 199n4

Handbook for Women Travellers, 106
hashtag activism, 246–47
hermaphrodite, 9, 33, 35
heteronormativity, 9, 40, 48, 190
heterotopia, 46;
heterotopic space, 34, 48
Highway, 82, 87–88, 96, 118–122
hijra, 9, 33–42, 46–48;
Hindi cinema, 8–11, 93–94, 96–99, 101, 103, 107, 111, 143
Hindi print media, 203–206, 216;
journalism, 205
Hollaback, 246
honor, 80, 86, 96, 99, 109, 160–61, 192, 211;
killing, 85, 86, 123

immoral, 96, 194–95, 233, 236
intersectionality, 87, 131, 146, 195
India's Daughter, 63
Intrepid Travel, 232–33
inviting, 107, 117, 125, 166, 175, 225, 237

Kahaani, 118–122
Kashmir, 34, 92n24, 121, 203
Keeling, Scarlett, 19, 21, 244n2
Kolkata, 7, 12, 39, 77, 116, 118, 120–21, 189, 196, 199nn1–4, 203, 247,

legitimate, 4, 107, 236
leisure, 80, 122, 173, 217, 227
liberalization, 16, 77–78, 81
loiter, ix, x, xiii, 2, 4, 6, 122, 168, 170, 194, 231, 245, 248
Lonely Planet, 223, 227, 238
lone woman, 11, 24, 74, 131

male companions, 10–11, 131–32, 135, 139, 143, 146
male-dominated, 3, 5, 38, 57, 101, 103, 106, 118, 126, 224

Index

male gaze, 5, 7–8, 12, 19, 26–29, 95, 100, 116, 137, 144, 185, 187, 190–92, 195, 237, 245
Mardaani 2, 5, 10, 95, 98–103, 105–106, 110–111
margins, 34, 47–48, 60, 84, 93
mediascapes, 77, 79
Meet to Sleep, 168, 182, 246
megacities, 10, 73, 77, 78
middle-class, 25, 27, 37, 78, 81, 120, 162, 169, 174, 189
The Ministry of Utmost Happiness, 8, 33–34, 37–40, 45, 48
Ministry of Women and Child Development, 247
minorities, 115, 127, 132, 139, 142, 166, 175
misogyny, 5, 7–8, 12, 19, 26–27, 29, 95, 100, 116, 137, 144, 185, 187, 190–92, 195, 237, 245
modernization, 93
moral code, 80, 157
motherhood, 94, 98, 145, 155, 162
Mr. and Mrs. Iyer, 10, 132, 135–41, 144, 146
Mumbai, ix, xi, 2, 4, 6–7, 22, 26, 74, 77, 81, 152, 156, 158, 166, 174, 181n2, 199n4, 203, 245, 246

narrative, x, xi, xii, xv, 1–6, 8–9, 12–20, 22–28, 36, 54, 62, 73–79, 88–93, 101–111, 121–22
National Crime Records Bureau, 4, 51, 205, 226
National Geographic, 227, 232
national highway, 84, 88, 125
nationalism, 39, 140, 206
National Women's Commission, 29, 247
NCRB. *See* National Crime Records Bureau
neoliberalism, xii, 39, 73, 130n1, 190–92;
  neoliberal India, xv, 2–5, 8–10, 12–14, 16n3, 24, 34, 37–39, 43, 48, 116–117, 124, 135

NH10, 82, 84–85, 123–27
nightlife, 76, 84
night shifts, 12, 185–87, 189, 192–94
Nirbhaya, 1–2, 5, 8, 11, 16n2, 19–21, 38, 81, 87, 107, 141, 166, 169–70, 173, 179, 199n3, 208, 236, 244n1, 245, 247
nocturnal, 22, 187, 192, 195
non-binary, 33–39, 40, 48

OTT. *See* over-the-top
over-the-top, 5

patriarchy, 3–4, 13, 21, 26, 38–39, 58, 63, 66, 87, 96, 109, 133, 161, 166–67, 186–87, 191, 205, 209, 212, 216, 223, 225, 227, 229–230, 235–36, 239
Piku, 118–122
Pinjra Tod, 168, 182, 246
Pink, 5, 82–84, 87, 123–27
Pink Taxis, 247
pleasure, xi, 10, 13, 79, 95, 102–3, 111, 115, 122, 126–28, 132, 144, 167, 238
popular culture, 2, 5, 13, 176;
  Indian, 166, 179
postcolonial, 140
Priya's Mirror, 53–57, 59–64, 66–67
Priya's Shakti, 9
protests, 19, 81, 169, 170, 245–46
provocation, 96, 106
public transport, 6, 23, 101, 173, 186, 193–94, 203, 217, 225, 234, 246
punishment, 51, 53, 61, 67, 103, 117, 125, 173, 236

Qareeb Qareeb Singlle, 118, 120–24
QQS. *See* Qareeb Qareeb Singlle
Queen, 79, 96, 128
queer, 33–34, 39–40, 42, 46, 48

race, 29, 132, 139, 140–42, 146, 213
rape culture, 7, 12, 55, 173, 177, 179, 209, 246;
  myths, 6
Roy, Arundhati, 8, 33–48

The Sea of Innocence, 8, 19, 20–21, 24, 28–29
sexism, 12–13, 178, 201, 246;
    sexist public spaces, 104, 205
sex workers, 166, 174–76
She, 5,11, 165–66, 169, 174–75, 177–79
Sir, 153, 156, 157, 164
sisterhood, 42, 109
SlutWalk, 168, 246
small cities, 202–03, 206, 210, 211, 213, 217;
    journalism, 216
social media, xvi, 13, 63, 225–26, 232, 234, 246–47
social norms, 64, 66, 117, 211, 230
The Space between Us, 158, 160, 162–63
space theorists, 2, 11, 13, 96
stigma, 6, 12, 37, 60, 187
stigmatization, 111, 229
street harassment, 4, 7, 21, 23, 25, 153, 246
surveillance, 39, 196, 210, 237
survivor, 107–8, 123, 186, 193, 246;
    victim-survivor, 9, 51–53, 55–58, 60–62, 64, 67

TEPK. *See* Toilet Ek Prem Katha
Toilet Ek Prem Katha, 123–27
tourism, 20, 22, 78–80, 116, 232
toxic masculinity, 9, 51–53, 63, 66, 144
transgender, 8, 34, 39, 40
transgress, 3, 80, 209, 215, 224
transgressions, 73–74, 167, 190
trauma, 54, 56, 60–61, 66, 109, 118, 141, 176
travel blog, 232–33;
    blogger, 226, 234, 238

Udhaharanam Sujatha, 153, 156–57
Umrigar, Thrity, 153, 158–61
UN Habitat, 37, 115,
United Nations, 54, 115
UN Women, 54, 230, 233
urban India, 4, 24–25, 77, 119

urbanization, 43, 202, 212, 216, 217;
    peripheral, 8–9, 33–34, 42–45, 48

victim-blaming, x, 6, 8, 29, 117, 121, 125, 134, 168
vulnerability, 1, 3, 5–6, 8–12, 20, 22, 27, 53, 58–59, 71, 95, 100–101, 107, 127, 131–32, 143, 151, 153–54, 160, 165, 173, 177, 179, 187–88, 193, 195, 199n5, 205, 211, 226, 228, 233, 246

Wanderlust, 232
web series, xii, 5, 11, 13, 166, 177. *See also* Delhi Crime; She
western, xvi, 2–3, 10, 16n1, 19, 40, 79–80, 102, 120, 139, 145, 168;
    women, 20, 96
westernization, 96, 191
white woman, 25
"Why Loiter," 245–46
women journalists, 12, 201–207, 209–11, 213–17, 219n1
women's movement, 10, 58, 95–96, 101, 169, 177, 236
women solo travelers, xii, 13, 97–100, 105, 223–28, 230, 232–36, 238–39;
    tips for, 13, 223, 233
women's safety, xv, 1, 3–6, 10, 13, 16, 22, 51, 58, 60, 82, 100, 126, 128, 132, 186–87, 195–96, 208, 235, 247
working women, 12, 94, 101, 123, 183, 210, 211
World Health Organization, 226
World Nomads, 232
workplace, 42, 103–4, 133, 152, 160, 190, 193–94, 204–6, 216;
    harassment, 58, 199

Yeh Jawaani Hai Deewani, 118–19, 121–22
YJHD. *See* Yeh Jawaani Hai Deewani
young women, x, 7, 21–22, 27, 75, 83, 100–101, 107, 116, 231, 245

About the Editors

Srirupa Chatterjee is Associate Professor of English in the Department of Liberal Arts at IIT Hyderabad, India. Her research interests include American literature, gender and body studies, film and media studies, and travel narratives. She has published research papers in journals such as *Critique: Studies in Contemporary Fiction, South Asian Popular Culture, Papers on Language and Literature, LIT: Literature Interpretation Theory, English Studies, Women: A Cultural Review, Journal of Language, Literature and Culture, ANQ: A Quarterly Journal of Short Articles, South Central Review, Notes on Contemporary Literature,* and *The Explicator.* Her forthcoming works include edited volumes titled *Women's Body Image in Contemporary Indian Literature and Culture* and *Gendered Violence in Public Spaces: Women's Narratives of Travel in Neoliberal India* (Lexington Books) and monographs entitled *Body Image in Contemporary American Young Adult Literature* and *Body Image: An Introduction.* Email id: srirupa@la.iith.ac.in.

Swathi Krishna S. is Assistant Professor of English in the School of Humanities, Social Sciences, and Management at IIT Bhubaneswar, India. Previously, she was Assistant Professor in the Department of Humanities and Social Sciences at IIT Ropar, India. Her research interests include contemporary American literature, women's literature, road narratives, feminist theory, gender studies and gender-based violence. Her essays have appeared in *Critique: Studies in Contemporary Fiction, LIT: Literature Interpretation Theory,* and *The Explicator,* among others. Her forthcoming works include a co-edited volume entitled *Gendered Violence in Public Spaces: Women's Narratives of Travel in Neoliberal India* (Lexington Books). Email: swathi@iitbbs.ac.in; swathikrishnasmic@gmail.com.

ABOUT THE CONTRIBUTORS

Pronoti Baglary is a writer, photographer and independent researcher based in Paris, France. She completed her MA and MPhil from the Centre for the Study of Social Systems in Jawaharlal Nehru University, New Delhi. She has also been a Senior Research Fellow at JNU where she worked on issues of reproductive health and fertility among women in New Delhi. Her areas of interest include urban sociology, feminist perspectives on women's health, and explorations of women's everyday lives in the city. Email: pronotibaglary@gmail.com.

Rima Bhattacharya is an Assistant Professor in the Department of Humanities and Social Sciences at the Indian Institute of Technology Kharagpur, India. Previously she was an Assistant Professor at IIT Jodhpur. She has published papers in journals like *Media Watch, Journal of Men's Studies, Neohelicon, Journal of Language, Literature and Culture, American Notes and Queries* (ANQ), *South Asian Review, Journal of Commonwealth Literature, International Journal of Comic Art, Economic and Political Review, Indian Journal of Gender Studies, British and American Studies*. Her areas of research interest are postcolonial literature, Asian American literature, and diasporic literature. Email: rima.b.mukherjee@gmail.com; rima@hss.iitkgp.ac.in.

Jana Fedtke is Assistant Professor in Residence in the Liberal Arts Program at Northwestern University in Qatar. Her research and teaching interests include data justice, science and technology in fiction, gender studies, and transnational literatures with a focus on South Asia and Africa. Dr. Fedtke's work has been published in, for example, *Online Information Review, Asian Studies, Journalism Practice, South Asian History and Culture*, and *Asexualities: Feminist and Queer Perspectives*. Email: jana.fedtke@northwestern.edu.

Kiranpreet Kaur Baath, presently working at the University of Wolverhampton as Research Associate and Lecturer with Centre for Sikh and Panjabi Studies, has earned her doctorate in African studies and Anthropology from the University of Birmingham in January 2022. Her thesis focused on the performance of identity and selectivity of voice and silence in construction of travel narratives is to be published by a leading academic publisher in 2024. She is an active member of Royal African Society, Hakluyt Society and Fellow of Royal Asiatic Society. Other than undertaking academic writing for various high impact journals and newspapers, she has also published a book that is a collection of poems in the Punjabi language, and has undertaken commissioned translation projects. Her debut novel is to be published in March 2023. She is also a regular contributor to Panjabi media through her weekly slots on the Akaal Channel which is aired globally with millions of viewers. Her program "Kirdar- E-Khalsa" in Panjabi language has been running successfully since July 2022; and has telecasted two seasons of "The Kids Show" in English language. Email: kpkaur629@gmail.com.

Uttara Manohar is an Assistant Professor in the School of Communication Media and Theatre Arts at Eastern Michigan University. Her research examines representations of gender and gender-based violence in fictional and non-fictional media. Her work has been published in peer-reviewed journals like *Sex Roles*, *Feminist Media Studies*, *International Journal of Intercultural Relations*, and *Communication Education*. Email: umanohar@emich.edu.

Madhuja Mukherjee is Professor of Film Studies at Jadavpur University, India. She extends her archival research into art-practice, curatorial-work and filmmaking. Mukherjee is the author of *New Theatres Ltd.* (2009), editor of *Aural Films, Oral Cultures* (2012), and of the award-winning anthology *Voices of the Talking Stars* (2017). She co-edited: *Popular Cinema in Bengal* (2020) and *Industrial Networks and Cinemas of India* (2021). She is editing an issue for *South Asian History and Culture* journal on single screens in India. She is the creator of the Bengali graphic-novel *Kangal Malsat* (2013); and is editing a graphic-narrative volume titled *Body Matters*. She is the co-writer of the film *Qissa* (Punjabi, 2013); her first directorial feature-film *Carnival* (2012), had its World Premiere at the *41st International Film Festival Rotterdam* 2012, and her second feature-film, *Deep6* (2021), had its World Premiere at the *26th Busan International Film Festival* 2021. Email: madhuja001@gmail.com.

Ditto Prasad is Assistant Professor in the Department of English at CMS College Kottayam (Autonomous), Kerala, India where he teaches post-graduate students, literary theory and film studies. His research focuses on discourses of feminism and narratology in contemporary cinema. He has presented research papers in conferences across India and has contributed modules to e-PGPathshala, a project by the Ministry of Human Resource and Development, India. He is a senior soft skills trainer for the Additional Skill Acquisition Program (ASAP), a project by the Government of Kerala, India. He serves as the College Chaplain and has a new-found interest in thanatology. Email: dittoprasad@gmail.com.

Shreya Rastogi is a Doctoral Scholar in the Department of Liberal Arts at IIT Hyderabad. Her research interests are contemporary American literature, literary theory, spatial theory, and gender and body studies. Rastogi's recent research has appeared in *English Studies* and *South Central Review*. Email: la18resch11001@iith.ac.in.

Sucharita Sen is a History Innovation Fund Post-Doctoral Research Fellow at the University of Auckland, New Zealand. She completed her PhD from Victoria University of Wellington, New Zealand. Her articles have appeared in *South Asia: Journal of South Asian Studies, Society and Culture in South Asia, Studies in People's History* and *Rupkatha Journal on Interdisciplinary Studies in Humanities*. Her select awards include a gold medal in M.A. (Political Science) from Presidency University, Kolkata, India, and a Certificate of Excellence from Oxford University Press (India) for her contribution in *Tell Me Your Story Review*. Email: sucharitasen13@gmail.com.

Dr. Nidhi Shrivastava completed her PhD in the department of English and Writing Studies at the University of Western Ontario (now Western University) in London, Canada. Her research focuses on the #MeToo movement, Hindi cinema, censorship, the figure of the abducted and raped women, Indian rape culture, and the 1947 partition. She co-edited the volume titled *Bridging the Gaps Between Celebrity and Media* with Jackie Raphael and Basuli Deb. She has also contributed various book chapters and her journal articles have been published in *South Asian Review* and *Intellect Press*. She is currently co-editing a volume, *Reimagining #MeToo in South Asia and the Diaspora* and working on her monograph, *"India's Daughter": Representation of Women and the 1947 Partition in Hindi Cinema And Television*. Email: shrivastavan@sacredheart.edu.

Ranu Tomar is Assistant Professor at Sharda School of Media, Film and Entertainment, Sharda University, Greater Noida, Uttar Pradesh, India. She has a doctorate in media and cultural studies. Dr Tomar has authored a book titled *Gender in Hindi Print Media in Central India: Lived Experiences of Women Journalists in Cities of Madhya Pradesh* (2022). Her research interests cover feminist research methodology, gender, media, communication, and development. Dr Tomar is a reviewer for the Gender and Communication Section of International Association for Media and Communication Research (IAMCR) and the Feminist Studies Division of International Communication Association (ICA). Dr. Tomar belongs to Bhopal, Madhya Pradesh, India. Email: ranutomar2010@gmail.com.

Bonnie Zare is the Director of Women's and Gender Studies and a Professor of Sociology at Virginia Tech. Her research focuses on Dalit literature as well as discourses of identity, feminism and activism in contemporary India. Zare's articles have appeared in *Women's Studies International Forum*,

Humanity and Society, and *South Asian Review* among others. With Nalini Iyer, she is the co-editor of *Other Tongues: Rethinking the Language Debates in India*. Since 2008 she has been collaborating with organizations to secure the future of low-income girls in Telangana and Andhra Pradesh. Email: bonzare@vt.edu.